KOREA UNDER
NEW LEADERSHIP

KOREA UNDER NEW LEADERSHIP

The Fifth Republic

Harold C. Hinton

PRAEGER

PRAEGER SPECIAL STUDIES • PRAEGER SCIENTIFIC

Library of Congress Cataloging in Publication Data

Hinton, Harold C.

    Korea under new leadership.

    Bibliography: p.
    Includes index.
    1. Korea (South)—Politics and government—1960-
I. Title.
DS922.35.H56   1983   951.9'053   83-2238
ISBN 0-03-063284-6
ISBN 0-03-063283-8 (pbk.)

Published in 1983 by Praeger Publishers
CBS Educational and Professional Publishing
a Division of CBS Inc.
521 Fifth Avenue, New York, New York 10175 U.S.A.

3456789 052 987654321

Printed in the United States of America
on acid-free paper

PREFACE

On September 8, 1945, as a second lieutenant and military historian serving with Headquarters United States Army XXIV Corps, I became one of the first U.S. officers to land in Korea after the Japanese surrender. My ten-month stay served as an interesting introduction to the region, and I decided at that time to make this area the focus of my career. Japan, the defeated enemy, held little attraction for me. When I asked my Korean friends—English-speaking, of course— whether I should devote my graduate studies at Harvard, where I had already been admitted as a doctoral candidate, to Korea, they advised against it on the ground that Korea was only a small country. Instead they recommended China, and China it became, for the most part. But I have always retained a strong interest in Korea and have made eight visits to it since the first one.

At present Korea is more interesting than ever to me, and I believe it should be also to anyone with a sense of involvement, personal or vicarious, in the Far East. In no other Asian country has there occurred during the past few years a series of more dramatic developments, amounting to a successful revolution. The most important developments have been the assassination of a president, Park Chung Hee, who had ruled increasingly as a dictator for nearly two decades, and the emergence after a stormy interlude of a new generation of military and civilian leaders. These leaders pledged a constitutional government and collective leadership rather than one-man rule, although they were not prepared to tolerate a challenge from any rival elite. The efficiency with which all this has been accomplished has few parallels.

From these developments alone it could be inferred that the Koreans are a remarkable people; this impression is confirmed by an abundance of evidence, much of which is presented in this book. On the whole they are energetic and direct to a degree that contrasts rather sharply with the behavior patterns normally found in the Chinese and Japanese cultures and renders them relatively understandable and congenial to the Western mind.

These gifted and attractive people have nevertheless had a turbulent and sometimes tragic history. The reasons for this are essentially geopolitical. Although the most populous peninsula projecting from the east coast of the Asian continent, Korea is smaller and has generally been weaker than its neighbors, China, Japan, and

Russia, all of which have tried in modern times with varying degrees of success to dominate Korea. In fact, Korea has acted historically as a kind of land bridge linking China, Japan, and the Northeast Asian mainland. Yet while experiencing invasion and sometimes conquest, the Koreans have refused assimilation, remained highly homogeneous, and retained a distinctive culture.

To be sure, Korean culture is to a degree an offshoot of Chinese civilization. The Chinese impact reinforced a tendency, strong throughout the entire Far East, toward social discipline and political consensus as the norm. The first insight I had into Korean discipline and cohesion came in December 1945, when I witnessed in Seoul large demonstrations, obviously organized and led very effectively on very short notice, against the idea of international trusteeship for Korea; these were not Communist demonstrations, since the Communists were supporting trusteeship because it had been endorsed by the Soviet Union.

At the end of the nineteenth century, Korea passed from the Chinese orbit into the Japanese Empire, a much less tolerant entity. For half a century, the Japanese tried not only to dominate and exploit Korea but to assimilate the Koreans. From this ordeal they were delivered by the fall of Japan in 1945, which they greeted with greater joy than did any one else; U.S. war correspondents who had witnessed the liberation of Paris and Manila insisted that the Korean crowds were the most enthusiastic they had seen.

This rapture was soon tempered by the realization that their country had been partitioned without their knowledge or consent into Soviet and U.S. occupation zones separated by the 38th parallel. The brutality of the regime north of that line soon became obvious as hundreds of thousands of refugees streamed southward. In the South, the Koreans endured with understandable impatience the rather inept U.S. Military Government that had only a superficial understanding of their problems and sometimes treated them with contempt. U.S. personnel in Korea at that time were divided sharply into two schools, one of which believed the Koreans could make it and the other of which did not; I belonged emphatically to the first school and still do.

Having unavoidably failed to create the conditions for a parliamentary democracy in South Korea, the United States nevertheless terminated the occupation in 1948. A year later it withdrew its forces on the theory that South Korea was indefensible and probably not worth trying to defend. When this act of abandonment led directly to a North Korean invasion in June 1950, the United States to its belated credit reversed its stand, staunchly defended South Korea, and in cooperation with the South Koreans and some other contingents sent by various members of the United Nations ultimately liberated South Korea from the North Koreans and their Chinese allies, who however remained entrenched north of the 38th parallel. The United States then gave South Korea a defensive guarantee combined with military aid insufficient to give it military parity with North Korea, an adversary that has never accepted the idea of a "German" solution (live and let live) for Korea. The siege mentality inevitably created in the minds of many South Koreans by this menacing confrontation has contributed powerfully, especially during the presidency of Park Chung Hee, to an atmosphere of political tension and repression. Official and public opinion in the United States has tended to be critical, often very critical, of this situation, understandably except for the fact that the United States' Korean policy since World War II has been a major factor in the emergence of what is being deplored. On the other hand, in at least one important respect the United States did the best it could by creating a lesser evil rather than accepting a greater one: the only realistic alternative to Soviet occupation of North Korea in 1945 was Soviet occupation of the entire peninsula.

South Korea is highly unusual among the United States' allies. It maintains large armed forces and a high level of readiness as a matter of necessity, and with minimum complaint. It shows no inclination to compromise with, much less to yield to, the adversary; in return it asks that the United States refrain from dealing with the adversary to the disadvantage of South Korea.

This book has been written in an effort to increase the level of understanding of this important and complex country, especially in the United States. In the past the U.S. outlook on Korea has been formed to a large extent through contact with Korean intellectuals and political oppositionists, who have tended to believe, at least until recently, that in spite of the difficulties involved and the dangers faced by their country, a parliamentary democracy of the Western type not only can but should be introduced in South Korea. It is much more difficult for the U.S. public to understand the Korean political or military leaders who are partly responsible for the survival of their country and may be convinced, if not rightly then at least with considerable plausibility, that Korea cannot yet afford to risk the relaxation of unity and watchfulness that the adoption of the opposition's program would probably entail. It is important to understand this point of view, whether one agrees with it or not, because those who hold it are in power, whereas the opposition by definition is not. Korea should be viewed from both perspectives.

CONTENTS

Documents

INTRODUCTION:
KOREA'S UNIQUE DILEMMA

At the end of World War II, half a century of Japanese domination had prevented the world from knowing much more about Korea than its name. Even today, when this ignorance has considerably diminished due to a series of dramatic events that have occurred in Korea since the war, an understanding of those events can be facilitated by a brief sketch of the relevant background information.

A SKETCH OF KOREA

The area of Korea (approximately 85,000 square miles) is roughly equal to the combined areas of New York and Pennsylvania. It juts out from the mainland of Northeast Asia in such a way as to border on Manchuria and, for a short distance only, the Soviet Maritime Province, from which it is separated by the Yalu and Tumen rivers, and to divide the Yellow Sea from the Sea of Japan (or the Eastern Sea, as the Koreans call it). The peninsula extends from approximately 34 to 43 degrees north latitude and therefore has considerable north-south variations in climate, especially if one takes into account the mild climate of the beautiful island of Cheju Do, situated 50 miles south of the peninsula. Except for the western coast along the Yellow Sea, Korea is largely mountainous.

Korea is only moderately endowed with natural resources. The fact that these are very unevenly distributed, the industrial resources (coal, timber, hydroelectric potential, and so on) being in the north and the best agricultural land in the south, makes the country a natural economic unit and renders its division into two separate political entities since 1945 a double misfortune for the Korean people.

The Koreans are identified by certain physical characteristics, such as the eyelid fold, as belonging to the so-called yellow or Mongoloid race. Considering their numbers (about 49 million, including 34 million in the South and 15 million in the North, in 1980), they are highly homogeneous in physical traits and in language, although Korean does display some dialectal variations.

The early culture of the Koreans, which testifies to their nomadic origins in mainland Northeast Asia and perhaps before that in Central Asia, began to be modified in the early centuries of the Christian Era by contact with their two principal neighbors, China and Japan. Of the two nations, China, by virtue of its much higher cultural level as compared to Japan, was by far the greater influence, and from it Buddhism, Confucianism, the Chinese writing system and written language, and the essentials of the Chinese administrative system were adopted by the Koreans. Korea in turn helped significantly to transmit these basic features of Chinese culture to Japan shortly after receiving them from China.

During this period Korea was not yet politically united; it was divided among Koguryo in the north, Silla in the southeast, and Paekche in the southwest. In the seventh century the peninsula was united under Silla, and a flourishing Buddhist culture then developed. In the tenth century, power passed to the state of Koryo, based in the north and Buddhist like Silla but less culturally advanced. Koryo was weakened by a series of invasions from Manchuria, especially by the Mongols in the thirteenth century. In 1392 a new dynasty, the Yi, came to power with its capital farther south, at Seoul, and with an official culture that was strongly Confucian. Two hundred years later, the Yi barely survived a massive Japanese invasion aimed ultimately at the conquest of China.

As during other periods, Korea under the Yi dynasty displayed impressive creativity. In the fifteenth century, King Sejong devised a simple but ingenious phonetic writing system, which has become the standard system for writing the Korean language since World War II, although Chinese characters continue to be used as well. During the Japanese invasion, Admiral Yi Sun Sin developed an ironclad warship that inflicted heavy losses on the Japanese fleet.

Nevertheless, the Yi tended to decline into futility after the terrible trauma of the Japanese invasion. Korea became known in the West as the Hermit Kingdom because of an official isolationism paralleling that of contemporary Japan under the Tokugawa Shogunate. Korea was even less able than Japan to resist the efforts of the major powers, including the United States and Japan itself, to "open" Korea in the late nineteenth century, through treaties negotiated under pressure, to foreign trade, Christian missions, and therefore to foreign influence. For obvious geographic reasons and by virtue of its impressive progress in modernization, Japan rapidly moved to the fore among the foreign powers competing for influence in Korea. The efforts of Korea's nominal suzerain, the Chinese Empire under the Manchu dynasty, to oppose this trend brought on the Sino-Japanese War (1894–95) and the expulsion of Chinese political influence from Korea. Almost immediately afterward, however, tsarist Russia became active in the Far East including Korea, only to be excluded similarly from influence in the peninsula as a result of defeat in the Russo-Japanese War (1904–5). As the war was ending, Korea was proclaimed a Japanese protectorate, and in 1910 it was formally annexed to the Japanese Empire as its most important colonial dependency.

Japanese rule in Korea was harsh and exploitative. As a result of Japan's surrender in 1945, it was replaced by the Soviet military occupation of North Korea and the U.S. Military Government in South Korea. In the North the Soviet Union systematically and ruthlessly created a satellite regime controlled by Korean Communists subservient to themselves. In the South the United States attempted with much less success the far more difficult task of coaxing a Korean democracy into life. Since negotiations between the U.S. and Soviet commands supposedly aimed at unification failed because of the obvious Soviet intent to communize the South as well as the North, the United States in 1947–48 took the problem to the United Nations, under whose auspices elections were held in the South (but not the North) in 1948. The United States then terminated its occupation, which gave way to the independent Republic of Korea, and withdrew its troops in 1949. The Soviets felt compelled to duplicate this performance, at least in appearance. They terminated their occupation and withdrew their troops in 1948, but they left behind a full-fledged satellite, known officially as the Democratic People's Republic of Korea, with much stronger armed forces than those of South Korea.

In June 1950, with Soviet consent and support, North Korea invaded the South. Intervention by the United States, supported by some other members of the United Nations, in cooperation with the forces of the Republic of Korea, barely prevented the conquest of South Korea. But an invasion of the North in the fall of 1950, aimed at unifying Korea under the Republic of Korea, brought China into the war. In July 1953, after much hard fighting and much damage to both halves of the Korean peninsula, an armistice was concluded, but there was no peace settlement, and there has been none to date. Instead there has been an armed confrontation between the two Koreas, which accordingly have tended to resemble garrison states, the North, because it is Communist, much more so than the South.

KOREA AND GEOPOLITICS

Being a relatively small country sandwiched between much larger and more powerful neighbors, Korea has constantly been threatened with domination by one or more of them and has sometimes succumbed, but never without a struggle. The intensity of these struggles is paralleled by the fact that foreign influence, cultural and political, was accepted by the Koreans only when unaccompanied by efforts at domination. Thus the Koreans accepted nothing from the Mongols or the Japanese, who always came to conquer, but much from the Chinese at exactly those periods when they did not—in the early centuries of the Christian Era and again in the early modern period under the Yi.

Similarly, in recent times the United States has exerted a much greater influence, in a positive sense, on South Korea than the Soviet Union has on North Korea. By imposing satellite status on the North, Moscow earned such ill will that Kim Il Song, whom the Soviets had groomed as their puppet, took advantage of the Korean War and its aftermath to throw off Soviet control while continuing to control his colleagues and people with Soviet methods. At the popular level, U.S. troops fighting in North Korea in the fall of 1950 often found that local civilians willingly provided them with combat intelligence, and soon afterward many North Koreans wanted to be taken along when it became necessary to evacuate the North in the wake of the Chinese intervention in the war.

In the thirteenth and fourteenth centuries, both China and Korea suffered cruelly, as did much of the rest of Eurasia, from invasion and conquest by the Mongols. The earliest major blow to Mongol power was delivered by the Ming dynasty of China, which rose to power in 1368, expelled the Mongols from China, and fought a series of campaigns against them in Mongolia. In the process the Mongols also lost their grip on Korea, and this liberation combined with the enormous traditional prestige of Chinese culture rendered the Yi dynasty a willing and loyal member of the remarkable Chinese tribute system, which allowed maximum autonomy in practice to the tributaries as long as they acknowledged Chinese suzerainty in certain prescribed ways and adopted at least some features of Chinese culture.

One feature of the tributary system was the fact that the Chinese tried to protect their tributaries from invasion and conquest by others, a distinct advantage to the tributary because any other overlord was likely to be more demanding than the Chinese. Accordingly, the Ming sent an army to Korea to help stop and ultimately expel the Japanese army that invaded with devastating effect near the end of the sixteenth century. Almost three centures later, the Western powers, having already "opened" China and Japan to foreign trade and Christian missions through pressure and treaties, approached Korea with the same thing in mind. China, now under the Manchus but still regarded by the Yi as the suzerain power, tried with limited success to insist that at the minimum the foreigners should deal with Seoul through Peking.

The Chinese were least successful with the Japanese, the most assertive of the foreigners and the ones most interested in Korea for strategic reasons in addition to commercial ones. After the Japanese expelled Chinese influence from the peninsula in the Sino-Japanese War, tsarist Russia in a mood of misplaced confidence challenged Japan for supremacy in Korea and Manchuria. Aware that they were now dealing with a power much more formidable than the Manchu dynasty, the Japanese in 1896 offered to agree to the division of Korea into two spheres of influence separated by the 38th parallel, which comes fairly close to bisecting the peninsula evenly and would have left Seoul in the Japanese sphere. The Russians refused, and the policy of which this refusal was an important aspect soon resulted in a humiliating military defeat and something very close to a revolution at home. The Japanese celebrated their victory by proclaiming Korea a protectorate in 1905 and annexing the peninsula five years later.

For the Japanese, Korea was somewhat interesting as a source of agricultural exports but was valued more as a strategic springboard on the Asian mainland for the penetration and ultimate domination of Manchuria, North China, and possibly the Soviet Far East. In this spirit they always appointed as governor general a senior military man, usually an army general. Japanese colonial policy in Korea was consistently harsh and assimilationist and became increasingly so as the army grew more expansionist in the 1930s; northern Korea was industrialized to a degree in support of the Japanese military effort in Northeast Asia. During this period hundreds of thousands of Koreans went to Japan, voluntarily or under compulsion, and many emigrants (or their descendants) are still there; during World War II many other Koreans served in the Japanese armed forces in various theaters.

THE RISE OF KOREAN NATIONALISM AND COMMUNISM

Few Koreans accepted the imposition of Japanese rule willingly; some resisted it with arms, but of course without success. The most famous case of Korean resistance and protest was the large nonviolent demonstrations, in which Korean Christians were prominently represented, on March 1, 1919, on the occasion of the funeral of the last of the Yi rulers. Nonviolence did not appease the Japanese, who repressed the protest with great ferocity. After that there were no more such demonstrations, and Japanese policy toward Korea mellowed, but not for long.

As an offshoot of the March 1, 1919 movement, there arose a Korean nationalist movement in exile, with its main base in Shanghai. Although blessed with some prominent leaders, it was hampered by factionalism. Of the same general outlook as this group, but living in Hawaii or the United States, was Dr. Syngman Rhee, who had opposed the Japanese in his student days and had later taken a doctorate at Princeton under Woodrow Wilson.

Similarly anti-Japanese, but oriented toward the Soviet Union, was the Korean Communist movement, which also arose in the early 1920s. Never "monolithic" during that period, it contained eventually four distinct groups or factions: the domestic faction, which led a hunted existence, essentially underground, in Korea; the Manchurian faction, which emerged among the large Korean community that had been living in Manchuria since the mid-nineteenth century; the Soviet faction, which was directly controlled from Moscow and composed largely of members of the sizable Korean community first living in the Soviet Far East and then transported forcibly to Soviet Central Asia after 1937; and the Yenan faction, which worked with the Chinese Communists.

Although brave and energetic, none of these resistance elements had much of an impact on the Japanese position in Korea, which collapsed exclusively as a result of Japan's defeat in 1945 in World War II.

NORTH KOREA UNDER SOVIET OCCUPATION

As it had done in Mongolia 24 years earlier, the Soviet army entered North Korea in August 1945, accompanied by a cadre of trained indigenous Communists eager to take over. The Soviets gave them, as well as other cooperative Koreans, as much local power as was consistent with strict overall Soviet control and began promptly to create a satellite regime very similar in structure and functioning to those it was setting up in Eastern Europe.

In all their satellites the Soviets installed a "little Stalin" to run for them a regime that could be claimed as independent. Looking over the field of Korean Communists, they evidently decided that the Yenan faction was unacceptable for this purpose on account of its Chinese ties, that the domestic faction was too weak and in any case located partly in South Korea, that a member of the Soviet faction would be embarrassing, and that the choice therefore had to fall on a member of the Manchurian faction. It actually fell on a young man with some background as an anti-Japanese guerrilla who about this time took the name of an earlier and better known Manchurian Korean who had fought the Japanese, Kim Il Song. The Soviets must have hoped and believed that their selection would be pliable, and at first he evidently was. But the sequel was to suggest that Kim Il Song resented the high-handed way in which the Soviets treated him, as they did all their satellite leaders, and he became determined to throw off their control when and if an opportunity occurred.

Regardless of any feelings that Kim Il Song and other North Koreans may have had, the sovietization of North Korean life proceeded at a rapid rate. Agriculture was collectivized, industry was socialized, a massive police network and sizable armed forces were created along Soviet lines, and the Soviet Union and Stalin were constantly proclaimed to be the Big Brothers of the Korean people.

Moscow would very likely have proclaimed the formal termination of its occupation and withdrawn its troops from North Korea after a few years in any case, but this development was accelerated by the proclamation of the independent Republic of Korea under United Nations auspices on August 15, 1948. During the ensuing fall the Soviets set up what they termed the Democratic People's Republic of Korea, had it recognized by the other Communist states, and soon afterward withdrew their troops.

SOUTH KOREA UNDER U.S. OCCUPATION

The U.S. occupation of South Korea contrasted with the Soviet occupation of North Korea in every significant respect. The United States hoped to create an independent and democratic, as well as ideally a reunited, Korea, not a satellite of any kind. They regarded the Koreans as a liberated friendly people, whereas the Soviets in the North tended to treat them as enemy aliens. Apart from a few former missionaries, the U.S. officials brought no one with them who spoke Korean or knew much about the country; they relied at first on English-speaking Koreans to the point of being known as running an "interpreters' government," and when trained U.S. Military Government teams arrived in October 1945, they turned out to have been trained for Japan and to have been diverted to Korea only because the cooperativeness of the Japanese authorities rendered them unnecessary there. Also during the early weeks of the occupation, and much to the annoyance of the Koreans, the U.S. Military Government made considerable use of Japanese retained in their previous posts until repatriated beginning in October 1945. The U.S. officials in South Korea were under the command of General MacArthur in Tokyo, who interfered very little but also gave little in the way of support. The same was true of the State Department, even though the occupation was a highly political affair with important international aspects.

There were other, even more serious, problems. The division of the country and the control of the North, where the minerals and industries were located, by the Soviet Union constituted an economic and political disaster for the South, and there was no prospect of this situation coming to an end. The U.S. military, although well intentioned, were not trained or mentally equipped to deal with the inevitable upsurge of Korean political activity, especially because they disliked Syngman Rhee, who returned to Korea in October 1945 and became a gadfly to the Military Government in the process of building up his political following.

THE KOREAN WAR AND ITS AFTERMATH

In February 1946 the U.S. and Soviet military commands initiated discussions on possible unification of the two occupation zones. These failed because the Soviet side insisted that no Korean political party could even be consulted on, much less represented in, a provisional government for the entire country unless it accepted in principle the idea of international trusteeship for Korea that had been enunciated tentatively by the Big Four Foreign Ministers Conference at Moscow the previous December. Since only the Communists endorsed trusteeship, the Soviet position was completely unacceptable to the United States.

Because of this deadlock, the United States submitted the problem to the United Nations General Assembly in the fall of 1947. Since the resulting resolution calling for supervised elections in both halves of Korea could not be implemented in the North, they were held in the South only, and the General Assembly accepted this result as the best attainable. It was on this basis that the United States ended its occupation and recognized the independent Republic of Korea on August 15, 1948.

The new republic was in a weak internal condition and was faced by a menacing and much more heavily armed adversary to the north. As was to be expected, Pyongyang made no secret of its intent to "liberate" the South by whatever means were necessary. Until mid-1950, these means stopped short, but not far short, of invasion; they included propaganda appeals to opposition politicians and public opinion in the South, incitement of mutinies in the South Korean armed forces, and armed clashes along the 38th parallel. For its part, the U.S. government believed during this period that the Republic of Korea was doomed by internal weaknesses, even in the absence of an invasion from the North, and accordingly was not a "situation of strength" (Secretary of State Dean Acheson's phrase) that the United States should try to defend. U.S. forces were withdrawn from South Korea in 1949, and on January 12, 1950 in a celebrated speech, Acheson indicated that South Korea, as well as Taiwan and Indochina, lay outside the U.S. defensive perimeter in the Western Pacific and would have to rely on the United Nations if faced with external aggression.

There is no reasonable doubt that this seemingly authoritative statement aroused the keenest interest in Moscow and of course in Pyongyang. Stalin unquestionably wanted to round out Communist holdings on the Asian mainland, partly as a base for later pressures on Japan. If he could get control, even by proxy, of the excellent ice-free ports of South Korea, he could afford to accede to Chinese Communist requests for the return of the Manchurian ports of Dairen and Port Arthur, which had been held and used by the Soviets since 1945 under the cover of an agreement extracted from the former Chinese Nationalist government. In fact he did agree in

February 1950 to turn back Dairen and Port Arthur by the end of 1952. In the spring of 1950, he strengthened the North Korean army with heavy artillery, armor, and the like.

It is possible that Stalin intended the attack on South Korea to occur around the beginning of August 1950, when Moscow was scheduled to assume the chairmanship of the United Nations Security Council; if so, Kim Il Song "jumped the gun" when, for reasons of his own, he attacked on June 25. In any event, it does appear that friction between Moscow and Pyongyang started at that time and probably in that connection.

The military history of the war is well known and requires only the briefest summary here. The Republic of Korea's armed forces fought bravely but were rapidly pushed back. President Truman changed his mind promptly and committed increasingly powerful U.S. forces to the defense of South Korea, with the result that the North Korean offensive was stopped well south of Seoul in August, while the United States obtained political support from the United Nations for its actions. A U.N. counteroffensive featuring a spectacular amphibious landing at Inchon on September 15 drove the North Koreans back approximately to the 38th parallel by the beginning of October. Mainly at the insistence of General MacArthur, an advance deep into North Korea then began, but in late November it was pushed back by a powerful Chinese force. In early 1951 the United Nations armies rallied again, a little south of Seoul, but a decision was taken not to advance into North Korea again. After two Chinese offensives aimed at Seoul failed in April and May, the Communist side agreed to armistice talks.

Although very aggressively conducted on the Communist side, these talks had produced something seemingly close to an agreement by the end of 1951. In early 1952, however, the United Nations side introduced into the talks the politically sensitive question of the disposition of prisoners taken from the Communist side who did not want to return home; these were known to be numerous, and the Communists made a major issue of the prisoners. In fact, it was not until February-March 1953, when the newly installed Eisenhower administration threatened the Communist side with the use of nuclear weapons and the extension of the war to the mainland of China, that an agreement embodying the United Nations side's insistence on voluntary as opposed to compulsory repatriation became possible. An armistice agreement along these lines, with a ceasefire line running approximately along the 38th parallel, was signed on July 27, 1953 and is still in force.

The effects of three years of war were devastating for both Koreas. There had been enormous casualties, much destruction of property, and loss of production. The South became more than ever dependent on the United States for economic as well as military aid and support, and the South Koreans who survived the war at an age great enough so that they remembered it clearly were rendered totally immune to future political appeals from the North. As for North Korea, the chaos of the war, the presence of Chinese forces, and the death of Stalin in early 1953 loosened the Soviet grip without transforming Pyongyang into a Chinese satellite, and Kim Il Song was able to begin playing Moscow and Peking against each other, for example, by securing commitments from both in mid-1953 to identical amounts of economic aid.

With both parties so badly weakened, there was little likelihood of another war for a time, but the relationship between them naturally remained hostile and tense, if anything more so than before the war because of the extreme bitterness on both sides. There were frequent armed incidents, initiated by the North, along the misleadingly named Demilitarized Zone straddling the ceasefire line. From about 1965 to 1969, apparently in an effort to duplicate what the North Vietnamese were then doing in South Vietnam, North Korea launched an escalating campaign of infiltration and subversion against South Korea and its U.S. ally; two spectacular features of this campaign were a nearly successful commando raid on the Blue House (the South Korean presidential mansion) and the seizure of the USS *Pueblo*, both in January 1968.

After 1970 this campaign slackened, and secret high-level political contacts between the two sides began in 1971. The reason for this shift seems to have been the changes that were occurring at that time in Far Eastern international politics and, in particular, the obvious intent of the United States to withdraw from Indochina and improve relations with China; Peking for its part may have encouraged Pyongyang privately to assume a less bellicose posture toward South Korea. On July 4, 1972, it was announced that as a result of previously secret talks formal political discussions between North and South Korea would soon begin. They took place in 1972–73, but without significant results. The South wanted small concrete steps—exchanges of visits among relatives, for example—as steps toward a climate of mutual confidence and a reduction of tension; the North wanted to use the talks mainly to establish a political presence in the South that could be used to destabilize the South Korean political situation. Furthermore, the North began about that time to dig a series of now famous tunnels under the Demilitarized Zone; the most plausible explanation of this strange step, which has worried the South greatly since not all the tunnels have necessarily been discovered and intercepted, is that the North Korean military leadership was unhappy over the political contacts with the South and was therefore allowed or encouraged to do something, even if more or less covert, to enhance the North's capabilities for offensive military action in case the talks with the South should not succeed.

There has been no essential change in North-South relations since the mid-1970s. All is definitely not quiet on South Korea's northern front.

U.S. INTEREST IN KOREA

U.S. ties with Korea have a history of about a century. Their importance to both parties and to the world has mounted dramatically in recent years as a result of the U.S. commitment first to liberate Korea from Japanese rule and later to save South Korea from conquest by its Communist adversaries. In this way the momentum of Communist expansion in the strategically most sensitive region of Asia was checked. Since the Korean War, the security ties between the United States and the Republic of Korea have made an indispensable contribution to stability in Northeast Asia, a contribution all the more necessary because of Japan's reluctance to date to play an active role in ensuring the security of the region.

EARLY TIES

The so-called Hermit Kingdom, which had traditionally been an independent state acknowledging a tributary relationship with the Chinese Empire, was first compelled to open its doors to modern foreign contact by a treaty extracted by Japan in 1876 by means of considerable pressure.

The next treaty concluded by Korea was the achievement of a U.S. statesman, Commodore Robert W. Shufeldt, in 1882. This treaty was the result of diplomacy, not pressure. It rejected the Chinese claim to suzerainty over Korea even though it was acknowledged by the Yi dynasty, established diplomatic relations, and included most favored nation and good offices clauses. When Japan absorbed Korea into its empire in the first decade of the twentieth century, however, the United States refused to honor its obligation under the good offices clause and acquiesced in the Japanese action, only to decide during World War II that Korea deserved independence.

Under Japanese rule Korea was not encouraged to trade except with other components of the Japanese Empire, and United States-Korean trade therefore remained small. There were cultural contacts between the United States and Korea, mainly through the (largely Protestant) U.S. Christian missions that had begun to work in Korea before the Japanese occupation and remained under it, in spite of severe restrictions. In addition to strictly evangelical activity, these missions, like those (Catholic and Protestant) from other countries, of course engaged in medical and educational work. In fact, the missions were almost the only channel of contact between the United States and other Western countries on the one hand and Korea on the other during the latter's half century as an unwilling Japanese dependency.

WORLD WAR II AND AFTER

One of the major war aims of the Allied powers in World War II was the defeat of Japan and the dismemberment of its empire, and in this connection the question of independence for Korea naturally arose. At the Cairo Conference in late 1943, the participants—the United States, Britain, and Nationalist China—declared among other things that after the defeat of Japan Korea should be independent "in due course."

At the Yalta (February 1945) and Potsdam (July 1945) Conferences, the arrangements for the immediate postwar period were made by the United States, Britain, and the Soviet Union, and it was agreed in principle that there should be Soviet and U.S. occupation zones in Korea for the initial purpose of disarming and evacuating the Japanese. The only realistic alternative would have been Soviet occupation of the entire peninsula, since the United States lacked the manpower that would have been needed to occupy all of Korea in addition to Japan, and in any case the Soviet Union would almost certainly not have tolerated U.S. troops in an area directly adjacent to Soviet territory, a situation that existed nowhere else around the Soviet periphery.

The Soviet Union entered the war against Japan on August 8, 1945, after abrogating its neutrality pact with Tokyo, and almost immediately invaded North Korea from the Maritime Province.

Within about a week, rumors began to fly in Korea and elsewhere that Soviet troops were advancing rapidly toward the middle of the peninsula, and even that they were about to occupy Seoul.

Accordingly, in mid-August two colonels in United States Army G-3 (Plans and Operations) drew a zonal boundary along the 38th parallel, which lies not far north of Seoul, with the aim of implementing the previous agreement in principle on occupation zones and giving Japan some protection against possible Soviet pressures. This boundary was then communicated to and ultimately accepted by the Soviet Union, even though its forces in Korea advanced south of it in some places and were initially reluctant to fall back to it after the arrival of U.S. occupation forces (the Seventh Division at first, and later also the Fortieth and Sixth Divisions) in South Korea, which began on September 8.

DISENGAGEMENT

The ensuing U.S. Military Government of South Korea was a difficult, confused, and not very successful operation, except that it prevented mass starvation in an economy dislocated by war and the partition of the country into two occupation zones that did not trade with one another. After an election in South Korea sponsored by the United Nations, the United States terminated its occupation on August 15, 1948, in favor of the Republic of Korea under President Syngman Rhee. No such development was possible in North Korea, where the Soviets were still in control and refused the United Nations the opportunity to sponsor an election.

At that time there appeared to be little future for a U.S. role on the continent of Asia. The Chinese Nationalists were obviously losing their long civil war with the Communists, who in 1949 proclaimed a firm tilt toward the Soviet Union and (on October 1) the establishment of the People's Republic of China. As for Korea, the new Rhee government soon began to experience difficulties—economic hardships, leftist-inspired riots, pressures from North Korea, and the like—so serious that the Truman administration, with the concurrence of its military advisers, decided that South Korea was indefensible, not worth defending, and likely to collapse from internal stresses even without an invasion from the North. Accordingly, the remaining U.S. troops were withdrawn by the end of 1949, leaving behind a civilian relief program and a small military aid program for the benefit of a very lightly armed South Korean military establishment, really a constabulary. Like Taiwan at that time, South Korea was to be allowed to fall to its Communist adversaries if they chose to attack it and proved able to overrun it. In keeping with this policy, the House of Representatives almost failed to approve an economic aid appropriation for South Korea in January 1950.

REINVOLVEMENT

U.S. disengagement from the fate of South Korea precipitated an invasion on June 25, 1950, by the heavily armed and well-trained forces of North Korea, a Communist regime known to be a Soviet satellite. The startled Truman administration was unanimous in viewing the invasion not only as a threat to South Korea and Japan but as a probable forerunner of a general Soviet-directed offensive against non-Communist Asia, and possibly also against Western Europe. There was no real disagreement with the proposition that the previous decision not to defend South Korea must be reversed, and it was reversed. By the time South Korea was finally cleared of Communist forces and an armistice agreement was signed on July 27, 1953, some 35,000 U.S. and many times as many South Korean lives had been lost, and the United States was committed to the support of an independent, non-Communist, and hopefully democratic South Korean state to a much greater extent than ever before.

Simultaneously with the conclusion of the armistice agreement, the 16 U.N. members with troops in Korea signed a declaration, the terms of which had been basically agreed on as early as January 1952, to the effect that the consequences of another North Korean attack on South Korea would be "so grave that, in all probability, it would not be possible to confine hostilities within the frontiers of Korea."

On October 1, 1953, the United States and the Republic of Korea signed a mutual defense treaty, or treaty of alliance. It is typical of such U.S. treaties of that period in that it obligates each party to "act to meet" an attack on the other "in accordance with its constitutional processes," a qualification inserted in deference to Congress. The treaty can be terminated on one-year's notice; since no such notice has been given or is likely to be given, the treaty remains in force and will presumably remain in force for the indefinite future. Unlike the People's Republic of China in recent years, North Korea continues to display aggressive tendencies that require containment by the United States, and there is no significant school of U.S. political opinion that advocates terminating the mutual security treaty with the Republic of Korea for the purpose of improving relations with the latter's Communist adversary, as there was in the case of the now-lapsed mutual defense treaty with the Republic of China on Taiwan.

From the end of the war to about 1970, and in spite of the Republic of Korea's geopolitical handicaps including the nearness of Seoul to the Demilitarized Zone, the security of South Korea seemed to be comfortably assured by the United States-Republic of Korea alliance. The North made no overt move to take advantage of the year of confusion in the South that followed the fall of Syngman Rhee in April 1960, although fear that it might was a major reason for the military coup of May 1961. The increase in the rate of infiltration and the number of armed incidents in the late 1960s was not great enough to pose a truly serious threat to the security of the South.

THE NIXON DOCTRINE AND KOREA

By 1969, the first year in office of the Nixon administration, the impact of the Vietnam War on U.S. public and official opinion had begun to produce a significant reduction of the level of willingness felt by the United States not only to commit armed forces to combat on the mainland of Asia but even to maintain them there. According to the famous Nixon Doctrine, announced in mid-1969, the United States would "keep its treaty commitments" to its allies, but primarily with sea and air power rather than with ground forces as it had in Vietnam. The conduct of ground combat, including counterinsurgency, in the future would be the responsibility of the allies.

The logic of this policy inevitably bore on the presence of U.S. ground forces in South Korea. In September 1970 Vice-President Spiro Agnew visited the Republic of Korea and made it clear that one of two U.S. divisions stationed there, the Seventh, would soon be withdrawn, and in fact it left in 1971. Less formally, he indicated that the other division, the Second, would be out by 1975; this did not actually happen, probably because it might have had a dangerously negative effect on South Korean morale and the aggressive tendencies of North Korea in the context of the fall of non-Communist Indochina.

More or less by analogy with Vietnamization, the application of the Nixon Doctrine to South Korea included a program of

"Koreanization," or in other words of modernizing the Republic of Korea's armed forces, essentially with U.S. equipment paid for by Seoul. During the first so-called Force Improvement Plan (1971–75), however, South Korean defense expenditures, which were already heavy, rose at only a fairly slow rate.

The sense of urgency was considerably heightened on both sides by the fall of non-Communist Indochina in 1975 and a visit by Kim Il Song to Beijing in mid-April of the same year, even though he was disappointed in his hope that his Chinese allies would give him enough aid and support to enable him to do to South Korea what his Vietnamese colleagues were doing to South Vietnam. With the beginning of the Second Force Improvement Plan (1975–80), Seoul's defense expenditures began to grow at a much more rapid rate and were projected to reach $5 billion for the five-year period, a figure equal to 6 percent of GNP; the actual figure for 1980 was $3.9 billion, substantially higher than planned.

THE UNITED STATES AND KOREA IN THE POSTWAR PERIOD

In the years following the Korean War, contacts between the United States and Korea expanded at all levels. These contacts, to be sure, had not been negligible even before the war. There had been some Korean migration to Hawaii and the West Coast. Syngman Rhee and some other leaders of the movement for Korean independence had made their base on U.S. soil, and the movement in Korea itself had been considerably influenced by the Wilsonian principle of self-determination.

After the substantial relaxation of U.S. immigration restrictions in the mid-1960s, a sizable Korean community (about 400,000) began to emerge in the United States, mainly on the East and West coasts. Many of these immigrants were highly educated professionals and skilled workers who made a significant contribution to their new country of residence. Among the postwar organizations that stimulated cultural, educational, and scientific exchange between the United States and Korea were the Asia Foundation in San Francisco, the East West Center of the University of Hawaii, and the U.S.-supported Korean Institute of Science and Technology (the largest organization of its kind in the Far East). One of the most popular U.S. television serials, M*A*S*H, dealt with the Korean War and generally portrayed its Korean characters and their culture in a very sympathetic light. Much more controversy was inevitably attached to the dynamic Unification Church headed by the Korean Reverend Sun Myung Moon.

Partly because of the U.S. role as protector of South Korea and its main source of economic and military aid, the United States has exerted a much greater influence on the South Korean political system since 1945 than has any other country. This influence has gone beyond mere superficialities and has extended to constitutions and elections. The political opposition—the New Democratic party, the intellectuals and students, and elements of the Christian community— tended to feel a rather strong attraction for the substance of U.S. political life and to believe that it was not only desirable but possible to introduce a parliamentary democracy of the Western type into South Korea in the reasonably near future; the establishment, remembering the turbulence following the fall of Syngman Rhee in 1960 and the menacing proximity of North Korea, disagreed.

For obvious geographic, cultural, historical, and economic reasons, Japan rapidly assumed a leading position in South Korea's external economic relations once the political relationship between the two neighbors was normalized in 1965. On the other hand, the United States too continued to play an important role in the remarkable growth of the South Korean economy beginning in the early and mid-1960s. U.S. grant aid, both economic and military, was phased out during this period as unnecessary, but U.S. development loans and private trade and investment continued on a significant scale.

The application of the Nixon Doctrine to Korea, and especially the withdrawal of the Seventh Division, worried the Park government and led it to consider how it would improve its image and increase its influence in the United States as a safeguard for the future of its most important external relationship. It fell in readily with a suggestion, made in complete innocence by a senior and respected U.S. official, that it ought to cultivate Congress and not merely the executive branch. The result was a systematic but poorly conceived and inevitably counterproductive campaign to woo members of Congress through methods that included outright bribery. The campaign lasted for most of the first half of the 1970s, and the exposure, investigation, and repercussions occupied much of the second half of the 1970s. Before it was over, the Koreagate affair, as it was generally called in the United States, became very disconcerting to the U.S. public.

During roughly the same period, another issue that unfavorably affected the U.S. image of South Korea was the record of the Park government on human rights. The role of the KCIA under President Park in containing opposition and punishing dissidents was well known, both within Korea and abroad, and was frequently brutal. During the 1970s feeling on this question in the United States, by no means all of it on the part of the left, mounted fairly rapidly, especially among educated people, but it was often overlooked that the level of human rights was much lower in North Korea—which, of course, was not a U.S. ally.

Public opinion polls taken in the United States in the late 1970s showed that, for reasons that included the memory of the Korean War, the continuing presence of U.S. troops in South Korea, and the Koreagate and human rights issues, the U.S. public's image of South Korea was rather unfavorable as compared with its image of other allies of the United States.

THE CARTER ADMINISTRATION AND KOREA

The administration of President Jimmy Carter was a rather populist one, at least by contrast with its Republican predecessors, and there was nothing surprising in the fact that from the beginning it took a dim view of the Park government and wanted to reduce the level of the U.S. commitment to the security of the Republic of Korea. President Carter himself was evidently influenced by the issues mentioned in the preceding section, the human rights question in particular, and probably also by a dislike acquired from his naval background for the idea of ground forces engaging in land warfare.

Well before coming into office, President Carter had begun to advocate the withdrawal of the Second Division from South Korea, a step that as we have seen had been decided on by the Nixon administration but then shelved during the Ford administration. Some of Carter's advisers wanted a complete withdrawal of the U.S. military presence in South Korea, evidently as a preliminary to a cutting of the U.S. security tie with the Republic of Korea. In the spring of 1977 the Carter administration announced its intention of pulling out the Second Division by 1982, on the ground that the international environment was not threatening to the Republic of Korea and that its armed forces had reached or would soon reach the point of being able to cope with a North Korean attack with no more than sea and air support from the United States; the withdrawal was to be implemented in stages and was said to be subject to revision if events required. The decision to withdraw the Second Division was supposedly to be compensated by an acceleration of military sales to the Republic of Korea, but the credibility of this pledge was impaired by Congress's slowness to act on account of the Koreagate scandal and the announcement in May 1977 of new regulations barring the sale of major new weapons to foreign countries except for those having "major defense treaties" with the United States; South Korea was not included in this category.

From the beginning the plan to withdraw the Second Division was controversial, except of course in North Korea. In South Korea both the government and the opposition objected strongly. The Japanese and several other Asian governments were far from enthusiastic. Major General John K. Singlaub, chief of staff of United States Forces Korea, was forced to retire in the spring of 1977 for having said to a U.S. reporter that withdrawal of the Second Division would increase the chances of another war in Korea, a view that was evidently shared by most if not all of his colleagues.

At about that time, U.S. military intelligence, no longer compelled to focus on Indochina, began to reassess the strength of the North Korean armed forces. The conclusion was that they were considerably stronger than had previously been realized; they included, for example, two armored divisions whose existence had been unknown prior to the intelligence reassessment. Important figures in both the executive branch and in Congress, notably Chairman John Glenn of the Subcommittee on East Asian and Pacific Affairs of the Senate Committee on Foreign Relations, urged in 1978–79 that in the light of these findings the Carter administration reconsider its decision to withdraw the Second Division. President Park undoubtedly argued along the same lines when President Carter visited Seoul at the end of June 1979.

Bowing with reluctance to the more or less inevitable, Dr. Brzezinski announced on July 20, 1979, that the withdrawal of the Second Division would be postponed at least until 1981, or in other words until after the next U.S. presidential election.

Much as President Carter disliked President Park, he and his administration were not pleased with the developments in South Korea that followed Park's assassination on October 26, 1979. As in 1960–61, the United States officially indicated a strong preference for civilian leadership and a dislike for the rise to power of a military elite, which in turn was inevitably irritated by its realization of the U.S. attitude. In particular, the U.S. government objected to the use of some South Korean combat troops in a political role in December 1979 without the prior permission of General John Wickham, the

U.S. commander of the recently established Combined Forces Command. The United States continued to display a negative official attitude toward the trend of South Korean politics during the ensuing year, and especially toward the proclamation of martial law in May 1980 and the sentencing to death for sedition later in the year of the well-known opposition leader Kim Dae Jung, whom President Carter publicly urged the South Korean government to spare.

THE REAGAN ADMINISTRATION AND KOREA

President Reagan indicated before his election that he would not openly press foreign governments on human rights as the Carter administration had done and also, at least by implication, that he would try harder to cooperate with U.S. allies. His election was understandably welcomed in Seoul, at least in official circles.

Between his election and his inauguration, Reagan publicly urged that Kim Dae Jung's life be spared, and in order to prevent this stand from being mistaken in Seoul for pure posturing he communicated the same message privately to the South Korean government through an aide. There is little doubt that this view, reinforced by similar expressions from leaders of other governments including the Japanese, had an influence on President Chun Doo Hwan, who for reasons of both domestic and foreign policy wanted an invitation to visit the United States although he was understandably unwilling to put himself in the position of paying a price for it, such as the commutation of Kim Dae Jung's sentence. The outcome was as satisfactory to both sides as could be imagined: on January 21, the day after his inauguration, President Reagan invited President Chun to visit the United States; on January 24, President Chun announced the lifting of martial law and the commutation of Kim Dae Jung's sentence to one of life imprisonment.

Accordingly, Chun's visit to Washington (February 1-3, 1981) took place under circumstances that were as favorable as possible. In the communiqué issued at the end of the visit, the U.S. government stated that it had "no plans to withdraw U.S. ground forces from the Korean peninsula" and promised to sell South Korea "appropriate weapons systems and defense industry technology," to "remain a reliable supplier of nuclear fuel, generation equipment, and power technology," to give favorable consideration to South Korea's "special needs for rice imports" (because of the unusually cold and wet summer weather of 1980), and (as the Carter administration had also pledged) not to establish contacts with North Korea without the participation of the Republic of Korea or without reciprocation by the Soviet Union and the People's Republic of China (North Korea's allies) toward Seoul. The two sides agreed to improve their consultation and cooperation in a number of fields, and President Reagan accepted an invitation to visit South Korea at some mutually convenient time.

Not long afterward, indications began to appear that the Reagan administration would authorize the sale of F-16s to the Republic of Korea, as Seoul had wanted for some time.

The atmosphere of United States-South Korea relations had improved enormously since the end of the Carter administration. In such an atmosphere, it would be easier for people in the United States to remember what the essentials of the U.S. interest in the Republic of Korea are: the geopolitical and strategic importance of the Korean peninsula to the entire Northeast Asian region; the "credibility" of U.S. commitments, weakened by the U.S. disengagement from Indochina and to a lesser extent by its disengagement from Taiwan; good faith with a country and people for whose survival as a non-Communist independent nation the United States assumed ultimate responsibility in 1950; and the role of the Republic of Korea as a major trading partner of the United States.

THE UNITED STATES AND KOREA IN 1982

Following a visit by Secretary of Defense Weinberger to South Korea in late March 1982, the first major event in the celebration of the centennial year in U.S.-South Korean relations, which was largely ignored in the United States' but not in the South Korean media, was a visit in late April by Vice-President Bush. Under tight security precautions due to demonstrations by the opposition, he brought messages of support and of continuing hope for political liberalization. On May 11 President Reagan addressed a message to the South Korean people including the statement that "We will stand by our friends in Korea."

In late June newly appointed Foreign Minister Lee Bum Suk visited Washington for talks with newly resigned Secretary of State Alexander Haig. It appears that the U.S. government declined to involve itself in the South Korean-Japanese loan negotiations then in progress.

2

KOREA'S POLITICAL DEVELOPMENT

As would be expected on the basis of Korea's location, its political development has been a process of interaction between its own tradition and influences exerted by its neighbors, among which in recent years the United States must logically be included.

THE KOREAN POLITICAL TRADITION

Presumably because of Korea's comparatively small size and relative ethnic and cultural homogeneity, and in spite of the existence of a high level of village autonomy of the kind normal in Asia, regionalism has not been an important influence on Korean political development. Korea was probably the most centralized and uniformly administered state in traditional Asia. On the other hand, it did not possess a fully autocratic political system, in the sense that the king was neither divinized like the Japanese emperor nor considered at least potentially absolute like the Chinese emperor. As a rule power was exercised collectively rather than individually. There was a strong aristocracy, and competing cliques of nobles and officials, normally based on personal loyalties, struggled for power and influence. Indeed, factionalism entered the lifeblood of Korean politics at an early date and has never really been eliminated. There was no feudal military class as in Japan. Unity was maintained to an impressive degree, but more on the basis of social consensus than on centralized political power.

The relative lack of strong central leadership, combined with geographic proximity to China and the enormous prestige of traditional Chinese culture, opened Korea to influence from its huge and self-confident neighbor to the west. From the early centuries of the Christian Era, and most of all in modern times under the Yi dynasty, Buddhism, Confucianism, the complex Chinese writing system, the comparably complex Chinese civil service system, as well as other features of Chinese culture exerted a profound effect. Since even countries subject to little or no Chinese influence other than political and military, such as Mongolia, were often tributaries—meaning protectorates, more or less—of the Chinese Empire, it was practically inevitable that Korea, which experienced such a wide range of Chinese influence, should have been a regular Chinese tributary. This was especially the case under the Yi dynasty, whose later kings in fact tended to become overly dependent on their Chinese connection for their legitimacy and therefore insufficiently creative and responsive in their approach to the political needs of their own people.

By the end of the nineteenth century, Korea had grown so weak, politically and militarily, that it could offer little resistance to annexation by Japan in 1910 except for some stout but ineffective guerrilla warfare and a peaceful nationwide demonstration for independence in March 1919. Japanese rule gained only minimal acceptance from the Koreans; in 1936, for example, the Japanese flag on the shirt of a Korean who had won the marathon at the Olympic Games was obliterated from the photographs published in two Korean newspapers, which were promptly suppressed by the Japanese authorities. Since the Koreans neither accepted Japanese rule nor had the opportunity to govern themselves, either in the traditional manner or some other, their political development marked time or if anything retrogressed. Most Koreans wanted liberation from Japanese rule and independence; the only possible source from which they could come was the victory of the Allied powers over Japan in World War II.

NORTH KOREAN COMMUNISM

Everywhere the Soviet army went at the end of the war, it set up not independent but satellite regimes. Only two of these succeeded in breaking away from Soviet control to any significant degree during Stalin's lifetime. One was Yugoslavia, which had an independent-minded guerrilla leadership and did not border on the Soviet Union; the other was North Korea, which had a similar leadership and, although it did border on the Soviet Union, was the only one of the satellites, then or later, to get involved in a major war fought at least partly in the Soviet interest and to gain in the process the necessary leverage and freedom of maneuver, largely due to Chinese intervention in the war.

As in the other satellites, the Soviet occupation authorities in North Korea worked through local agents, who of course were for the most part Communists or at least leftists. In the finest Korean tradition, however, the Korean Communist movement was highly factional, the main groupings as of 1945 being the Manchurian, Soviet, Yenan (or Chinese), and domestic factions. The Soviets selected as their instrument a young ex-guerrilla chosen from the Manchurian faction, who took the name of Kim Il Song. The Soviets of course gave orders to him—a situation with which later developments were to indicate that he was never happy—and he in turn, under their supervision, gave orders to the political mechanisms at whose head the Soviets placed him. As in all Communist countries, these were essentially two in number: the ruling party, the Korean Workers Party, formed in 1949 through the formal amalgamation of the four factions, and the state, known officially as the Democratic People's Republic of Korea, established in 1948 at about the time of the Soviet military withdrawal.

The Korean War (during which Moscow needed him or at any rate Kim Il Song and his Chinese allies together roughly as much as he needed Moscow) and Chinese intervention in the war gave Kim Il Song his opportunity to begin freeing himself from Soviet domination. By the end of the war, through a series of masterly and ruthless maneuvers that must have earned him at least grudging respect from Stalin, he and his personal supporters, who were mostly drawn from the Manchurian faction, had eliminated the leadership of the domestic faction and made an impressive start at purging or at least curbing the Soviet and Yenan factions. This process was completed in the late 1950s, when the beginning of the Sino-Soviet dispute, even though it was virtually unperceived in the non-Communist world, made it difficult for either Moscow or Peking to exert much influence on North Korea and easier for Kim Il Song to play them against each other, or perhaps more accurately to maneuver in the political gap that was opening up between his two giant patrons.

The termination of decisive Soviet influence on North Korea did not lead Kim Il Song and his colleagues to revert to a more traditional or otherwise more acceptable political system. As Communists, they had learned from the Soviets how to operate the most effective and self-perpetuating totalitarian system the modern world has known: a "proletarian" dictatorship by a Communist party apparatus, supported by a massive political police and powerful armed forces.

In the mid-1950s, Kim Il Song launched a campaign for "self-reliance" (*chuch'e*, literally self-identity) for North Korea. This campaign is still in effect, at least as a slogan. Among its main features have been a colossal "cult of personality" focused of course on Kim Il Song; a further tightening of his personal political control over his regime; an ambitious—in fact, overambitious—economic development program stressing self-reliance in theory but in practice heavily dependent on foreign (ultimately non-Communist as well as Communist) credits and technology; and an increasingly awe-inspiring military buildup under the umbrella of alliances—defensive, to be sure—concluded with the Soviet Union and the People's Republic of China in mid-1961.

This military buildup has been so impressive that the question of its probable purpose or purposes naturally arises. One obvious possibility is the deterrence of a South Korean attack, with or without U.S. support, a highly improbable contingency but one whose likelihood may be significantly overestimated in Pyongyang. Another, more plausible, is the capability to exploit aggressively any military opportunity, such as a U.S. withdrawal or a "revolutionary" situation in South Korea. Third, the buildup may be intended to frighten the United States into withdrawal. Fourth, it may be designed to exert psychological leverage on South Korea and render it ultimately amenable to an accommodation on the North's terms; if so, the buildup has been counterproductive to date in this respect. Fifth, the buildup may reflect the considerable political influence of the North Korean military leadership and its frustration at the failure to achieve unification so far. Sixth, the buildup may be seen as compensation for the unreliability (as it is undoubtedly perceived in Pyongyang) of Soviet and Chinese support as a source of influence on Moscow and Peking and as a form of insurance for North Korea's survival in the event of a Sino-Soviet war. It is very likely that most, if not all, of these possible motives are in fact operative.

The North Korean military buildup and the extremely hostile political attitude toward the government in Seoul that accompanies it have been reciprocated, at a somewhat lower level of intensity, by the South, and the result has been a tense confrontation that is a constant threat to the peace not only of Korea itself but of the entire region. This threat cannot be eliminated under present conditions, but it is clear that neither South Korea nor any of the major powers wants another war in the peninsula. In the case of Germany, a somewhat similar, although actually less threatening, situation was eased in the early 1970s because the Soviet Union, which had continued to maintain troops in East Germany and had therefore managed to retain ultimate control, pushed the East Germans into an accommodation (the "German solution") with West Germany and into diplomatic relations with the United States. In the case of North Korea, there has of course been no Soviet military presence since 1948, no Soviet control since about five years after that, and therefore no possibility as yet of a "German solution," acceptable though it would be, at least as an interim situation, to South Korea and its foreign friends including the United States.

POLITICS UNDER SYNGMAN RHEE

South Korea was never a U.S. satellite after 1948, nor were its politics ever as intensely authoritarian as those of the North. On the other hand, neither were they those of a Western-style democracy.

Syngman Rhee, the first president of the Republic of Korea—or, to put it differently, president of the Republic of Korea during the period of the First Republic—was the best known and most influential single South Korean leader of his time both at home and abroad. He was in his mid-70s when he took office in 1948, a point in his favor considering the Korean respect for age. A man of great ability and profound familiarity with the political tradition and institutions of the West, he nevertheless believed firmly that Korea was not yet ready for Western-style democracy and, being of a basically authoritarian temperament, he tended to behave in a high-handed way toward his own people and above all toward his rivals. Bitterly anti-Japanese, he nevertheless tolerated in the police force men who had served under the Japanese and who retained much of their harshness. Rhee was anti-Communist to the point of doing his best to suppress any form of leftist activity in South Korea with brutal police methods and advocating a "march north" at the earliest opportunity to reunify Korea by force. Although basically opposed to the existence of political parties in Korea, he found that the constitution, which was parliamentary at least in form, made it advisable for him to establish (although not until November 1951) and lead the Liberal party, which remained essentially his personal following. The party developed no real life or program of its own and did not survive his fall in 1960.

Under extreme stress but with sharply intensified U.S. support, the Rhee government performed relatively well during the early months of the Korean War, and it benefited greatly from the inevitable upsurge of patriotic and anti-Communist feeling that occurred at that time in the South. In April 1952 the Republic of Korea was able to hold its first local elections.

On the other hand, once it was clear that South Korea would not be overrun from the North, serious friction began to develop between Rhee and the National Assembly, which started a move to amend the constitution so as to limit Rhee's immense power. In October 1951 Rhee struck back by launching a campaign for an amendment providing for the election of the president by direct popular vote rather than as heretofore by the National Assembly, which he feared would not reelect him (in 1952). This proposal aroused strong opposition and split even the Liberal party, and the assembly rejected the amendment by a wide margin in January 1952. There followed an all-out political struggle, culminating in the proclamation of martial law in some southern areas of the republic in May. Under intense pressure and intimidation, the assembly extended Rhee's term in June and amended the constitution in July to provide for direct election of the president. The Liberal party then nominated Rhee for a second term. He won overwhelmingly in August, even when allowance is made for considerable irregularities in the voting. The crisis had vindicated Rhee in a sense, but at a high cost in the eyes of other South Korean politicians and his U.S. allies.

Another crisis, less violent but perhaps even more serious in its implications, occurred in 1954. Rhee and his supporters in the National Assembly managed to pass, actually without the required two-thirds majority, a constitutional amendment removing the previous two-term limit on a president's tenure. This episode tended to polarize South Korean politics even more than before. Rhee and his followers sincerely believed that they were working for stability, not merely for Rhee's personal power, and that stability was vitally necessary in view of the shortcomings of the Korean political tradition and system and the continuing threat from the North; his opponents were trying not only to limit his power and preserve or increase their own but to foster parliamentary government and, at least in theory, democracy as well, if necessary at some cost to stability at least in the short run. In 1955 the opposition parties, except of course for the (illegal) leftist ones, united to form the Democratic party.

In the 1956 presidential election, the Democratic party and other anti-Rhee elements succeeded in eating into Rhee's majority and in actually defeating his vice-presidential candidate, Lee Ki Boong, who lost to the Democrat Chang Myon. In the National Assembly elections of May 1958, the Democrats won slightly more than one-third of the seats. The aging and increasingly autocratic Rhee and the more dictatorially minded of his supporters responded, beginning later in 1958, with a series of high-handed measures, both legal and extralegal, designed to crush the opposition in the name of national security.

Rhee and his supporters were so alarmed at the growing strength of the opposition that they doubted whether Rhee would win a free election in 1960 to a fourth term. Accordingly, they resorted to blatant rigging of the election, which was held on March 15. This time Lee Ki Boong, although seriously ill, was "elected" as Rhee's vice-president, and Rhee himself of course also "won."

The following month, April, seems to be a favorite time for student demonstrations everywhere in the Northern Hemisphere, and in South Korea there was plenty for students to demonstrate against. Virtually for the first time in the republic's history, there were student demonstrations. The government retaliated with violent police repression that caused hundreds of casualties, the army remained essentially neutral, the demonstrations grew more violent, and on April 26 Rhee resigned. The First Republic had come to an end under conditions that were not encouraging for the political future of the country.

THE 1960–61 REVOLUTION

The immediate successor to the Rhee government was an interim regime headed by Ho Chung, a supporter of Rhee who had been appointed foreign minister only shortly before. During his brief tenure the constitution was amended by the National Assembly to institute a cabinet rather than a presidential form of government, the idea being that a cabinet system would be more effective in preventing a dictatorship.

The real successor to Rhee, however, or in other words the Second Republic, did not emerge until after the National Assembly elections of July 1960, which gave the Democratic party a majority of over two-thirds; Rhee's Liberal party had almost collapsed.

United only by its opposition to Rhee, the Democratic party now began to engage in factional quarrels that prevented it from gaining the respect even of anti-Rhee elements such as the students. It was only by a narrow margin in the new National Assembly that

Chang Myon became premier in August 1960. Although an honest and intelligent man, he was cautious, short on political experience, and therefore a weak leader in relation to the demands of the situation.

The next several months saw a further polarization of South Korean politics and society. The Chang government stood almost helpless in the middle, with his own party split into two contending factions, while tension grew between the (non-Communist) left (intellectuals and students as well as politicians) and the right (mainly former Rhee supporters and some of the military leadership). Chang would not ally with either side and retained the support of neither. The left resented his unwillingness to take action against the Rhee supporters through retroactive legislation. The economy was in very poor condition as a result of war, inflation, and mismanagement by the Rhee regime; and Chang's measures to improve it (such as a public works program and a currency devaluation), even though supported by special U.S. aid allocations, did not have time to pay off. In the new and heady atmosphere of freedom, there was considerable labor unrest and almost continuous demonstrations for several months. It was during this period that the two divergent trends in South Korean politics that have dominated it ever since emerged: the desire for freedom and the demand for order.

Many of the students, excited by their key role in the overthrow of Rhee, became politically active again. They tended to believe that South Korea's ills were caused not only by Rhee but but U.S. influence and by the partition of the country, and they showed a strong interest in unification through contacts with the North. Pyongyang naturally welcomed this development and on November 24, 1960 proposed a North-South conference to bring about a confederation of the two Koreas, each to have an army of not more than 100,000 men. Although the Chang government promptly rejected this idea, the student activists reacted with approval, and their enthusiasm evoked a strong reaction from the right. The early spring of 1961 was a period of considerable political disorder.

The radicals consciously tried to hold their activities below the level that would evoke what they most feared, a military coup, but they miscalculated. A portion of the military executed a coup on May 16, 1961, due to the combination of a weak government, student activism, and the attempted involvement of the North in the situation, in addition to discontent with government by civilian politicians that had begun to emerge among the military in the late Rhee period and of course the normal temptation to translate potential political power into actual control.

THE THIRD AND FOURTH REPUBLICS

This being the first time the South Korean military had assumed power, the coup had aspects of a revolution and was referred to as such by its leaders. Under the umbrella of martial law, which lasted until late 1962, political parties and demonstrations were banned, and some political figures prominent under the First and Second Republics—but not Syngman Rhee, who had left the country—were tried and executed or imprisoned for corruption, rigging the 1960 presidental election, and similar offenses. Pressures for conformity were exerted on the press and to a lesser extent on the students, who had acquired considerable political importance since early 1960.

The official attitude of the United States toward these events was one of explicit displeasure at the forcible displacement of a civilian by a military regime and at the use of Korean troops under the U.N. Command, which was headed by a U.S. general, in connection with the coup. U.S. objections probably had something to do with the regime's announcement in August 1961 that a civilian government would be installed in mid-1963.

The general who rapidly emerged as the leader of the Third Republic was Park Chung Hee. As a young man he had served in the Imperial Japanese Army, an experience that probably contributed to the strong authoritarian tendencies he displayed when in power. As it was explained to me in the early 1970s by a well-informed non-Korean source, he preserved and enhanced his personal power by using one lieutenant after another without allowing any of them to become his heir apparent, much less his rival. This was especially true with respect to the director of the Korean Central Intelligence agency (KCIA), which was created shortly after the coup as a security service with not only external but also sweeping domestic responsibilities and powers; together with the army, it formed Park's main power base. In 1964 the founder of the KCIA, a powerful military figure named Kim Jong Pil, was eased out of office, essentially so that he would not become a threat to Park; a decade later it was the turn of KCIA Director Lee Hu Rak, who had also served as chief secretary to President Park, for basically the same reason.

At the end of 1963, at the time martial law was lifted, political parties were allowed once more and naturally began to be formed. The ruling elite established its own party, the Democratic Republican party, and its leaders, including Park, retired from the army to be able to take part in politics as civilians. This move was apparently part of a conscious effort not to repeat the experience of Burma, where the military leadership under General Ne Win had seized power in 1958, returned it to a civilian government under U Nu in 1960, and felt compelled to resume it in 1962. After some serious controversies with the opposition parties over the procedure and timing of the installation of a civilian government, a presidential election was held in October 1963. Park, the Democratic Republican party's candidate, won with 47 percent of the popular vote; the principal opposition candidate, the respected civilian Yun Po Sun, got 45 percent, and if the opposition parties had united behind him he would presumably have won. National Assembly elections in December 1963 gave the Democratic Republican party a large majority.

One of the first problems to which Park turned his attention as president was the state of the economy, which after more than a decade of political turmoil and war, and in spite of massive U.S. aid, was racked by shortages, renewed inflation, slow growth, and large negative payments balances. By this time the Japanese economy had begun its spectacular recovery from its own ordeal, and it was in that direction that the Park government turned for help, in spite of the intense anti-Japanese feeling still present in Korea. Negotiations with Japan began in 1964 and resulted the following year in the establishment of diplomatic relations and the conclusion of a commercial agreement, which was followed by a rapid growth of Japanese trade with and investment in South Korea that, together with the Park government's policies and able Korean entrepreneurship, generated a process of impressive export-based economic growth. In both countries there was strong political opposition, especially on the part of South Korean students and Japanese opposition parties, to the South Korean-Japanese rapprochement. In the South Korean case, the Park government thought it necessary to declare martial law in July 1964, but the political situation became much calmer in late 1965.

Another important development of 1965 was the Park government's decision, taken under U.S. prodding, to send troops—two divisions, as it turned out—to fight in Vietnam. Although of course this step did not alter the outcome, the two divisions performed well. Since Seoul had chosen to support the United States in this way in the expectation of enhancing the U.S. sense of commitment to the security of the Republic of Korea, there was especially good reason for the disappointment felt in South Korea when the Nixon administration began in 1970 what it intended at that time to be the complete withdrawal of U.S. ground forces from South Korea.

In preparation for the presidential election of 1967, the opposition parties merged to form the New Democratic party, with Yun Po Sun as its candidate. Park won again by a much larger margin than in 1963, and the Democratic Republican party won 130 of the 175 seats in the National Assembly. In 1969, using as a pretext the tense atmosphere created by intensified North Korean pressures such as the attempted raid on the Blue House in January 1968, Park succeeded by irregular methods in getting the constitution amended by the National Assembly to permit him a third term. This he won in 1971 by 53 percent of the popular vote (a margin of almost 1 million votes) over the New Democratic party candidate Kim Dae Jung, who won 45 percent, after a campaign in which Park indicated that he would not seek a fourth term and would groom a capable successor.

This promise was not kept, not only because Park had acquired a strong taste for personal power but also because he believed that he alone could steer the Republic of Korea safely through the treacherous waters that he thought he saw ahead. As his statements during this period indicated, he was dissatisfied with the level of political order and the rate of economic growth in South Korea, especially against the backdrop of what appeared to him to be an unstable and dangerous international environment. The Nixon administration's decision to withdraw all U.S. forces from Vietnam and U.S. ground forces from South Korea and its interest in improving Sino-U.S. relations, which Peking reciprocated, had begun to alter significantly the international climate in the Far East. The U.S. commitment to South Korea seemed less dependable. North and South Korea came under pressure, partly from the logic of events and partly from their allies acting behind the scenes, to negotiate with each other. In the South Korean case, public opinion also played a part; for some years one of the main charges against Park by the opposition and the students had been that he was doing too little toward unification with the North.

In 1971–72 North-South talks accordingly got under way, secretly and at a high level, and resulted in a dramatic joint announcement issued on July 4, 1972. Although the public negotiations that followed this announcement were abortive, the episode left Park with a suspicion that South Korea might be at a disadvantage in a prolonged political contest with the North unless it were more tightly and effectively controlled from the top than it had been until then.

Park could not base the political changes that he considered desirable on a constitutional amendment, because the Democratic Republican party at that time had less than a two-thirds majority in the National Assembly. In October 1972, accordingly, he proclaimed martial law, suspended most of the constitution, forbade political activity, closed the universities temporarily, and imposed press censorship. Public expectation of a restoration of constitutional government by the end of the year, on the basis of promises made by Park at least partly because of U.S. pressure, was severely disappointed when he unveiled instead a new order based on the Yushin (Revitalizing Reform) Constitution. Under the new constitution, the president was permitted an indefinite number of six-year terms, was to be chosen indirectly by a popularly elected electoral college known as the National Conference for Unification, from which members of political parties were barred, and had the power to nominate to the National Assembly one-third of its total membership (73 out of 219 seats at that time). He could also dissolve the assembly at will and take emergency measures on his own authority. In a referendum held a month later, 92 percent of the voters approved the new constitution and thus brought into existence the Fourth Republic. Park then lifted martial law and was elected president without opposition in December. The National Assembly elections of February 1973 gave the opposition parties a total of 42 percent of the popular vote as compared to 39 percent for the Democratic Republican party; the latter won half of the elected seats (73), however, because the opposition vote was divided and was concentrated disproportionately in the cities. With the support of the 73 appointed members, the government controlled a large majority of the total seats.

For all practical purposes Park was now a dictator, potentially for life. As usual in such cases, he tended to become more isolated, suspicious, and dictatorial; the opposition, which still existed, became increasingly disaffected while remaining essentially powerless. In August 1973 Kim Dae Jung was abducted from Japan by the KCIA and placed under house arrest on the charge of election violations, but in reality on account of his increasingly outspoken opposition to President Park. This episode produced a crisis in South Korean-Japanese relations, and another resulted from the assassination in 1974 of Park's popular wife by a Korean resident of Japan. After that Park grew more isolated than ever. Having already sacked the director of the KCIA, Lee Hu Rak, after the Kim Dae Jung affair, Park now increasingly entrusted effective control over security matters to his personal bodyguard and chief of the presidential security force, a hardline fanatic and martial arts expert named Cha Chi Chol.

For the next four years, Park's regime maintained its control with relatively little trouble, although it was shaken by the fall of Indochina in 1975 and then by President Carter's emphasis on human rights and his decision to withdraw the Second Division from South Korea. Trouble began again in 1978, when Park insisted on being elected to another presidential term, his second under the Yushin Constitution. There was a growing feeling, even on the part of many of his former supporters, that he had held office too long. The December 1978 National Assembly elections accordingly gave the New Democratic party, now led by Kim Young Sam, more elected seats than the Democratic Republican party, but the appointed members together with independents recruited into the Democratic Republican party still provided the government with an overall majority. There could be no doubt that there existed widespread opposition to Park and the Yushin Constitution. The question was whether, how, and when it could make itself effective.

3

ECONOMIC AND
SOCIAL TRANSFORMATION

Development, or modernization, is normally a destabilizing process in many respects, although it is probably less destabilizing than a relative absence of development in a situation of population growth and rising expectations. Much of the instability that marked the history of the Third and Fourth Korean Republics arose from a remarkably rapid developmental surge, which would probably have been even more remarkable if it could have embraced the whole of the peninsula instead of only half of it. From the standpoint of economic growth, the Republic of Korea joined the so-called Gang of Four—the dynamic Far Eastern economies, aside from the uniquely gigantic one of Japan—the others being Taiwan, Hong Kong, and Singapore.

ASSETS AND LIABILITIES

When Korea was divided in 1945, the industrial raw materials, heavy industry, hydroelectric potential, and timber passed largely to North Korea; the South inherited mainly some excellent natural harbors, the best agricultural land, considerable light industry, and well over half of the population, including most of those with modern skills in the services, as distinct from manufacturing, and several hundred thousand refugees from North Korea. U.S. aid alone prevented the impact of partition and war on this slender economic base from creating a catastrophe for South Korea during the 1950s and the early 1960s.

On the other hand, the picture was not entirely bleak; in some ways it resembled that of Japan in the early stages of its modernization.

There was great social cohesion arising from the combined influence of indigenous tradition and Chinese influence. The literacy rate was relatively high, and the agricultural labor force was disciplined—when not overexploited—industrious, and teachable, or more precisely capable of being retrained for industrial work. The politico-economic elite was able, energetic, and ambitious. The shortage of raw materials forced the elite to think of the export of processed goods rather than primary products, and therefore of economic transformation and industrialization, as the only available route to national development and power.

DEVELOPMENT STRATEGY

For several rather obvious reasons, it was inevitable that in South Korea, as in nineteenth century and for that matter contemporary Japan, the government should be heavily involved in planning and carrying out development, even though in both cases a large sphere was left to private initiative. There was, however, at least one basic difference between the Japanese and South Korean cases. In Japan, the Meiji leadership decided for political reasons against foreign borrowing and foreign investment and therefore had no choice but to squeeze the capital for early industrialization out of agriculture; one consequence was a large number of peasant revolts, which were ruthlessly suppressed. In South Korea, President Park, who was a man of humble peasant origins and evidently empathized with the rural population, considered such an approach both undesirable and unnecessary. Substantial private assets, illegally accumulated before 1961, were confiscated and provided the government with a valuable working fund. Credits could be obtained from the United States and other foreign sources, especially the World Bank, and direct investment would be forthcoming from the United States and (after 1965) from Japan, under conditions that did not endanger Korean independence. The other side of this coin was a problem of debt service, which has been a serious, although so far manageable, one for South Korea.

Another problem was that, although agriculture was not exploited as a major source of investment capital, neither was it given much constructive attention during the 1960s. While industry surged in the second half of the 1960s, the rural sector lagged badly, and much of the population of the countryside flooded into the cities in the hope of finding better conditions, but often with the effect of creating worse ones through urban overcrowding, a situation that is too common in developing countries. In the early 1970s, however, the government began to pay more attention to village life and agriculture, with good results.

Energized by government planning, protection, and participation, including credits on favorable terms to preferred types of industry, by able entrepreneurs, technology imports, and (after 1965) U.S. and other foreign credits and Japanese direct investment, the South Korean economy achieved and maintained an average annual GNP growth rate approximating the very high rate of 10 percent from the early 1960s until the late 1970s; annual per capita GNP rose to about $1,500, a highly respectable figure for an Asian country.

Like many other countries developing rapidly along more or less capitalist lines and with substantial reliance on foreign borrowing, South Korea acquired an inflation problem as well as considerable inequalities of income (Taiwan is one of the few such developing areas that has succeeded in maintaining reasonable income equality). A specific cause of inflation in the South Korean case was a tendency, especially in the late 1970s, for firms to grant wage increases in excess of government recommendations and of rises in productivity, presumably as a means of insuring against labor troubles during a period of skilled labor shortage. Inflation of course raised the prices of South Korea's exports, eroded its competitive position, and required currency devaluations from time to time.

An even more serious source of difficulty, it appears, was the Park government's response to the sharp increase in oil prices after 1973. Instead of stressing conservation and retrenchment like most other industrial countries dependent on imported oil, South Korea decided on an intensified export offensive across a rather wide range of manufactured, and especially heavy industrial, products. Some of these, such as heavy machinery and petrochemicals, were essentially noncompetitive in foreign markets, and the problem already created by inflation and higher oil prices tended to be made worse rather than better. Another round of price increases by OPEC at the end of the 1970s made South Korea's economic situation still more difficult. Then a pair of blows fell in 1980, following although not as a result of devaluation of the won by one-third early in the year: a poor harvest caused by unusually cold and wet summer weather, and serious political disorders. The GNP for 1980 showed a negative growth rate of about 5 percent. The South Korean economy was in trouble.

AGRICULTURE

In the late 1970s South Korea became roughly self-sufficient in basic food grains. In this and other respects, agricultural progress was impressive; in real terms, farm household incomes almost trebled between 1965 and 1977. To a considerable extent, this situation resulted from inputs so familiar that they need only be mentioned: expansion of the irrigated area, fertilizers, mechanization, and so on. But two specific features of South Korea's agricultural development, both of them attributable to the Park government, deserve fuller discussion: reforestation and the New Community Movement.

U.S. viewers of "MASH" have an impression of the Korean landscape as one dominated by virtually deforested mountains. By the mid-1970s, however, the mountains were no longer bare. What must be one of the most successful reforestation programs in history, with incalculable and at least semipermanent benefits not only for the ecology and agriculture of the country but for the entire economy, had made the difference. The rural population had been mobilized to plant trees on the mountainsides and deterred by stiff penalties from cutting down more than the permitted quotas. This was possible because at the same time the rural population was provided, through such means as electrification and light industrial development, with alternative sources of fuel and construction material.

The New Community Movement (in Korean, *Saemaul Undong*) was about equally remarkable. It was launched by the Park government in 1971 to promote development and avoid discontent in the rural areas by encouraging self-help and cooperation, supplemented by an increased level of investment from both public and private sources. Farmers were urged and helped to reclaim land, improve roads, raise livestock, grow cash crops, start local industries, upgrade housing, install electricity, and the like.

INFRASTRUCTURE AND ENERGY

Most of South Korea's 15 seaports, the two most important of which are Pusan and Inchon, acquired greatly improved facilities under the Third and Fourth Republics; the merchant fleet was similarly enlarged and modernized. Korean Air Lines became a major international operation. The rather good railway net left by the Japanese had already been repaired after the Korean War; during the Park regime it was expanded and to a considerable extent electrified, although it suffered to some extent, as in other countries, from competition from buses and trucks. The highway network was vastly improved, Seoul for example being linked by expressways with Inchon, Pusan, and other key cities. In 1974 Korea became the first Asian country outside Japan to operate a subway system (in Seoul). (There are now subways in Beijing, Pyongyang, and Hong Kong as well.)

One of the major economic policies of the Park government was to encourage the consumption of oil, rather than South Korea's fairly modest resources of anthracite coal; refining began in 1964. The result was that by the end of the 1970s oil accounted for about 60 percent of all energy consumption, and coal for about 30 percent, the rest being derived mainly from wood and charcoal and to a very small extent from hydroelectric and nuclear power. As already indicated, the economy acquired a massive Achilles heel in the form of dependence on imported OPEC oil, most of it from Saudi Arabia.

Like other countries in a similar situation, South Korea inevitably acquired an interest in nuclear power. Its ambition for something more than a modest level of development in this field, however, fell afoul of the official U.S. concern over the possibility of nuclear weapons proliferation, as Japan was to do later. Even though the Republic of Korea ratified the Nonproliferation Treaty in March 1975 and is not known to have had any plans for acquiring nuclear weapons, it was compelled shortly afterward by U.S. pressure to cancel an order for a French plutonium reprocessing plant.

INDUSTRY

Under effective governmental encouragement and private management and with the support of a highly teachable and generally disciplined labor force, the industrial sector of the South Korean economy developed rapidly in the 1960s and 1970s along lines that resembled, on a smaller scale of course, the experience of Japan. At first the emphasis was on labor-intensive light industries oriented toward the export market. Later (approximately from 1970) the emphasis shifted to capital- and technology-intensive industries, also oriented to a considerable extent toward the export market. As a relatively late starter on industrialization, South Korea had the advantage of a large pool of available foreign (mainly U.S. and Japanese) technology to draw on and adapt to its own needs, and it did this with great effectiveness.

Probably the pride of the South Korean industrial edifice is the government-sponsored Pohang Iron and Steel Company, which went into production in 1973 at Pohang, which lies on the best natural harbor on the east coast of South Korea. As of 1981, its capacity was 8.5 million metric tons per year. It is larger than any steel mill in the United States and almost as advanced as the most sophisticated mills in Japan. Its output has competed successfully with Japanese steel in some foreign markets.

FOREIGN TRADE

As already indicated, export expansion has been the basis of South Korea's development strategy; from the early 1960s to the late 1970s, exports grew at the phenomenal annual rate of about 40 percent. As for the composition of exports, the main categories to date have been textiles, electronics, footwear, steel, plywood, ships, and synthetic resin products; as for direction, the United States has been the biggest customer (about 30 percent), followed by Japan (20 percent), Western Europe (about 15 percent), and the Middle East (10 percent).

On the import side, raw materials (especially oil, iron ore, rubber, wool, logs, and copper ore) have accounted for a little over half of the total, and capital goods for about one-third. Japan has been the major supplier (about 40 percent of all South Korean imports, mainly capital goods), followed by the United States (20 percent, mainly raw materials) and the rest of Asia including the Middle East (also 20 percent). In spite of occasional U.S. complaints about barriers to U.S. trade and investment, South Korea has generally had an unfavorable trade balance with the United States.

From the early 1960s until the late 1970s, when South Korea's exports got into some trouble, its foreign transactions showed a favorable trade and payments balance. In 1980, however, inflated prices for South Korean exports, competition from other exporters (not only Japan and the rest of the Gang of Four but also the People's Republic of China), and the unfavorable image created abroad by political disorders in South Korea, plus higher OPEC prices, contributed to a trade deficit for the year of approximately $5 billion. In 1981, exports began to pick up, probably on account of devaluation, energetic efforts to diversify markets, and greater political stability.

EDUCATION

South Korea's highly developed educational system, in conjunction with study abroad (mainly in the United States and Western Europe) by many thousands of Koreans, has contributed indispensably over the years to the emergence of a large and highly competent elite in all fields related to economic and social transformation. The foundation of the system is six years of free compulsory education. All schools and colleges, private as well as public, are subject by law to a high degree of supervision and control by the Ministry of Education.

In its impact on the students, the South Korean educational system resembles the Japanese to a significant extent, but not completely. In both cases students, if they go to college, pass from a very demanding and competititve primary and secondary school environment into a considerably more relaxed one in which for a few years they can enjoy themselves, join voluntary associations, and perhaps demonstrate in a way that was impossible before and that they know will be out of the question once they start their careers. They may come into contact with and be influenced by Marxist ideas. In Japan this is easier and more common because of the large number of academic Marxists on the faculties. In South Korea, however, it is much more likely to come from reading and from thinking about the desirability of unification with the North. It is difficult for students to learn about unification but quite possible for them to cherish optimistic illusions about it, since they have no personal memory of the Korean War and little understanding of communism in practice.

In Japan a highly militant student organization known as the *Zengakuren* emerged in the 1960s and engaged in massive violent demonstrations until it was crushed by the police; a decade later there were more violent demonstrations aimed at preventing the opening of Narita Airport near Tokyo. If this is true in Japan, where students have few real grievances, it is not surprising that there have been student demonstrations in South Korea, where the students can logically consider that they have grievances quite apart from any objections they may feel to the political and social order as a whole. Their curricula and college administrations are subject to some political control through the Ministry of Education. By law the police can enter the campuses without a summons from or the permission of the administrations. Able-bodied male students are required to take military training, not very demanding to be sure, and after graduation to serve for three years as conscripts in the armed forces

or else in some officially approved public service occupation, sometimes while under military discipline.

Under these circumstances, it is not surprising that South Korean
college students have demonstrated, usually at times of political tension, and sometimes with considerable violence. Since such demonstrations run counter to the traditional Korean emphasis on "Confucian" social and political consensus, brought down one government
(in 1960), and undeniably tend to whet the "revolutionary" appetite
of the North Koreans, it is also not surprising, however regrettable it
may be, that the South Koreans have generally suppressed these
demonstrations with severity. Even so, in no case does the repression
appear to have been as brutal as, for example, in Mexico City in
1968 or Sri Lanka in 1971. Furthermore, official closing of some or
all colleges is definitely not the norm in South Korea, whereas it has
been fairly close to the norm in some countries of southern Asia.

4

KOREA IN CRISIS

Park Chung Hee's insistence on being elected to a second term under his Yushin Constitution in 1978, when he had already held office for three years longer than Syngman Rhee, created the impression that he intended to hold on to the presidency indefinitely. The discontent created by this situation expressed itself in widespread criticism of and sporadic demonstrations against the Yushin Constitution, open opposition to which had been banned under emergency decrees issued by President Park. A major political crisis was the result.

THE CHALLENGE FROM THE
NEW DEMOCRATIC PARTY

National Assembly elections were held in December 1978, for the first time in five years. Another first was the fact that the New Democratic party won a 1 percent plurality of the popular vote. Even though this result was not accurately reflected in the new assembly, where the government had a substantial majority consisting of the elected Democratic Republican party members and the Yujonghoe (the appointed one-third of the total membership), the New Democratic party understandably began to play a more active role suited to its status as the major opposition party and its support from the electorate.

This trend became especially noticeable after the election of a new and vigorous president of the New Democratic party, Kim Young Sam, in May 1979. In June he angered the government by proposing that he meet with Kim Il Song, with or without the participation of representatives of the Democratic Republican party.[1] At the end of the same month his importance, or at any rate his own sense of it, was enhanced by President Carter's insistence on meeting him during the presidential visit to South Korea. Kim Young Sam's behavior during this period suggested to some observers that he hoped that a combination of the New Democratic party's popular base, unrest among students and other antigovernment elements, official U.S. favor, and perhaps acceptance by North Korea as the spokesman for the South might enable him to challenge the Park government or even bring it down in somewhat the way that the Rhee government had been overthrown in 1960. He indicated that he hoped for the political neutrality of the army, also as in 1960, if such a crisis developed. Kim's statements along these lines, which grew stronger as the confrontation between the New Democratic party and the government unfolded, obviously constituted a serious challenge to President Park, as well as a violation of various constitutional and legal prohibitions against activity of this sort.

In August 1979 some 200 female textile workers, who had been discharged by their employer as a result of bankruptcy and had then been evicted by police from their dormitories, moved into the headquarters of the New Democratic party, which welcomed them and took up their cause. On August 11 the police stormed the headquarters and evicted the women again; each side accused the other of precipitating a confrontation over this issue for political purposes. Two days later, in a move evidently engineered by the government's inner circle, some members of the New Democratic party filed a suit against Kim Young Sam alleging his election as party president to be invalid because of irregularities in the voting. The case was heard with unusual promptness, and on September 8 a court order barred Kim from the leadership of the New Democratic party. Shortly afterward Kim gave an interview to the *New York Times*, in which he said that the "minority dictatorial regime" of President Park, which he compared by implication with that of the Shah of Iran, was "on its last legs" and urged the United States to withdraw all support for it.[2] Partly at least in retaliation for this interview, Kim was expelled by the National Assembly on October 4, in a vote that was boycotted by the opposition. At this point the Carter administration, which profoundly disapproved of the government's pressures on Kim, recalled Ambassador William Gleysteen for "consultation." All opposition members, including even those who had opposed Kim Young Sam's personal leadership of the New Democratic party, resigned on

October 13 from the National Assembly, which then went into recess; whatever their individual feelings, the views of their constituents apparently left them no choice.

At that time violent demonstrations against the police by about 5,000 students, unemployed workers, and others began in Pusan, Kim Young Sam's hometown. Some 200 persons were arrested, and martial law was proclaimed throughout the city on October 17, for the first time since 1972. It was severely enforced by paratroopers. The demonstrations nevertheless continued and spread, not to Seoul where police controls were too strong for that to happen but to the southern city of Masan, a fact of symbolic importance since it was the death of a student there in April 1960 that had triggered the disorders that compelled Syngman Rhee to resign.

Meanwhile, on October 17, U.S. Secretary of Defense Harold Brown had arrived in Seoul with the dual mission of assuring the Republic of Korea and the world that the U.S. commitment to South Korean security was still valid—a credible proposition in the light of President Carter's decision of the previous July to suspend the withdrawal of the Second Division at least until 1981—and of urging President Park, in an unpublished letter, to improve his record on human rights.

The Park government's control of the situation had not been destroyed, but it was sufficiently in danger so that there were almost bound to be disagreements within the top leadership over the issue of whether repression was an adequate answer to the problems that it was facing.[3]

THE DEATH OF A PRESIDENT

One man who evidently thought that repression was not the answer was Kim Jae Kyu, who had been director of the KCIA since 1976 after being minister of construction. Although a boyhood friend of President Park, he turned increasingly against the president for some combination of personal and political reasons. In early 1978 he had tried to arrange a meeting between Park and the respected elder statesman Yun Po Sun, who had been president of the Second Republic, but the Blue House refused.[4]

Their differences were brought to a head by the October 1979 demonstrations in Pusan and the stern measures taken against them at least partly on the insistence of Cha Chi Chol, who considered Kim too soft in his attitude toward the demonstrations where Kim considered Cha too repressive. Apparently believing that Park was about to purge him as he had previous KCIA directors, Kim invited Park and Cha to dinner on the evening of October 26 at a restaurant in the KCIA compound, presumably with the purpose of killing them unless Park could be persuaded to get rid of Cha. After Cha had abused Kim for some time for his alleged mishandling of the Pusan situation, Kim shot and killed first Cha and then Park, and other KCIA agents under orders from Kim killed four other members of the president's entourage.

Kim then went to Army Chief of Staff Chung Seung Hwa, who was dining elsewhere in the KCIA compound, told him that Park was dead—but not that he had killed Park—and urged Chung to declare martial law. Apparently Kim hoped to precipitate a military takeover, regardless of what happened to him. The military soon became suspicious and arrested Kim and the others involved in the assassinations as well as Park's secretary Kim Kye Won, who had been present at the shooting.[5] Seven of the conspirators were sentenced to death by a military court on December 20; the sentence of Kim Kye Won was subsequently commuted to one of life imprisonment.

AFTERMATH OF THE ASSASSINATION

Elements of the opposition, notably among the students, welcomed the assassination of President Park and regarded Kim Jae Kyu as a hero. The establishment including the military leadership, on the other hand, tended to view the assassination as a crisis that might threaten not only their own positions but the entire political system and indeed the security of the state if the North Koreans decided to try to exploit the situation. The example of Iran after the fall of the Shah was present in some minds, Korean and foreign. The North Korean aspect of the problem did not materialize, probably in part because the United States issued a warning to Pyongyang and sent an aircraft carrier to the area; the North did no more than increase the rate of infiltration into the South and engage Seoul in some fruitless discussions, presumably in the hope of further destabilizing the Southern political system. The internal aspects of the problem were less easy to manage.

After an initial misstatement to the effect that Park had been killed in an accidental shooting, the government began to react swiftly and effectively to the challenge facing it. It issued further, accurate— as far as can be determined—bulletins on the assassination. Premier

Choi Kyu Hah, a man with an academic and diplomatic background, became acting president in accordance with the Yushin Constitution. Martial law was proclaimed and was to be administered by a Martial Law Command headed by General Chung Seung Hwa; the restrictions imposed at that time included press censorship and a ban on public meetings, the fairly numerous violations of which by students and others were punished by arrest. At the end of October the army took effective control of the KCIA.[6] The population as a whole remained calm.

The opposition naturally protested and demanded the end of martial law, as well as the prompt scrapping of the Yushin Constitution. What it got was considerably less than that, because the establishment preferred to retain the Yushin Constitution, although only for the time being, as a stabilizing measure; the military leadership, which was acquiring increasing political power and influence under the umbrella of martial law, reportedly agreed in late October that the Yushin Constitution must go eventually.[7] Choi Kyu Hah was elected unopposed, although over opposition protests, to the presidency by the government-dominated National Conference for Unification, the electoral college under the Yushin Constitution, on December 6; this meant that he was eligible to serve out the unexpired portion of Park's term (until December 1984), but in fact he had already made it clear that he did not intend to do that. On December 7, the day after his election and two weeks before his inauguration, he rescinded President Park's Emergency Decree Number 9 of May 13, 1975, which had forbidden all criticism of the Yushin Constitution. About 70 political dissidents including Kim Dae Jung, who had been arrested under the provisions of this decree, were released on December 8 and promptly resumed political activity. Kim urged President Choi to form a "neutral," meaning presumably coalition, government of national unity.

The repercussions of the Park assassination had by no means died away. The investigation, which was conducted by the army's counterintelligence organization, the Defense Security Command, headed at that time by Major General Chun Doo Hwan, investigated reports that General Chung Seung Hwa had colluded with Kim Jae Kyu, a close friend of his, before the assassination. Eventually, Chung was charged with not having taken sufficiently prompt action against Kim after the assassination. In the investigators' opinion, General Chung also evaded their inquiries in a suspicious manner. Accordingly, he was arrested on December 12 after a firefight and in March 1980 was sentenced by a military court to ten years in prison.[8]

General Lee Hui Sung succeeded Chung as army chief of staff and martial law commander.

Like the Park assassination, this affair had rather extensive implications and repercussions. Chung Seung Hwa was by no means the only general arrested in mid-December 1979; in fact, the episode had aspects of a successful coup by one element of the military leadership against another. The core of the new military group including its real "strongman," General Chun Doo Hwan, were graduates (in 1955) of the Eleventh Class of the Korean Military Academy (the first four-year class) and therefore significantly younger and presumably more professionally competent than those whom they displaced. The new group lost no time in putting their own members, or other officers acceptable to them, in key positions, one of them of course being Lee Hui Sung.[9] Their rapid rise and assertiveness worried the opposition and the U.S. government, which also objected to the fact that units of the Ninth Division, commanded by General Roh (or No) Tae Woo (Eleventh Class, Korean Military Academy), had been moved into Seoul in connection with the coup and without the permission of General John Wickham, commander of the Combined Forces Command.[10]

On December 18 General Lee issued a "special announcement," really a manifesto, reflecting the views of the new military elite. It denied any intent to interfere in politics ("Politics is outside the realm of the armed forces"), denounced corruption on the part of civil servants and unethical behavior by those in business, and enjoined the public against any sort of activity that might incite the North Koreans. This document appeared to reflect an outlook that, although unquestionably patriotic, was at best simplistic.[11] It remained to be seen whether the new military group would keep the armed forces, including themselves, out of politics as promised, or if not whether they would mature politically beyond the level of sophistication suggested by the December 18 manifesto.

For the next several months the politics of the Fourth Republic proceeded along two tracks, not necessarily parallel. On one track, the civilian, the emphasis lay on the regeneration of political party activity following the 1978–79 crisis and on the search for a new constitution to replace the Yushin Constitution. The Democratic Republican party elected as its new president the formidable Kim Jong Pil, the founder of the KCIA, who although sometimes out of favor with President Park had managed to retain considerable political influence and accumulate an enormous private fortune, partly it appears from presents and bribes offered by Japanese firms eager for favors of one kind or another. The New Democratic party remained under the presidency of Kim Young Sam. The recently released Kim Dae Jung, the third of the "three Kims," had his civil rights restored in February 1980 and then tried to reenter the New Democratic party and regain its presidency from Kim Young Sam but failed; he then began to make his political base increasingly among actively dissident elements such as those within the student organizations.[12] As for constitutional revision, the National Assembly created in late November 1979 a 28-member committee (7 from the Democratic Republican party, 7 from the Yujonghoe, 13 from the New Democratic party, and 1 from the Democratic Unification party) to deal with this question. Acting Premier Shin Hyon Hwack's government also began work on a draft constitution. There was disagreement as to whether the government under the new constitution should be presidential or cabinet in form and whether it should have strong emergency powers predicated on the assumption of a threat from the North.[13] As for the public, a newspaper poll taken in March 1980 showed the largest single bloc of respondents (40 percent) as considering the government's most urgent task to be the maintenance of social stability.[14]

On the other track, the military, the main theme was the rapid growth in the real power of the group that had taken action on December 12, 1979 and in particular of Chun Doo Hwan. In mid-April 1980, while retaining control of the Defense Security Command, he was appointed director of the KCIA, which had been in a state of reduced activity and semidisgrace since its previous director had assassinated President Park. At the end of April Chun gave his first press conference, in which he stated that in the future the KCIA would stop interfering with the government and other public organizations and would confine itself to the collection of anti-Communist intelligence.[15] Although General Chun and his colleagues had agreed to the restoration of Kim Dae Jung's civil rights, they disliked and distrusted him because of what they considered his leftist tendencies and associations in the past. They were also concerned over the apparently intensified efforts of the North Koreans to stir up political disorder in the South and over continuing restlessness on the part of students. They were soon to become even more concerned over these problems.

THE CRISIS OF THE FOURTH REPUBLIC

Students demonstrations began on March 28 in Seoul and various provincial capitals; the most violent ones occurred in the southwestern city of Kwangju, the capital of Cholla Namdo and a traditional center of political opposition. Although the demands made by the demonstrators at that time related mainly to university matters, they soon became political; as everyone knew, the twentieth anniversary (April 19) of the beginning of the movement that had overthrown Syngman Rhee was approaching.

Early in April the North Korean media began to take favorable notice of the demonstrations. A rally was held in Pyongyang on April 18, the eve of the anniversary, at which the students were urged by a speaker to "wipe out the fascist Yushin system and set up a new democratic regime."[16] Subsequent North Korean statements spoke in similar terms, while denying any intent to invade South Korea.[17]

Meanwhile, large-scale student demonstrations and riots were continuing in the South, in spite of official warnings to stop and efforts by the police to contain the students. On May 17 a group of student leaders gave the government an ultimatum to lift martial law by May 22 or face a new wave of demonstrations.

The military leadership, and the Martial Law Command in particular, had been growing increasingly concerned over the demonstrations and over labor unrest that broke out at the same time. They too remembered the spring of 1960 and the ensuing period of instability. They were worried by the contacts between some of the activist students and Kim Dae Jung, whom they regarded as an irresponsible and dangerous leftist demagogue having, at least in the past, some North Korean sympathies. They feared that Pyongyang was trying to exploit the situation or soon would be, by infiltration or even by actual attack; there were rumors of North Korean troops massing near the Demilitarized Zone. They expected a strong reaction by dissidents, especially students, to the execution of Kim Jae Kyu, which took place as scheduled on May 24. By the middle of May, they had apparently decided to take action and were waiting only for the return of President Choi from a trip to the Middle East.

The crackdown took the form of a declaration of "extraordinary" martial law, effective May 17. The difference between this state of affairs and the earlier version of martial law lay essentially in the fact that the military—the Martial Law Command, the Defense Security Command, and the Special Forces, in particular—now intended not only to maintain order but also to exercise a predominant influence on politics. Accordingly, the entire cabinet resigned on May 20 in token of its acceptance of responsibility for failing to prevent the

Kwangju disorders and was replaced the next day by one more acceptable to the military and headed by Acting Premier Pak Chung Hun. The proclamation of extraordinary martial law was accompanied by the arrest of Kim Dae Jung and six other politically prominent individuals. On May 27 President Choi appointed a 25-man Special Committee for National Security Measures, 14 of whose members were military leaders; the chairman of its Standing Committee was General Chun Doo Hwan.[18]

The main center of opposition lay in Kwangju, which is located not far from Kim Dae Jung's birthplace, the southwestern port city of Mokpo. On May 18 a crowd of about 2,000, most of them students, demanded the end of martial law, the sacking of General Chun, and the release of Kim Dae Jung. They were dealt with severely by paratroopers, but the latter were then driven from the center of the city by superior numbers. This episode, which profoundly shocked the government, turned rapidly into an insurrection that then spread to other towns in Cholla Namdo, although not beyond. The retaking of Kwangju by the army on May 27 put an end to the revolt, at a cost in lives somewhere between 200 (the approximate official estimate) and 400 (the approximate opposition estimate) and also to the series of student demonstrations that had begun two months earlier. The colleges were closed by government order for the time being.

While work on constitutional revision proceeded along lines laid down in the early weeks of the post-Park period, President Choi lent his authority to a campaign by the Special Committee for National Security Measures aimed at renovating the country's political life. At the head of the target list were the "three Kims," all of whom were widely considered to be presidential timber, and all of whom had been arrested on May 17. In mid-June Kim Jong Pil was released after resigning the leadership of the Democratic Republican party and agreeing to turn over his private fortune of $36 million to the state and stay out of politics. Kim Young Sam, who had been merely under house arrest, was released after resigning the presidency of the New Democratic party and announcing that his political career was over. Kim Dae Jung was in much worse trouble, since he was officially considered to bear considerable responsibility for the spring 1980 disorders; in July criminal proceedings on charges of sedition were begun against him before a military court. At a lower level of notoriety, some 8,000 civil servants, executives of state corporations, and journalists were dismissed for corruption and the like during the summer of 1980, and 172 journals of various kinds were closed down.[19]

Clearly the dominant political trend of the period since December 1979 had been the rapid growth in the power of the army and of General Chun Doo Hwan as the rising figure in the military elite. Under these conditions it was logical, and almost inevitable, that Chun should sooner or later become president in succession to Choi Kyu Hah, who was a civilian without a power base and without much in the way of leadership qualities. Choi, who had already promised not to serve out his full term, made no difficulty over his own departure; he resigned the presidency on August 16, 1980, although without bringing the Fourth Republic to an end. This he obviously did in order to pave the way fror the formal installation of General Chun, who had turned over the directorship of the KCIA to another general at the end of June, was promoted to full general on August 6, received the endorsement of the chiefs of staff and ranking commanders of the armed forces for the presidency on August 21, retired from the army on August 22, and was elected unopposed to the presidency by the National Conference for Unification on August 27.[20]

NOTES

1. *Asian Wall Street Journal*, June 26, 1979.

2. *New York Times*, September 16, 1979.

3. See Chong Sik Lee, "South Korea in 1979: Confrontation, Assassination, and Transition," *Asian Survey* 20 (January 1980): 63–69; *Washington Post*, October 22, 1979.

4. *New York Times*, October 27, 1979.

5. For test of Martial Law Command report of November 6, 1979, see Document 1; excerpts in *New York Times*, November 7, 1979. See also "Murder and Mystery End," *Asiaweek*, November 9, 1979, pp. 34–37; Ron Richardson, "Anatomy of a Failed Coup," *Far Eastern Economic Review*, November 16, 1979, p. 16.

6. *New York Times*, October 29, 1979.

7. *New York Times*, November 2, 1979.

8. For text of Ministry of National Defense report on Chung case, see Document 5.

9. *Asian Wall Street Journal*, December 18, 1979; *Christian Science Monitor*, December 20, 24, 1979.

10. Compare "South Korea: Recent Developments," *Gist*, Department of State, May 1980.

11. For commentary see *Washington Post*, December 19, 1979.

12. Compare *New York Times*, March 13, 1980 on the "three Kims."

13. *New York Times*, April 17, 1980.

14. *Washington Post*, March 17, 1980.

15. *New York Times*, April 30, 1980; *Washington Post*, April 30, 1980.

16. Pyongyang Domestic Service broadcast, April 18, 1980.

17. For example, Korean Central News Agency statement, May 14, 1980.

18. David Rees, *Crisis and Continuity in South Korea*, London: Institute for the Study of Conflict, *Conflict Studies*, no. 128, March 1981, pp. 19–20.

19. Ibid., pp. 22–24.

20. Ibid., pp. 25–26.

5

THE TRANSITION TO
THE FIFTH REPUBLIC

The transition from the Fourth to the Fifth Republic occurred not only under martial law but under a new leadership that was to a high degree military. The emergence of this new elite has naturally had important effects; these amount, and are intended to amount, to something of a revolution in the political life of South Korea.

THE NEW LEADERSHIP

Chun Doo Hwan was born in 1931 in a village in the southeastern province of Kyongsang Namdo. He was educated in the city of Taegu and in 1951, a year after the outbreak of the Korean War, entered the Korean Military Academy. That was also the year in which the Rhee government took the advice of General James Van Fleet, the newly appointed commanding general of the United States Eighth Army, to lengthen the curriculum of the academy from two years to four. The Eleventh Class, which entered in 1951 and graduated in 1955 and was to produce a number of military and political leaders including Chung, was therefore the first four-year class. The academy was then at Chinhae, on the southern coast not far from Pusan; today it occupies a handsome campus near Seoul.

Although graduating too late to fight in the Korean War, Chun served in a variety of line and staff assignments, one of the most challenging of which was as a regimental commander in Vietnam. In early 1978, as a general officer, he assumed command of the First Infantry Division and played a prominent role in the discovery of a third tunnel dug by the North Koreans under the Demilitarized Zone, two others having been found a few years earlier. After a year in that assignment he was given the Defense Security Command, which is responsible for military counterintelligence, since he had demonstrated special competence in analyzing and countering North Korean infiltration tactics. A year and a half later he was president of the Fourth Republic.

This brief summary is enough to show that Chun has real military ability and the confidence of at least an important segment of the country's military leadership. His record in office and the impressions of foreigners who have talked with him at intervals since he became politically prominent also suggest an ability and a willingness to learn rapidly about the immensely difficult art of politics. The real test of his political talents, of course, will be his entire political record and the judgment of his own people and future historians.

Chun's public statements, the texts of some of which are among the documentary appendixes to this book, indicate a keen awareness of the dangerous external environment in which the Republic of Korea lives, the North Korean threat being of course the most important aspect. On the other hand, he also realizes that the powerful influence of external forces of Korean life, today as in the past, has had beneficial as well as harmful effects. He is conscious of both the strengths and the limitations of the Korean tradition, including its political aspects. He believes that Park Chung Hee made important contributions to South Korea's development but stayed in office too long and was too repressive, especially toward the end of his career. Chun favors a strong presidential system, but with relatively short tenure for the president. Because of the corruption and conflict that have accompanied Korea's efforts to adopt and adapt Western political institutions in the past, he believes that the president should be elected indirectly, and that there should be more than two major political parties to avoid the bilateral confrontation that marked the history of the Democratic Republican and New Democratic parties under the Third and Fourth Republics. He considers that Korea's traditional and external environment do not permit the full level of freedom for political opposition, press criticism, and the like that exists in some other countries, mainly of course in the West. With this important qualification, Chun sees as the desirable goal for South Korea what he calls a "just democratic welfare state."

As anyone in the same situation would normally do, Chun brought into the Blue House as staff assistants some known and trusted junior associates from his previous career, and since he was a general they were colonels in some cases. These colonels have been accused in the foreign press of restricting access to him, shielding him from unwelcome views, and influencing his outlook. These charges appear to contain more plausibility than accuracy. Much of the criticism along these lines appears to be of Japanese origin and to reflect an analogy, obviously speculative and probably misleading, with the political situation in pre–World War II Japan, where activist colonels did indeed exert great influence, and a more plausible analogy with the so-called human curtains that surrounded President Rhee, and President Park during his last years.[1]

It is probably more significant that as soon as he entered the Blue House Chun appointed to his staff some first-rate civilians. The most important was his secretary general or chief of staff, Kim Kyung Won, a political scientist and a Harvard Ph.D. who had also served in staff capacities under Presidents Park and Choi.[2] Among the other such appointments was Chun's chief economist, Kim Jae Ik, a Stanford Ph.D.

Outside the Blue House, Chun appointed to various key positions military men who were graduates of the Eleventh Class, Korean Military Academy, or who at any rate had supported him in his rise to power. An excellent example is Roh Tae Woo, who took over the Defense Security Command; in this capacity his power, which would have been great even in relatively normal times, was especially so under martial law. Like President Chun, these men appear to have embarked on the political phase of their careers with very little knowledge or understanding of politics but, being intelligent, to have learned rather rapidly. A good example is the fact that they somehow brought themselves to accept the advisability of sparing the life of Kim Dae Jung, when they would have preferred that he be executed.

Outside these elite ranks, the political scene was partly emptied by the ouster of thousands of people, military and civilian, who were officially considered guilty of some sort of corrupt activity under the Third Republic or extreme opposition under the Fourth Republic, or both. Many other prominent individuals were not dismissed, and the continuity of leadership among the Third, Fourth, and Fifth Republics has been greater than has been generally realized outside Korea and than was expected by at least some foreign correspondents based in Korea.

THE POLITICS OF MARTIAL LAW

At his inauguration President Chun reaffirmed the basic political timetable announced earlier by Choi Kyu Hah: a new draft constitution would be completed in time to be submitted to a referendum by the end of October; martial law would be lifted and a new presidential election and a National Assembly election would be held under the new constitution in the first half of 1981. There would be some restrictions on campaigning designed to prevent, if possible, the bitterness and violence, as well as the widespread vote buying, that had marked some previous presidential election campaigns, and presumably also to facilitate the victory of the government party.[3]

Chun's cabinet, which was announced on September 2, 1980, was headed by Premier Nam Duck Woo, a U.S.-trained economist who had been deputy premier and minister of the Economic Planning Board under Park; it included seven holdovers from the previous cabinet and 13 new ministers, only two of the total number being retired generals.[4] The Special Committee for National Security Measures was replaced in late October 1980 by a body known as the Legislative Assembly for National Security, which had 81 members, only 10 of whom had been members of its predecessor.[5]

Since the National Assembly had been dissolved and the election of a new one was not contemplated for the duration of martial law, there was a need for some other body to exercise legislative functions. This body was to be the Legislative Assembly for National Security. Although not elected and not entirely composed of individuals commanding public confidence, it did include representatives of various walks of life. During its lifetime of about four months it passed, at the government's initiative, considerable important legislation. Approximately 560 individuals were banned from politics until June 30, 1988, a restriction that would prevent them from taking part in elections during President Chun's term or in the election that would determine his successor.[6] A law was passed authorizing the formation of new political parties, subject to certain requirements. Procedural legislation was passed governing the composition of the National Assembly, the number of election districts, and the like. Enabling legislation was passed for the benefit of various ministries. Finally, some legislation, fairly moderate in the eyes of the establishment although too rigorous to suit the opposition, was passed to provide a "storm barrier" against possible future disorders, especially student unrest, and against antigovernment campaigns in the media, or in effect to provide the government with a stronger legal basis for and more effective means of maintaining order without declaring martial law again.

It was clear from the early weeks of Chun Doo Hwan's presidency that he wanted the new political party system to be very different from the old and that he was likely to get his way, which he did. The new parties began to emerge during the period between the end of November 1980 and the middle of January 1981. During those weeks it became increasingly apparent that, in deference to Chun's wishes, there would be more than two major parties, including a government party; one of the opposition parties would be a moderate social democratic party. The official rationale was that this multiparty system would avoid the former confrontation between two major parties that had existed during much of the previous history of the Republic of Korea; the opposite side of the coin, as pointed out by critics, was that it would be easier for the government and its party to cope with three opposition parties than with one.

During the last months of 1980, the KCIA continued to maintain a relatively low profile, many of its formal internal security functions having been taken over by the Defense Security Command for the duration of martial law. In an effort to improve both the efficiency and the public image of the KCIA, some fresh blood was injected at the upper levels from the military and from the legal profession.[7]

The media were "purified" to a considerable extent, although not completely, of commercialism and foreign influence of types deemed undesirable, for example imported television films if too violent or considered otherwise unsuitable.[8] Similarly, even people who had not been as corrupt and therefore still active in public life were required to attend political orientation lectures from time to time.[9]

The colleges reopened in the fall of 1980 and were much quieter than in the previous spring, although by no means entirely so. There were some demonstrations, off campus as well as on, and for a few weeks in October–November the Korean Theological Seminary and Korea University were closed. A few hundred students were arrested, and several officers of administration at several of the universities and colleges were forced to resign for having allegedly promoted or at least tolerated the disorder.[10]

The violence of the previous spring was scheduled to receive what the authorities regarded as its just punishment. In the late summer of 1980, several hundred students and others who were considered to have played active parts in the turbulence of that period were tried, secretly and in groups, by military courts sitting at or near the two main centers of disorder, Seoul and Kwangju, and were generally given prison sentences; there were five death sentences.[11] These could be appealed, and there was the possibility of pardon by the president.

By far the best known and most controversial of the trials held during that period was that of Kim Dae Jung and 23 of his supporters on the charge of sedition. On July 4, 1980, the Martial Law Command began to pave the way for the trial by publishing a report on its investigation of this case, which had been conducted under conditions that Kim was reportedly to complain during the trial had included some harsh treatment of himself.[12] In this report and in other governmental statements published in 1980 with the obvious aim of cutting his image down to what the government regarded as its proper size, Kim was accused of having pro-North Korean sympathies and some North Korean connections in the past and of having tried to overthrow the Fourth Republic under President Choi and come to power through inciting student demonstrations.

By Western standards the charges against Kim Dae Jung, even if correct, were more political than criminal, and he was not allowed due process; the Department of State termed the charges "farfetched." On the other hand, it can be argued plausibly that the real core of the accusation against Kim was his involvement in the student disorders of April–May 1980, that the political sensitivity and illegal nature (under martial law) of such student activism were well known, and that Kim was therefore knowingly risking reprisals when he made his base in the student organizations after failing to gain control of the New Democratic party.

Kim was sentenced to death on September 17, 1980,[13] but even though his appeal was subsequently rejected there were reasons to believe that he would not actually be executed. There was a good deal of feeling in South Korea, especially on the part of the opposition, against the death penalty for Kim. The same feeling was virtually unanimous abroad, especially in the United States, Japan, and Western Europe, so much so that it appeared possible that South Korea might suffer economic reprisals at the hands of those important trading partners if Kim were executed. On the other hand, the South Korean military elite, so far as can be determined, was strongly in favor of Kim's execution. If he were to be spared, they would have to be peruaded somehow to agree to or at least tolerate a commutation of his sentence.[14]

THE NEW CONSTITUTION

On September 19, 1980 President Chun presented to the nation the official draft of a new constitution, which was labeled as amendments to the Yushin Constitution but was really a replacement for it, together with an official explanation of the differences between the two documents.[15]

The main body of the new constitution applied essentially to the future period that would begin with the lifting of martial law. But appended to the constitution proper were some important and controversial supplementary provisions dealing with the remainder of the transition period. Article 6 conferred on the Legislative Assembly for National Security the powers and functions of the old National Assembly, pending the election of a new National Assembly no later than June 30, 1981. Article 7 dissolved the existing political parties but authorized the formation of new ones not less than three months before the next presidential election, so that they could nominate candidates for the presidency.

The main body of the constitution contained a number of important and sometimes controversial provisions. Probably the most controversial was Article 39, which provided that the president was to be elected indirectly, by a popularly elected electoral college, rather than directly by the voters; the reason for President Chun's preference for the indirect method has already been given. The president was authorized to take "emergency measures," but only with the positive concurrence of the National Assemby (Article 51), rather than simply on his own authority as under the Yushin Constitution (Article 53). The latter document (Article 59) placed no restrictions on the president's power to dissolve the National Assembly, whereas the new constitution (Article 57) limited the exercise of this power to the period beginning one year after the "formation" of the National Assembly (presumably after each general election), and no National Assembly could be dissolved twice for the same reason. The president was limited to a single seven-year term of office (Article 45), as against an indefinite number of terms as under the Yushin Constitution (Article 47). If the new constitution were amended—the procedure for amendment being a two-thirds vote of the National Assembly followed by approval in a national referendum (Article 131)—in order to extend the presidential term or permit the president to serve more than one term, the change would not apply to the president in office at that time (Article 129); this restriction was obviously designed to guarantee that President Chun would not try to imitate Presidents Rhee and Park by prolonging his tenure of office even if, contrary to his promise, he should feel tempted to try.

The National Assembly's term was reduced from six years to four. The prime minister was to be appointed by the president with the consent of the National Assembly (Article 62). The assembly could require the president to dismiss the prime minister and the cabinet, but not within the year following the prime minister's appointment

(Article 99). Local autonomy, which had been abolished in 1961, was to be restored (Articles 118–19).

In form at least, this was a recognizable, modified, combination of the presidential and parliamentary systems, with emphasis on the presidential aspect. But as in all such cases, the form was less important than the spirit and manner in which the constitution would be implemented, something that would become clear only with the passage of time.

Before going into effect, the new constitution had to be submitted to a referendum, which took place on October 22, 1980. The officially announced result was that 95.5 percent of all eligible voters voted, and that of those who did 91.6 percent voted in favor of the new constitution. Regardless of the question of its statistical accuracy, this result is neither very meaningful nor very surprising. The voters knew that the government favored and indeed had sponsored the new constitution and that the alternative to the latter was a continuation of the unpopular Yushin Constitution.

The referendum brought the new constitution into effect in principle, but it did not put an end to martial law. For that a decision by the president was required.

THE END OF MARTIAL LAW

The adoption of the new constitution brought into being the Fifth Republic. It was generally expected that President Chun would lift martial law soon afterward, about March 1981. Instead, it ended two months earlier than that, and its termination came as one of a series of important and rather dramatic policy initiatives.

One consideration that probably influenced the Chun government to lift martial law and hold elections earlier than previously scheduled was a desire to prevent potential disorder during the coming spring. the main traditional time for political violence in South Korea. In addition, and as has usually been the case in modern times, Korean politics and policy making during the transition period continued to be affected, although not necessarily determined, by external developments. As before in recent years, these tended to originate principally with the threatening adversary, North Korea, or the sole ally, the United States.

On the North Korean front, Kim Il Song was grooming his son Kim Chong Il, evidently a man with an aggressive and headstrong personality, as his successor. From the South Korean point of view, it would be better to try to work out some sort of political agreement with the father, a relatively known quantity, while he was still alive and in charge, than to wait for the advent of the son.

As for the United States, the normal South Korean desire for good relations was intensified by special considerations. The following year, 1982, would be the one hundredth anniversary of the first treaty between the two countries, and the approach of the centennial tended to create an atmosphere appropriate to efforts at improvement of Korean-U.S. relations. More important, the election of Ronald Reagan was welcomed in Seoul as likely to lead to a U.S. policy less demanding on the issue of human rights and more supportive of allies than the Carter administration had been.

On January 12, 1980 President Chun addressed his first New Year's message to the Korean people.[16] Much of the statement was devoted to a recapitulation of his domestic program and a reiteration of his pledge to lift martial law in the near future. In addition to that, he proposed an exchange of visits between himself and Kim Il Song, each visiting president to have his safety guaranteed by his host and to be free to travel where he liked. Without referring to Reagan, Chun mentioned in favorable terms the approaching centennial of the first Korean-U.S. treaty.

Meanwhile, Reagan, although of course not yet in office, had been far from idle with respect to Korea. Shortly after his election, he had his foreign policy aide, Richard Allen, make an unattributed statement to the effect that the execution of Kim Dae Jung would harm Korean-U.S. relations.[17] Allen then began a series of private talks with high South Korean officials to show that this position was a serious one and not a propaganda gesture.[18] The message evidently had an effect in Seoul, especially since it was reinforced by similar views being expressed in other places, Japan and Western Europe in particular. President Chun could not be asked or expected to give, even in private, a flat pledge to spare Kim Dae Jung's life in exchange for something that both he and Reagan wanted, a visit by Chun to the United States shortly after Reagan's inauguration. But obviously Chun could increase the likelihood of an invitation to Washington by reiterating in private earlier informal assurances from Seoul that Kim would not be executed. It was probably something like this that happened, and it must have happened shortly before President Reagan's inauguration; the invitation was announced and accepted on January 21, the day after the inauguration.[19]

Two days later, the South Korean government announced that at President Chun's initiative Kim Dae Jung's death sentence, which had just been confirmed by the Supreme Court, was being commuted to one of life imprisonment. Presumably in an effort to make clemency more acceptable to those who had wanted the death penalty, it was stated, although denied by elements of the opposition, that Kim had apologized for what he had done and had requested clemency. At the same time the prison sentences of 11 others were reduced.[20]

This important announcement created an appropriate atmosphere for another one. On January 24, 1981 President Chun announced the lifting of martial law, while pointing out that the need for stability and order was as great as ever.[21]

NOTES

1. Compare Shim Jae Hoon, "Chun Banks on Young Blood," *Far Eastern Economic Review*, December 12, 1980, pp. 22–23.

2. *Korea Newsreview*, August 30, 1980, p. 13.

3. See Document 13.

4. *New York Times*, September 3, 1980; *Washington Star*, September 3, 1980.

5. Shim Jae Hoon, "Chun Sets His Priorities," *Far Eastern Economic Review*, September 12, 1980, p. 13.

6. *Korea Herald*, November 4, 1980.

7. For example, General Kim Song Jin, Eleventh Class, Korean Military Academy, was appointed deputy director of the KCIA soon after Chun's inauguration (*New York Times*, September 8, 1980).

8. *Washington Post*, August 24, 1980.

9. *Washington Post*, September 4, 1980.

10. Chong-Sik Lee, "South Korea in 1980: The Emergence of a New Authoritarian Order," *Asian Survey* 20 (January 1981):137–38.

11. *Christian Science Monitor*, October 15, 1980.

12. See Document 8. For commentary see *Washington Post*, July 4, 1980.

13. *Washington Post*, September 17, 1980.

14. Ron Richardson, "Clemency Could Prove Costly," *Far Eastern Economic Review*, September 26, 1980, p. 10.

15. See Document 12.

16. See Document 16.

17. See *New York Times*, November 18, 1980.

18. Rowland Evans and Robert Novak, "'Secret' Diplomacy with the South Koreans," *Washington Post*, February 4, 1981.

19. Shim Jae Hoon, "After the Gloom, a New Deal from Chun," *Far Eastern Economic Review*, January 30, 1981, p. 20.

20. See Document 9.

21. See Document 10.

6

THE FIFTH REPUBLIC

As the Republic of Korea left martial law behind, the major political problem remained: how to combine, in some workable and if possible optimal form, freedom and stability under the extraordinarily difficult conditions created by the threat from the North. The solution being attempted under the Fifth Republic clearly stressed stability, and the outlook for its viability appeared reasonably good, far better than could have been predicted with any confidence a few months earlier. The commutation of Kim Dae Jung's death sentence did not convert the opposition, but it relaxed public and foreign opinion to a considerable degree. The success of President Chun's visit to the United States greatly enhanced his prestige, and specifically his image as a statesman capable of keeping this most vital of South Korea's external relationships in good working order, certainly better than had been possible under his predecessor, or Reagan's.

ELECTIONS UNDER THE NEW CONSTITUTION

Under the provisions of the new constitution and the timetable already laid down by President Chun, three elections took place shortly after the lifting of martial law: one for the presidential electoral college (February 11, 1981), one of the president by the electoral college (February 25), and one for the National Assembly (March 25). The results were predictable and basically similar to what had generally happened under the Third and Fourth Republics: popular acceptance, for the sake of stability and in the absence of any real alternative, of the leading political figure and his overall program, balanced with impressive support for the opposition, even though there was little likelihood of its coming to power, as a check on the leader and the establishment.

The holding of these elections was predicated on the existence of a group of very new political parties. The government party was known as the Democratic Justice party; its president and presidential candidate was of course Chun Doo Hwan. The party that was to emerge as the strongest opposition party was the Democratic Korea party (led by Yoo Chi Song). Well behind these two in political strength and electoral appeal were the Korean National party (led by Kim Chong Chul) and the Civil Rights party (led by Kim Eui Taik).[1]

The 5,278 members of the electoral college were chosen by 78.12 percent of the registered voters, a turnout that compared closely with the norm for previous presidential elections, although of course it was considerably lower than the one for the referendum of October 1980. The Democratic Justice party won 3,676 (69.7 percent) of the seats, independents (actually committed in almost all cases to vote for the Democratic Justice party candidate) 1,123 seats (21.27 percent), the Democratic Korea party 411 seats (7.79 percent), the Korean National party 48 seats (0.9 percent), and the Civil Rights party 20 seats (0.37 percent).[2] When one allows for the fact that nearly all the independents voted for Chun Doo Hwan, the vote in the electoral college was virtually the same; Chun received 4,755 votes (90.23 percent).[3] He was inaugurated for a full seven-year term on March 3, and the Fifth Republic officially came into existence.[4]

Under the terms of the electoral law, two types of seats were at stake in the ensuing general election for the National Assembly: 184 elected seats, and 92 seats to be allocated on the basis of a kind of proportional representation, in such a way that the party winning a plurality or majority of the elected seats would be allotted two-thirds (61) of the proportional seats, the balance of the latter to be divided proportionally among the other parties winning at least 5 seats each. The outcome was that the Democratic Justice party won 90 elected seats (a little under half the total number of elected seats) and was allotted 61 proportional seats (total 151 seats, a clear although not overwhelming majority of the entire assembly, and a significantly smaller bloc of votes than would be needed to amend the constitution over the opposition of the other parties), the Democratic Korea party 57 elected seats and 24 proportional seats (total 81 seats), and the Korean National party 18 elected seats and 7 proportional seats (total 25 seats); the remainder (19) of the elected seats were split among the Civil Rights party (2), the Democratic Socialist party (2), the New Political party (2), the Democratic Farmers party (1), and independents (11).[5] A second socialist party, the Socialist party of Korea, led by the internationally known Kim Chol, won less than 2 percent of the popular vote and was therefore compelled under the law to disband, with the option of reconstituting itself later under another name.[6] The election campaign had been a fairly spirited one, even though its overall result had never really been in doubt; one of its most interesting features was the relatively poor showing of Yoo Chi Song, the leader of the Democratic party, in his campaign for a seat in the assembly.[7]

The National Assembly convened on April 11 for a brief inaugural session. The Democratic Justice party had already selected as speaker, Jung Nae Hiuk, a former general, minister of defense, and member of the now defunct Legislative Assembly for National Security.[8] President Chun's address to the National Assembly argued in favor of cooperation between the executive branch and the assembly, rather than conflict as at earlier times in the republic's history, and insisted that his desired goal of stability was not to be equated with stagnation.[9] At an assembly session held in May for the purpose of permitting members to interpellate the government, Prime Minister Nam Duck Woo stated that the government had no intention at that time of supporting a revision of the constitution, in particular its controversial provision for indirect election of the president, or the electoral law, to both of which the opposition objected.[10]

THE CONTINUATION OF DISSIDENCE

In addition to the opposition as represented in the National Assembly, there continued to be manifestations of political dissidence outside the framework provided by the new constitution.

In late March 1981 Kim Young Sam, although barred from politics and in fact still under house arrest, managed to give an interview to the *New York Times* for the second time in 18 months. He said that the army should stay out of politics and criticized the new constitution and the electoral law as devices for ensuring control of the political system by President Chun, his colleagues, and his party. This view was evidently shared by the dissidents—opposition politicians, journalists, students, clergy, and so on—whose permanent core numbered about 2,000, but was regarded as exaggerated by some, although not all, foreign observers.[11]

In late May 1981, presumably as a way of commemorating the events of the previous spring, sizable student demonstrations against the government erupted on several campuses in Seoul. They did not attain the proportions of 1960 or 1980, however, and generally did not spill off the campuses onto the streets. As a result the police presence on the campuses, already substantial, was increased, an unknown number of arrests were made, and several universities were threatened with closure if the demonstrations continued. By early June they had largely subsided.[12]

The important Christian wing of the dissident movement continued to believe that there were insufficient guarantees under the existing political system for human rights, their own in particular. The Catholic community, including a number of actively dissident priests, was distressed by the imprisonment of certain of its coreligionists, prominent among them being Kim Dae Jung.

THE "POLITICS OF RECONCILIATION"

In rebuttal of the dissidents, the government could and did point to its commitment to what it called, hopefully but somewhat wishfully as yet, the "politics of reconciliation."

In a step that was traditional in Korea on such occasions but was perhaps also designed to meet foreign criticism (by Amnesty International, for example), the government marked President Chun's inauguration, as he had already announced on February 20, with an amnesty affecting 5,221 persons, some of whom had been sentenced to prison for involvement in the disorders of 1979–80, including the assassination of President Park and the Kwangju affair. A total of 3,385 prisoners were released, either unconditionally or on parole; 646 others had their life sentences reduced to 20 years or their lesser sentences cut in half; 167 individuals already released and considered to have repented had their civil rights restored; and 1,023 overseas South Koreans, previously barred from the country as security risks, were to be allowed to enter it as well as to leave it again. Among those convicted for involvement in the plot to assassinate President Park, Kim Kye Won had his life sentence reduced to 20 years; General Chung Seung Hwa was released. Kim Dae Jung, whose sentence had already been commuted, was not affected by the amnesty.[13]

At the end of March the Supreme Court confirmed the sentences of 83 individuals found guilty of involvement in the Kwangju disturbances. The government thereupon commuted their sentences in a

similar way: three death sentences were commuted to life imprisonment, seven life sentences were reduced to 20 years, 13 lesser sentences were cut in half, 57 persons were released, and three others
already released had their civil rights restored.[14]

THE "POLITICS OF DIALOGUE"

In keeping with the traditional Korean emphasis on consensus for
the sake of stability and as a restraint on the countervailing tendency
toward factionalism, President Chun clearly preferred to govern with
the cooperation, rather than against the opposition, of the other
political leaders and parties. If this differs from the Western concept
of politics, with its preference for institutionalized opposition, it also
differs from President Park's tendency to seek confrontation with
the opposition.

On February 20, 1981, after his election but before his inauguration, Chun held a round table discussion with a group composed of
two former presidents (Yun Po Sun and Choi Kyu Hah) and the leaders of the five major political parties. The meeting did not generate
much controversy, but it was the first of its kind in Korean history.
President Chun reported on his trip to the United States and his
recent proposal for a meeting with Kim Il Song. He insisted that "We
must establish a precedent for changing the government through
peaceful and legal means," rather than through the violence that had
marked previous transfers of power in the history of the Republic of
Korea. He urged that the terms "ruling party" and "opposition" be
done away with and said that "We must not sling mud at one another
in the upcoming National Assembly election campaign." Chun agreed
with a demand by Yoo Chi Song and Yun Po Sun for an amnesty but
rejected a proposal for the restoration of full political rights to banned
politicians and a criticism of the proportional allocation of additional
seats in the National Assembly to the party winning the largest number of popularly elected seats.[15] A similar meeting was held four
months later.[16]

In accordance with Article 66 of the new constitution, a 26-man
body of presidentially appointed elder statesmen known as the
Advisory Council on State Affairs came into existence in April 1981
under the ex officio chairmanship of the immediate former president,
Choi Kyu Hah. The opening session was attended by President Chun,
Prime Minister Nam, and most members of the cabinet. Chun reiterated his pledge to observe the constitutional prohibition against serving more than one term as president.[17]

It was officially hoped that the National Assembly would act as a forum for dialogue, rather than confrontation, between the government and the opposition. The government guaranteed that it would allow sufficient time for the National Assembly to consider and debate bills presented by the government, including the budget. In return, the floor leaders for the opposition parties agreed, or at least appeared to agree, not to engage in obstruction or confrontation.[18]

POLITICAL PROBLEMS AND PERFORMANCE IN 1982

The second full calendar year of the Fifth Republic, 1982, saw the Chun government compelled to deal with political problems that, while mostly not of its own making, tested its capacity for building the stable, just, prosperous order to which it aspired. The year began with the first of a series of cabinet reshuffles, this one being mainly economic rather than political in cause and purpose; the economy was not recovering as fast as had been hoped.[19]

For a variety of reasons, including the assassination of Egyptian President Sadat on October 6, 1981, President Chun felt it advisable to take additional steps both to conciliate public opinion and to enhance security against possible disaffection. On January 5 he lifted the curfew (midnight to 4:00 a.m.), except in areas along the Demilitarized Zone and portions of the coast;[20] the result was public approval, accompanied by some increase in crime. On March 2 Kim Dae Jung's sentence was reduced to 20 years, and the terms of 2,862 other prisoners were also cut or cancelled.[21]

The opposition, the active elements of which centered in the Christian churches and some elements of the student population, was not to be won over by measures such as these. They demanded drastic liberalization, to a degree that the government considered would be dangerous to stability and security in view of the continuing threat from the North, and they claimed to see the United States as supporting the government, a perception possibly exaggerated as a result of the publicity accompanying the centennial celebration in 1982 of the establishment of U.S.-South Korean relations. On March 18, accordingly, three young people fire bombed the U.S. Cultural Center in Pusan, completely destroying the first floor, killing one Korean male (by smoke inhalation), and severely burning two young Korean women. From June to August, 16 individuals were tried under the National Security Law for committing or supporting this act; two were given death sentences, two life sentences, and the others varying terms of imprisonment.[22]

Both the government and the active opposition perceived this episode as symbolizing wider issues, including the government's legitimacy and of course its relations with the United States, and something of a test of strength followed the fire bombing. There were numerous arrests in various cities after the bombing.[23] The beginning of the trial of the 16 was anticipated by student riots in Seoul, mainly at Yonsei University.[24]

Meanwhile, there had occurred two other misfortunes that, while not really political in nature, inevitably had political repercussions unfavorable to the government's image. In mid-April a subway tunnel under construction collapsed in Seoul, with ten deaths. On April 26 a policeman went berserk in Kyongsang Namdo Province and fatally shot 56 people and wounded 37 others before taking his own life.[25]

The latter disaster, which shocked public opinion and seemed to many to reflect on the entire internal security system, led promptly to another cabinet reshuffle. The most important change was that the Home Ministry, which controls the police, was taken over by Roh Tae Woo, a close colleague of President Chun and one of the "strong men" of the regime; his mission was presumably to make whatever changes in the police system seemed to be needed.

In mid-May the biggest political scandal to date under the Fifth Republic, the so-called curb loan scandal, broke. Since early 1981 Chang Yong Ja, a woman distantly related by marriage to President Chun (her husband's brother was Mrs. Chun's uncle), and her husband had netted a huge sum—approximately $300 million—by trading on their connections, evidently without the knowledge of the president and his wife. They had done this by buying secured promissory notes at much less than their face value from firms needing cash and then reselling them earlier than promised. The disclosure of this scheme had a strong adverse impact on the major banks, some corporations, the stock market, and on public confidence in the government. From opposition quarters there came demands for President Chun's resignation, and some allegations that the money made by the guilty couple had gone into the treasury of the ruling Democratic Justice party. The official investigation, which involved the arrest of 31 individuals and culminated in a trial beginning in July, gave no support to this charge; all the defendants were found guilty, and 24 were given prison terms.[26]

In order to restore public confidence in the government, President Chun reshuffled his cabinet twice more, in late May and in late June. The second of these involved the appointment of a new premier, Kim Sang Hyup, who had been born in Cholla Namdo Province near

Kwangju and had just been serving as president of Korea University, a respected private institution in Seoul. Clearly his appointment was intended to please at least the moderate elements of the opposition.[27]

Since President Chun's pledge not to seek a second term had been an important part of his personal political program from the beginning, and since rumors had begun to circulate that he would nevertheless try to succeed himself, he reaffirmed his pledge in mid-July not to seek reelection.[28]

Meanwhile, the active opposition had been trying to extend its antigovernment and anti-United States activity into the labor force. With this aim a Christian organization, the Urban Industrial Mission, encouraged protests on the part of the workers affected by the closing of a computer component assembly plant owned by a U.S. firm, Control Data. The government responded with a campaign of propaganda and pressures directed against the Urban Industrial Movement, which it evidently perceived as subversive threat to stability within the labor force.[29]

THE SEARCH FOR ECONOMIC RECOVERY

For the South Korean economy, 1980 had been a bad year, partly on account of political turmoil and a resulting falling off of foreign investment, import orders, and earnings from tourism, but even more from economic causes already discussed (in Chapter 3) that reached back into the 1970s. There had been a devaluation of the won, the effect of which in raising the price of imports—without correspondingly stimulating exports—had been accentuated by the strengthening of the dollar. There had been inflation of about 40 percent, on the heels of two decades of inflation averaging about 14 percent per year. Agriculture had been hit hard by a cold, wet summer. Unemployment stood at about 5 percent of the labor force. GNP registered an absolute decline of 6.2 percent.

There is no doubt that this state of stagflation and its adverse effects on the general level of economic well-being intensified the normal Korean desire for stability through consensus as the best guarantee of ultimate prosperity, among other things, and increased the level of popular support for the Chun government, which was committed precisely to a search for stability and prosperity through consensus. On the other hand, this linkage between economics and politics also meant that if the Chun government failed to improve the state of the economy, it risked a serious erosion of its political support.

Well aware of the economic challenge and its political implications, the new leadership began to address the problems of the economy in early 1980. The initial idea, as might be expected from military leaders with little economic knowledge or experience, apparently was that the government should play the leading role, as it generally had under the Third and Fourth Republics, but presumably without President Park's tendency toward impulsive one-man decision making with occasional unfortunate results. Accordingly, the initial thrust of official economic thinking and planning was in the direction of compelling each of the large conglomerates to spin off all subsidiaries not involved in the main line of activity of the conglomerate, of purchasing compulsorily much of the unused land that many South Korean firms had been holding as a hedge against inflation, and of making additional government credits available to the undercapitalized heavy industrial sector.[30]

The political leadership soon began to realize, however, that both the economy and its problems had outgrown the government's capabilities for managing them. The commercial banks would have to be returned to private control. Industry would have to be permitted and encouraged to play a more active role in planning and carrying out economic recovery, although its role could not be as great as in the larger and more mature industrial economy of Japan. In September 1980, accordingly, the Korean Federation of Industries was asked by the government to work out a plan for the industrial sector. The result, which took several months to complete, was rather similar to the earlier official plan, with the main differences that the expert knowledge and active cooperation of the business community had been enlisted, and that there was to be reduction in the level of government subsidies to industry. Firms and conglomerates were to be reorganized and consolidated in such a way as to eliminate, or at least reduce, excessive duplication of activity and products and thereby achieve greater efficiency. An improved export position was seen as the leading edge of economic recovery.[31]

There was a general realization that no significant economic gain, including a rebuilding of export competitiveness, was possible without a curbing of inflation. The government hoped for no more in this respect than a reduction of the inflation rate to 10 percent by 1983.[32] Price stabilization was one of the major goals propounded by President Chun in his first talk as president of the Fifth Republic to the government's Economic Planning Board, the others being improvement in the quality of exports and diversification of foreign markets. The government launched a program for encouraging austerity in consumption, entertainment, and so on, on the part of officials and business leaders, partly in the hope of making a lower level of wage increases acceptable to the labor force.[33] At the same time, under a newly passed Antitrust and Fair Trade Act, the government was to give up progressively its positive power to set prices, while retaining the right to prosecute firms that increased prices to a degree considered by the government to be unjustified. The government also engaged in considerable "jawboning" of business to encourage the holding down of price increases.[34]

One of the most convincing signs of the basic soundness of the South Korean economy was the fact that, in spite of its problems and the probability that debt service would already require about $5 billion per year during the 1981–85 period,[35] foreign banks were not only willing but eager to make new loans to South Korean firms. To encourage foreign loans and foreign investment, the government in early 1981 adopted new regulations making it significantly easier for foreign investors to buy land, trade on the stock market, and invest directly; the preferred type of foreign investment, from the official South Korean point of view, was in projects involving large-scale high technology of types difficult for Korean firms to handle unaided.[36]

Although a $5.5 billion foreign trade gap was expected for 1981,[37] there were bright spots in the export picture, as there had been all along. Construction projects carried out abroad—especially in the Middle East—with South Korean equipment, building materials, and labor continued to be a significant foreign exchange earner. South Korean industry was beginning to produce oil rigs for export, and a South Korean firm was scheduled to begin a joint offshore drilling operation with Pertamina, the Indonesian oil monopoly, near East Java in late 1981. The quality of South Korean textiles, still an important export item, was being improved. On the other hand, the color television industry, hampered at home by the government's refusal until December 1980 to permit domestic television broadcasting in color, was faced with import quotas in the United States. There was the serious overall problem that the brand names of South Korean exports, unlike at least some of their Japanese equivalents and competitors, had not—or not yet—acquired recognition and acceptability in major foreign markets.[38]

Restrained official optimism was generated in Seoul by the fact that in the first quarter of 1981 the previous downward trend of GNP was reversed; there was 1.2 percent growth in real terms over the same quarter in 1980, a bad year of course. For the second quarter the rate was about 4 percent. The improvement, which was generally recognized as representing only a small beginning of a process that would require considerable time to achieve real success, was furthermore very unevenly distributed; there was a considerable decline in all types of construction, housing being the field in which the need for new construction was the greatest.[39]

As 1982 began, the government's economic stabilization program was doing better than in 1980, which had been a year of negative growth whereas the GNP grew 7.1 percent in 1981. Inflation had been cut by about two-thirds (to 14 percent) in 1981. In spite of late rains, the harvest in 1981 had been good, so that some rice imported from the United States in the expectation—based on inadequate data—of a poor harvest turned out not to be needed. Import prices were generally stable or declining.

On the other hand, the economy was not doing so well as had been hoped. Uncertainty as to the future and the shortage of available funds were holding down investment by firms. Consumer demand was off. Workers' real incomes were declining. Export prices were up, partly because the won had been allowed to appreciate along with the dollar, with a depressing effect on orders from abroad. The rate of import growth was declining. Trade liberalization and the reduction of barriers to foreign investment were proceeding, but only slowly.[40]

In the hope of getting more momentum into the economy, the president reshuffled the cabinet in January 1982 and pressed on with the effort to shift the bulk of South Korea's exports from the light industrial to the heavy industrial sector. In June, for example, he dedicated a huge heavy machinery complex at Changwon, near Pusan, which was operating at only 35 percent of capacity and whose future viability obviously depended on large, but as yet hypothetical, orders from abroad.

The stabilization program had kept down the growth of the money supply and made it difficult for firms wishing to expand to raise the necessary capital from the banks. Accordingly, an entirely unofficial curb loan market had developed to help meet the demand for funds. The massive scandal involving it that erupted in mid-1982 inevitably compelled the government to take action (in July) to regularize what now began to be called the nonbank financial market under official controls.[41]

More important than that, the government began to place its emphasis on stimulating rather than on stabilizing the economy, although it also attempted to devise a program that would ensure reasonable price stability under the new conditions.[42] At the end of

June, the government cut interest rates on deposits (approximately) from 12 to 8 percent, interest rates on bank loans from 14 to 10 percent, and corporate taxes from 33–38 percent to 20 percent; the rate of growth of the money supply was also increased.[43]

It would take time, of course, to see what the effects of this policy shift would be. Miracles were obviously not to be expected, and problems of course continued; the rains were late in 1982, for example, as they had been in 1981.

There appears to be a great deal of truth in the view expressed by a highly competent British analyst: "In the short term the Fifth Republic will be allowed to consolidate. It is the working of the economy over the next decade, in the context of the present world recession, which will determine the fate of the country's security and new constitutional structure."[44]

NOTES

1. *Korea Herald*, February 10, 1981.
2. *Korea Herald*, February 12, 13, 1981.
3. *Korea Herald*, February 26, 1981.
4. For Chun's inaugural address, see Document 17.
5. *Korea Herald*, March 27, 1981.
6. Shim Jae Hoon, "How Much Democracy Does Socialism Need?" *Far Eastern Economic Review*, May 15, 1981, p. 43.
7. Shim Jae Hoon, "Chun Wins Another One," *Far Eastern Economic Review*, April 3, 1981, pp. 18–19.
8. *Korea Herald*, April 2, 1981.
9. *Korea Herald*, April 12, 1981.
10. *Korea Herald*, May 8, 1981.
11. *New York Times*, March 25, 1981.
12. *Washington Post*, June 4, 1981.
13. *Korea Herald*, February 21, 1981; *Korea Herald*, March 3, 1981.
14. *Korea Herald*, April 4, 1981.
15. *Toward a Politics of Dialogue: Round-Table Talks with President Chun Doo Hwan, February 20, 1981* (Seoul: Korean Overseas Information Service, February 1981).
16. *Korea Herald*, June 13, 1981.
17. *Korea Herald*, April 21, 1981.
18. *Korea Herald*, June 2, 1981.
19. Hikaru Kerns, "Chun Replaces the Scholars," *Far Eastern Economic Review*, January 22, 1982, pp. 40–41.
20. *New York Times*, January 6, 1982.
21. *Korea Herald*, March 3, 1982; *New York Times*, March 4, 1982.
22. *Washington Post*, March 20, 1982; *Korea Herald*, August 12, 1982.
23. *Washington Post*, March 21, 1982.
24. *New York Times*, June 10, 1982.

25. *New York Times*, April 28, 1982.

26. *Washington Post*, May 17, 1982; *Wall Street Journal*, May 25, 1982; *Korea Herald*, July 8, 1982; *Washington Post*, August 9, 1982.

27. *Korea Herald*, June 25, 1982.

28. *Korea Herald*, July 18, 1982.

29. *Wall Street Journal*, August 24, 1982.

30. *Christian Science Monitor*, December 18, 1980.

31. *Christian Science Monitor*, March 18, 1981.

32. *Korea Herald*, January 30, 1981.

33. *Christian Science Monitor*, March 18, 1981.

34. "Exports Up; So Why Aren't Industries Expanding?" *Far Eastern Economic Review*, May 15, 1981, p. 48.

35. *New York Times*, May 19, 1981.

36. *Korea Newsreview*, April 25, 1981, pp. 17–18.

37. *Christian Science Monitor*, March 18, 1981.

38. *Christian Science Monitor*, March 18, 1981.

39. *Korea Herald*, May 14, 1981.

40. *Wall Street Journal*, December 21, 1981; *Economic Trends Report* (Seoul: American Embassy, April 1982).

41. *Korea Herald*, July 29, 1982.

42. *Korea Herald*, July 3, 1982.

43. *Wall Street Journal*, June 29, 1982.

44. David Rees, *Crisis and Continuity in South Korea*, London: Institute for the Study of Conflict, *Conflict Studies*, no. 128, March 1981, p. 32.

7

THE REPUBLIC OF KOREA
AND ITS EXTERNAL ENVIRONMENT

Today as in the past, Korea is located at the center and focal point of Northeast Asia, a region universally recognized as possessing immense strategic and economic importance. South Korea's strategic significance can be easily seen if one imagines what would happen if it were to fall under Communist domination, meaning the control of North Korea backed by the Soviet Union. In the first place, the security of Japan would be seriously threatened, as many Japanese have long realized. Secondly, the chances of bottling the Soviet Pacific Fleet up in the Seas of Japan and Okhotsk in the event of war would be greatly reduced, and conversely if the port of Chinhae were to fall into North Korean/Soviet hands the naval capabilities of the Soviet Union in the Pacific, already enhanced by its new facilities at Camranh Bay, would be further increased. South Korea's economic significance derives from the dynamism that its economy has displayed since the mid-1960s, its current difficulties notwithstanding, and the important role as an exporter of industrial products and technology, notably to non-Communist Asia and the United States, that it is capable of playing; the Republic of Korea is already the United States' twelfth largest trading partner.

Until recently, South Korea has suffered from a degree of diplomatic isolation, evidently because it has been preoccupied with its confrontation with North Korea and its partnership with the United States and because it is not a member of the United Nations. The Fifth Republic, however, has launched an energetic campaign, with impressive results, to improve South Korea's international contacts and standing, especially in Asia.

THE ASIAN CONTEXT

Since about 1970 the most striking, and probably the most important, feature of Far Eastern international politics has been the growing power and assertiveness of the Soviet Union, which have derived directly from Moscow's attainment of strategic parity (or better) with the United States. The main manifestations of this trend have been the massive Soviet buildup near the Sino-Soviet border since 1969; the steady growth of the Soviet Pacific Fleet and the improvement of its facilities at Vladivostok, on Sakhalin, at Petropavlovsk (on Kamchatka), and most recently at Camranh Bay; Soviet military and political support for Vietnam, especially in its invasion of Cambodia and its confrontation with China; and the invasion of Afghanistan.

To date, the country in East Asia that the rise in Soviet power and assertiveness has affected most heavily has been China. Regardless of its intentions, Beijing has been deterred by powerful Soviet pressures along the Sino-Soviet border from moving militarily in any direction. This is certainly one of the main purposes of the Soviet forces near the Chinese border; more broadly, Moscow profoundly distrusts China as a huge and dynamic neighbor and one of the few over which it has no positive political influence. Preoccupation with the Soviet threat and the search for ways of coping with it have induced at least two changes of great importance in Chinese foreign policy: a tendency to act as a force for stability in Asia rather than as one for troublemaking in the name of revolution, and a strong tilt toward the United States as the only possible adequate counterweight to the Soviet Union.

Both Moscow and Beijing have defensive alliances with North Korea dating from 1961, and each tries to stay on good terms with it, mainly in order not to drive it into siding with the other party to the Sino-Soviet confrontation. China, as both the weaker and the only true Asian one of the two adversaries, has been at once the more energetic and the more effective in cultivating Pyongyang; the Soviets for their part do not try very hard to hide their dislike of Kim Il Song and their hope for a "German solution" for Korea. But it is more significant that, because of memories of the Korean War and an awareness of the U.S. security commitment to South Korea, and in the Chinese case also because of a general desire not to see the new Sino-U.S. political relationship subjected to dangerous stresses, neither of the major Communist powers wants another war in the Korean peninsula, at least under current conditions. As a rule neither refers publicly to its alliance with North Korea; Beijing ordinarily does so only every five years, on each fifth anniversary of the signing of its treaty of alliance with North Korea (most recently on July 11, 1981). As is rather well understood in both Pyongyang and Seoul, and as was more or less confirmed during the Haig visit to China in June 1981, Beijing privately welcomes the U.S. military presence in South Korea as a stabilizing influence; it does not say so publicly for fear of worsening its relations with Pyongyang.

There is some concern in South Korea that, given the rising curve of Soviet assertiveness, Moscow might decide at some time in the future to give active support to an effort by Kim Chong Il to do what his father tried and failed to do in 1950. This is of course a theoretical possibility; whether it is anything more than that remains to be seen.

The U.S. tendency to react to "overinvolvement" in Vietnam by withdrawing militarily from Asia, and also to some extent from the Western Pacific, under the label of the Nixon Doctrine began to be reversed even before the end of the Carter administration due to concern over Soviet behavior in Asia and the Pacific, and elsewhere. This was the context in which the withdrawal of the Second Division from South Korea was "suspended" in 1979, even though the immediate potential adversary in that case was North Korea rather than the Soviet Union. The so-called swing strategy, under which U.S. naval forces in the Western Pacific were considered available for redeployment not only to the Indian Ocean but even to European waters, had been abandoned at least as far as the European aspect is concerned. The Carter administration initiated a modernization program for the Seventh Fleet, the instrument of U.S. naval power in the Western Pacific and the Indian Ocean. It is clear that the Reagan administration intends to continue strengthening the military presence of the United States in the Asian/Pacific region, for example by expanding the strategic relationship with China launched under the Carter administration.

Under the impact of defeat in World War II and the ensuing occupation, Japan adopted a "peace" constitution purporting to prohibit military activity as an expression of its tremendous national vitality and has concentrated on other things, economic growth in particular. Since the early Nixon period, and most recently in May–June 1981, the United States has urged Japan to do more for its own defense than successive Japanese governments have been willing to do. The Japanese political leadership has refused to make large increases in the defense budget and, while taking the U.S. commitment to Japan's security less and less seriously, has also for the most part regarded it as not really necessary because the Soviet Union, although greatly disliked, is not perceived as likely to attack Japan except in the unlikely event of a general war, in which Japan would probably be destroyed in any case. Even the recent strengthening of the Soviet military presence on the Northern Islands (the southern Kurils), which are claimed by Japan, and the invasion of Afghanistan have not, or have not yet, produced a consensus in Tokyo that there is enough of a Soviet threat so that Japan ought to do more to cope with it. The argument of the United States, supported by some Japanese including leaders of the Self Defense Forces, is that Japan needs better defenses against the Soviet air and naval threat to the approaches from the north and still more from the south (the vital sea lanes along which oil reaches Japan from the Middle East).

Given the absence of a national consensus on the need even for substantially improved defensive capabilities, Japan is not likely to play a significant strategic role outside its own immediate vicinity, at least for some time to come. The current Japanese slogan of "comprehensive security" has meant in practice a belief on Japan's part that others, principally the United States, should maintain stability and security in areas of interest to Tokyo, while Japan itself concentrates on making money through foreign trade and investment with the claim that it is contributing to the economic development of other countries.

The Japanese establishment still tends to regard Korea as a "dagger pointed at the heart" of Japan and would certainly be alarmed if North Korea were somehow to reunify the peninsula on its terms, especially if this were done by force; the Reagan-Suzuki communiqué of May 8, 1981 committed both parties to "promote the maintenance of peace on the Korean peninsula as important for peace and security in East Asia, including Japan," meaning that the Japanese government would continue to allow the United States to use its bases in Japan for the support and defense of the Republic of Korea.[1] Similarly, Japan does not want China to be attacked and defeated by the Soviet Union, but it is content to leave the problem to be managed by China itself with the support of the United States.

There is little reality in Moscow's charges that an anti-Soviet alliance is emerging among the United States, China, and Japan, with the anti-(Soviet) "hegemony" clauses that Beijing has managed to insert into its major diplomatic agreements with the United States and Japan as its visible symbol. To the very limited extent that such a combination exists, it is the result of Soviet assertiveness in Asia since about 1970. Beijing has had rather little success so far in getting other countries to align themselves with it in an anti-Soviet united front; the others generally do not feel the same sense of intense and continual confrontation with Moscow that the Chinese do and have more important political and/or economic relations with it than China does. Rather than a triangular anti-Soviet combination in the Far East, what has emerged is more in the nature of a four-power balance, in which no two of the six bilateral relationships are very much alike, but which seems to have considerable potential for maintaining peace and stability provided the Soviet Union is not allowed to build up a margin of military superiority—global or regional—large enough to tempt it irresistibly into seriously destabilizing adventures.

KOREA AND ASIA

Among the non-Communist Asian neighbors of the Republic of Korea, its most important relations are of course with Japan. Even apart from a strong element of mutual dislike inherited from the past, there are serious problems and issues between the two countries.

One of these is the fact that in the trade between them that began in the mid-1960s Korea has regularly run a deficit averaging in recent years about $3 billion per year; there is no sign of an early change in this situation. The large Korean community in Japan (about 600,000) has been discriminated against in a variety of ways, even though most of them have permanent resident status. Partly as a result of this discrimination, many Koreans in Japan have developed leftist and pro-North Korean sympathies, and the Japanese government has done little to prevent North Korea from establishing organizations among them. This is partly because even the conservative Japanese establishment likes to trade with North Korea and maintain other contacts with it, short of full diplomatic relations as yet, and does not take the North Korean threat to South Korea seriously enough to be willing to coordinate its policy toward Pyongyang with Seoul—another issue between South Korea and Japan. The Korean government, and the Chun leadership in particular, has felt that Japan was not doing enough for its own defense and for that of the region. Finally, Seoul resented Tokyo's efforts to prevent the execution of Kim Dae Jung, which included implicit threats of trade sanctions and the actual withholding of government credits; in December 1980 there were large meetings and demonstrations in South Korea in protest against Japanese "meddling" in the Kim case, and since political meetings were basically illegal under martial law it must be assumed that these were officially organized.

Following the commutation of Kim's sentence, the climate of South Korean-Japanese relations began to improve somewhat. The main reasons were apparently a belief on the South Korean side that the Chun visit to the United States had created a more favorable atmosphere for dealing with Tokyo, and on the Japanese side a feeling that the Fifth Republic had begun to stabilize itself and that Tokyo ought to try to keep abreast of the United States in establishing good relations with it. On his way home from the United States, President Chun said that he would be receptive if Japanese Premier Suzuki should propose a meeting between them.[2] Chun repeated this suggestion in a more positive way three months later.[3] Meanwhile, Japanese Foreign Minister Masayoshi Ito had attended President Chun's inauguration and held talks with South Korean Foreign Minister Lho Shin Young; soon after this meeting it was announced that Japan would sell South Korea 400,000 tons of rice on easy credit terms.[4] At about the same time, the Japanese government drafted legislation aimed at making it easier for certain Koreans living in Japan to be granted permanent resident status.[5] The attitude on both sides was still less than wholly cordial, however; in June 1981, for example, Seoul became indignant over a visit to Japan by a delegation of North Korean parliamentarians.[6] Over the next several months, the two sides failed to agree on a South Korean request for $6 billion in concessional credits, plus $4 billion in bank loans, over a five-year period, the rationale for this proposal being that the Republic of Korea was making an essential contribution to the security of the entire region including Japan. The trade balance between the two countries continued to run heavily in Japan's favor.

On the other hand, South Korean-Japanese relations did seem to be improving, one indication being the visit of Japanese Foreign Minister Sunao Sonoda and several of his cabinet colleagues to Seoul in September 1981. Another sign of a better atmosphere was the fact that Japan graciously accepted the choice of Seoul the following month as the site of the 1988 Olympic Games over the Japanese city of Nagoya, an event that evoked enormous enthusiasm in South Korea.

Unlike Japan, which once conquered Southeast Asia and appears to some to threaten it with economic domination, South Korea is not feared and resented in that region. On a much smaller scale, it has begun to develop an economic relationship with Southeast Asia comparable to Japan's: essentially capital, technology, and industrial products for raw materials. Like other countries, South Korea has observed with gradually increasing respect the rise of the Association of Southeast Asian Nations (ASEAN) as a viable regional organization. Accordingly, there was logic in the announcement in early May 1981 that, as a consequence of an invitation from Indonesia the previous November, President Chun would pay a two-week visit to the ASEAN countries in June–July.[7] The purpose of the visit on the South Korean side, apart from raising the level of trade, appeared to be to gain an increased understanding of South Korea's strategic problem and an acceptance of the Chun government's attitude on strategic questions, including the proposal for a North-South summit; this would not be an easy task, since the South Koreans view the Soviet Union as the overall threat to the region, but some of the ASEAN states, especially Indonesia and Malaysia, tend to see it as China.[8]

So far as can be judged from the public record, there was a general although of course not complete resemblance among the summit talks in the five countries. The ASEAN leaders endorsed the South Korean position on the linkage between the security of Northeast Asia and that of Southeast Asia, the principle of direct talks between the two Koreas (although not specifically the Chun proposal for an exchange of visits between President Chun and Kim Il Song), and the admission of both Koreas to the United Nations pending ultimate reunification of the country. The South Korean side expressed its approval and support for ASEAN as an organization, for its goal of a neutral Southeast Asia, and for its position on Cambodia (essentially, a call for a political settlement). Both sides agreed to expand their economic and technical relations, along lines already indicated.[9]

The main significance of the Chun visit to the ASEAN countries seems to be that it represented a possible beginning of an escape for the Republic of Korea from its previous sense of isolation from most of the world including much of Asia and its feeling of being trapped by the overwhelming presence of its neighbors including North Korea.

Although at first there was apparently little interest in South Korea in the concept of a Pacific Community,[10] such interest has recently begun to emerge. Like all the industrial states of the region, the Republic of Korea has both much to contribute to and much to gain from an expansion of political, economic, and cultural relations among the nations of the Pacific Basin.

THE NORTH KOREAN THREAT

When everything has been said about the Republic of Korea's interests and potential role on a wider stage, the fact remains that the main problem is still North Korea, and it will remain North Korea until there is some political settlement. Such a settlement is not now in prospect and probably requires the participation not only of the two Koreas themselves but of the four major powers with interests in the peninsula.

Regardless of Pyongyang's exact intentions, which are uncertain and presumably subject to change, its capabilities and dispositions strongly suggest a desire to be in a position to launch an attack against the Seoul area with minimum warning in the event of a serious crisis of some kind within the Republic of Korea. A large proportion of the North Korean armed forces are deployed in tactical formations very close to what is rather misleadingly called the Demilitarized Zone. No serious professional military analyst any longer doubts that those forces are offensively stronger, especially in armor, than those of South Korea, and by a significant margin. Plans now being implemented in the Republic of Korea, for example the purchase of F-16s from the United States, may narrow, close, or even reverse this gap in the mid-1980s, but for the present it is there.

A partial and approximate order of battle for the two sides, based on the best available published source,[11] would be as follows:

	North Korea	South Korea
Armored forces	2 divisions 2 independent regiments	2 brigades
Infantry forces	38 divisions (including 3 motorized)	18 divisions (including 1 mechanized)
Field artillery	20 regiments	30 battalions
Special forces	See below	5 brigades
Submarines	15	0
Missile attack craft	18	8
Bomber aircraft	85	0
Fighter bombers	0	222
Interceptor aircraft	420	0

Although the development is not reflected in published figures, there is reason to believe that the North Korean special forces have been rapidly built up in the past few years with Seoul as their main target, presumably in the event of major civil disorder in the South.

From a strategic point of view, South Korea's main problem has been its lack of an effective retaliatory deterrent to another attack by the North. The deterrent has been in the United States', not Korean, hands.

THE SECURITY OF THE FIFTH REPUBLIC

There have been some interesting indications that the Republic of Korea has been trying to outgrow its lack of a deterrent. In late September 1978, it unveiled what purported to be a medium-range ballistic missile (MRBM).[12] Little was heard in public after that about the MRBM or about the broader problem of a deterrent. Then, during the Chun visit to ASEAN, President Chun himself, echoed by some of his officials, began to say that if attacked again the Republic of Korea could and would destroy North Korea.[13] These statements naturally aroused speculation that South Korea had somehow acquired nuclear weapons, but foreign military analysts do not believe this to be the case. Whatever the exact position that the Republic of Korea may now occupy along the road to a nuclear weapons capability, and whether or not it seriously intends to be a military nuclear power, the statements appear to have a political purpose—to increase the psychological pressure on North Korea from various directions to agree to the Chun proposal for an exchange of visits. For the time being at least, the military deterrent to another North Korean attack still appears to rest in the United States' hands.

Under present conditions, the U.S. (not South Korean) deterrent, the joint defensive capabilities of the Republic of Korea and the United States, the relative political stability of South Korea, and the lack of enthusiasm on the part of North Korea's allies (especially China) for another war in the peninsula appear likely to continue to prevent such a war, as they have since 1953. But this cautious optimism is based on the assumption that the Republic of Korea and the United States will continue to strengthen their military positions with respect to North Korea and that they will keep their alliance in good repair.

FOREIGN AFFAIRS IN 1982

Foreign and security policy continued to absorb much of the attention of the Chun government in 1982, because the survival of both the country and the government depended to a considerable extent on the maintenance of at least a reasonably favorable external environment. Foreign statesmen were invited to South Korea in increasing numbers. In August 1982 President Chun traveled to Africa and Canada, with the same basic purposes as when he had visited the ASEAN states in 1981: political goodwill and improved economic relations.

Another initiative that grew logically out of the ASEAN tour was Chun's proposal, launched in May 1982, for a summit conference of all the Pacific countries, including presumably the Communist ones, within the next two years, as a stimulus to the Pacific Community concept that was gradually gaining favor in the region. The foreign response, although inevitably limited at first, was favorable as far as it went; it remained to be seen whether the proposal would really catch on.[14]

Although a role on the world stage was attractive, it was North Korea that remained the principal external problem. In his state of the nation address to the National Assembly on January 22, 1982, President Chun proposed a four-stage unification program, including the establishment of liaison offices and culminating in a joint constitution; each party was to retain its existing alliances.[15] This proposal was promptly rejected by Pyongyang.[16] Soon afterward the government of the Republic of Korea proposed, also without success, a series of contacts including the building of a highway between Seoul and Pyongyang, the opening to both parties of the ports of Inchona (in South Korea) and Chinnampo (in North Korea), exchanges of visits and missions of various kinds, and the like.[17]

The next several months saw three occasions that had at least potential or symbolic importance to North-South Korean relations but in fact produced nothing significant in this connection. One was Kim Il Song's seventieth birthday (April 16, 1982), the massive celebration of which in Pyongyang served mainly to suggest that the installment of his son Kim Chong Il as his successor was encountering both resistance at home and lack of enthusiasm abroad. The second was the anniversary (June 25) of the outbreak of the Korean War, on which occasion Chinese Defense Minister Geng Biao visited Pyongyang and gave somewhat stronger declaratory support to North Korea's positions on U.S. troop withdrawal from the South and on Korean unification than Chinese spokesmen had been accustomed to give on similar occasions in the past. It appeared, however, that Geng's enthusiasm reflected little more than a desire to smooth over some differences that had arisen in Sino-North Korean relations and to needle the United States in connection with its arms sales to Taiwan.

The third was the tenth anniversary (July 4) of the North-South statement of 1972 on unification.

By the beginning of 1982, Seoul's earlier hope for a $10 billion loan from Japan had been scaled down to $6 billion, the rationale for the proposal being not only economic but political: the cost and effort involved in South Korea's contribution to the security of Japan and the entire region entitled the Republic of Korea to special consideration from its wealthy neighbor. Tokyo rejected the security argument out of hand and informed Seoul in April 1982 that the most it could expect was $4 billion. During a series of further negotiations, notably when Foreign Minister Lee Bum Suk visited Tokyo in July on his way back from the United States, there were disagreements over terms. Seoul wanted the low interest rates usually accorded to developing countries; Tokyo insisted on more or less commercial rates, on the ground that South Korea was far from a poor country. It was not certain when or even whether these differences would be resolved.[18]

Around midsummer a huge storm blew up in South Korea and China over a new Japanese history textbook that described earlier Japanese aggression against Japan's neighbors as "advances" and the Korean independence movement of 1919 as a "riot." In both the offended countries this issue brought to the surface the powerful, historic, understandable anti-Japanese feelings that for decades had never been more than just beneath the surface.[19] Embarrassed by this reaction, the Japanese government agreed to change the offending passages;[20] it was clearly concerned among other things over the possible effects on its important trade with South Korea and China.

The same consideration influenced the leftist Mitterand government of France to revise an apparent decision to recognize North Korea. During a visit to Seoul by French Foreign Minister Claude Cheysson in early August, he was apparently given to understand that all South Korean-French commercial agreements would be cancelled in the event Paris recognized Pyongyang and replied that his government had no such intention at present.[21]

NOTES

1. Text in *New York Times*, May 9, 1981.
2. *Korea Herald*, February 7, 1981.
3. *Korea Herald*, May 16, 1981.
4. *New York Times*, March 11, 1981.
5. *New York Times*, April 5, 1981.

6. *Korea Herald*, June 14, 1981.

7. *Korea Herald*, May 8, 1981.

8. Rodney Tasker, "The Wooing of ASEAN," *Far Eastern Economic Review*, June 26, 1981, pp. 28–29.

9. Joint communiqués may be found in *Korea Herald* (1981) for the following dates: Indonesia, June 28; Malaysia, July 2; Singapore, July 3; Thailand, July 7; Philippines, July 9.

10. Compare Sung Joo Han, "Thoughts on the Pacific Community: A Korean View," in *Pacific Region Interdependencies*, Joint Economic Committee of Congress, 1981, pp. 84–86.

11. *The Military Balance, 1979–1980* (London: International Institute for Strategic Studies, 1979), pp. 68–69.

12. *Korea Herald*, September 27, 28, 1978; *Asian Wall Street Journal*, October 3, 1978.

13. *Washington Star*, June 27, 1981; *Korea Newsreview*, June 27, 1981, p. 6; *Korea Newsreview*, July 4, 1981, p. 6.

14. Shim Jae Hoon, "Chun's Grand Design," *Far Eastern Economic Review*, June 25, 1982.

15. *Korea Herald*, January 23, 1982; Shim Jae Hoon, "Chun's Unity Charter," *Far Eastern Economic Review*, January 29, 1982, pp. 8–9.

16. *New York Times*, January 27, 1982.

17. *Korea Herald*, February 2, 1982.

18. Compare *Korea Herald*, July 24, 1982.

19. *Christian Science Monitor*, August 5, 1982.

20. *Washington Post*, August 24, 1982.

21. Shim Jae Hoon, "Seoul Hangs Tough," *Far Eastern Economic Review*, August 13, 1982, p. 20.

8

CONCLUSION: A TENTATIVE APPRAISAL
OF THE FIFTH REPUBLIC

Since the Fifth Republic came officially into existence only at the beginning of March 1981, no real authority or finality can be claimed for an evaluation of its political system. Nevertheless, a necessarily tentative appraisal, by way of conclusion to this study, is probably better than none at all.

THE KOREAN PERSPECTIVE

There are two possible Korean analogues with which it seems logical to compare the Fifth Republic: North Korea and the Fourth Republic. Not much needs to be said about the first of these comparisons; readers who need to have it proved to them that the people of South Korea enjoy a significantly higher level of political development and freedom than the people of North Korea would not be convinced by any evidence or arguments that could be produced here, although they probably would be by a visit to both Koreas. In that connection, there is generally a positive correlation between the level of freedom that a government allows its citizens and the ease of access to its territory that it permits to foreigners; it is easy for a tourist or other foreign visitor to secure a four-year multiple entry visa to the Republic of Korea and travel almost anywhere in it, whereas he can get a visa for North Korea only if he has been officially invited and must then follow a very closely controlled itinerary.

Because of Soviet occupation and the "cult of personality" of Kim Il Song, who since the death of Tito (whose funeral he attended) has been continuously in power longer than any other major political leader, North Korea is one of the most totalitarian states in the world. The same would presumably be true of South Korea if the United States had permitted it to come under Soviet Occupation in 1945 or had not intervened to save it in 1950. As it is, South Korea has succeeded in reaching levels of political freedom and economic development (or at any rate living standards) that can be seen to be much higher than those of North Korea, although an exact comparison is difficult or even impossible. The point is reinforced, although not proved, by the fact the North Korean representatives who came to Seoul in 1972 for talks were amazed at the prosperity they saw, not only in comparison with what they had expected but in comparison with what they knew at home. Another approach to the comparison is to imagine what would happen if all barriers to movement between the two Koreas were somehow removed; whatever net flow occurred would be heavily from north to south, as was the case immediately after the end of World War II and during the Korean War.

The task of comparing the Fifth Republic with the Fourth is more complex. Obviously there are resemblances, such as the important role of the military and the constitutional structure (for example, the indirect election of the president and the ability of the government party to maintain a majority in the National Assembly by controlling a bloc of seats in addition to those won at the previous election). There are other, even more obvious, common characteristics that have marked South Korean governments at virtually all times since 1948: the strongly anti-Communist orientation; the admitted absence of a full-fledged parliamentary democracy of the Western type; general acceptance of the president and the political system, although not always or necessarily of the government party and the bureaucracy, by the majority of the public; and the restriction at most times of active and articulate political dissent to elements of a fairly small although far from insignificant proportion of the total population consisting of elements of the opposition parties, the press, the intellectuals, the students, and the Christian community.

In contrast to these general resemblances, there are significant, or potentially significant, differences between the Fourth Republic (especially in its last years) and the Fifth, to the extent that we may judge by the latter's brief record to date.

At the top leadership level, the difference is striking. Park Chung Hee ruled essentially and increasingly as a dictator relying heavily on his security services; he prolonged his own tenure as long as possible, made no observable arrangements for the succession, did not really try to acquire and practice political skills, and grew more and more isolated from the public by his own choice. Chun Doo Hwan came to power essentially as the representative of the most dynamic element of the military. Having no political experience or skills at first, he has rapidly acquired them and has moved with surprising speed to develop a true political base, first within the military leadership as a whole and then among the civilian population. Foreigners—including the author of this study—who have talked with him in the course of this development testify to the steepness of his learning curve. He has publicly criticized the length of Park's tenure and to all appearances has made it impossible for himself to serve more than one presidential term. Although under the Fifth Republic as under the Fourth there is no vice-president, it would be naive to assume that President Chun, who obviously cares deeply about the future of his country, desires that the succession to himself be the first orderly transition in the Republic of Korea's history but, distrusting the factional tendencies of Korean politicans, will make no effort to ensure that he is succeeded by an acceptable replacement. There has been speculation that the currently preferred successor is Roh Tae Woo, who held the assignment that Chun left in order to become president—the Defense Security Command—until July 1981, when he was promoted to full general, retired from the army, and was then appointed second minister of state in charge of security and diplomatic affairs, which however is not necessarily a powerful position.[1]

As compared with the Fourth Republic, the political role of the army in the Fifth is considerably greater, and that of the police (the KCIA, now the Agency for National Security Planning) somewhat less although certainly not negligible. This appears to be an improvement, inasmuch as the military leaders of any country are more likely than the police to give their highest political loyalty to the nation and to maintain close ties with the population, through the conscription system for example.

The fact that the Fifth Republic is less of a one-man show than the Third means greater overall efficiency, less corruption on the part of officials (or at least more energetic efforts to stamp it out), and more stress on consensus formation as against confrontation with the opposition. The other side of the coin is that the opposition has less freedom of maneuver. Many of its leaders are barred from political activity at least until after the next presidential election. The opposition—or more accurately, nongovernment—parties are tamer, or in other words they tend not to rock the boat because there is no point in doing so. The press is no longer formally censored as it was under martial law, but, at least until recently, it no longer criticizes the government as elements of it did under the Third Republic; there is only one news agency, the Yonhap (Allied) agency, although the press prints material from foreign wire services as well.

As for the economy, there appears to be a greater official willingness under the Fifth Republic than under the Third to avoid hasty top-level decisions and to admit economists and business leaders into the planning process and thereby allow greater scope for private initiative. In the long run, this is likely to result in a sounder economy—in relation to the unattainable possibilities, which are obviously constricted by such uncontrollable problems as rising oil costs and foreign tariff barriers—even though the near future will be difficult.

By proposing an exchange of summit visits with Kim Il Song, President Chun had gone a step beyond President Park in seeking a dialogue with North Korea. Chun made his first proposal along these lines even before the inauguration of the Fifth Republic; by that time he has already appointed as minister of national unification an able and experienced official, Lee Bum Suk, and given him and his ministry complete charge of dealings with North Korea.

THE ASIAN PERSPECTIVE

It was pointed out many years ago, with special reference to Southeast Asia, that in a region where communism is an entrenched threat and where political parties and parliamentary institutions of the more or less Western type are weak, immature, or nonexistent, the military not only consitute a valuable reservoir of modern skills but are likely to try to play an active role in opposing the Communist threat in its political as well as its military aspect. They are therefore likely to take a prominent part in politics,[2] and so they do, in one way or another, in most of the non-Communist countries of the region (that is, in Burma, Thailand, Indonesia, and the Philippines).

South Korea essentially fits the same description—Communist threat, weak political institutions—even though the threat is much more external than internal to the political system, and there has accordingly been a recurrent and similar tendency for the military to assume a prominent role in politics. At present, their role is dominant in the last analysis, although at least since the end of martial law their political functions have been exercised less overtly, less arbitrarily, less corruptly, and with more cooperation from civilian politicians than is normal in states where the military are considered to be politically influential or actually in control, as in the Southeast Asian countries just mentioned or some of the countries of the Middle East and Latin America.

Since World War II there have been three areas in the Far East to which the United States has devoted a great deal of effort, money, and manpower in order to prevent a Communist takeover: South Korea, Taiwan, and South Vietnam.

In the last of these cases, the effort was of course disastrously unsuccessful. This failure was due, not to a U.S. military defeat as many people believe, but to the fact that the United States withdrew undefeated because it was no longer willing to bear the costs and casualties associated with the attempt to protect the rather ineffective South Vietnamese government from its highly effective Communist adversaries, and the disaster occurred after the U.S. withdrawal and because of it. There is very little resemblance between this situation and that of South Korea in the recent past, at present, or in the foreseeable future. There is no significant Communist politico-military presence within South Korea, as there was within South Vietnam for a long time before the final collapse in 1975; the political system, economy, and armed forces of South Korea are much more vigorous and effective than their South Vietnamese counterparts were prior to 1975. As for the U.S. role, President Nixon, who withdrew the entire U.S. military presence from South Vietnam and the Seventh Division from South Korea, and President Carter, who started to withdraw the Second Division from South Korea, were not committed to a complete withdrawal from South Korea or a termination of the U.S. defensive commitment to it. The Reagan administration takes a more positive attitude toward the security of the Republic of Korea than its predecessors did.

Taiwan has grown prosperous and remained free of Communist control from a combination of the protection afforded by the Taiwan Strait, the talents of its people, an infrastructure inherited from the Japanese period, a reasonably effective—not truly democratic—government, considerable defensive military strength, and U.S. aid and protection. This combination of circumstances obviously resembles South Korea's, but with one important difference: the United States has abrogated its formal defensive commitment to Taiwan—although the Taiwan Relations Act affirms a continuing U.S. interest in the security as well as the prosperity of the island—severed diplomatic relations with it, and established formal ties with its Communist adversary. This was done, with inevitably negative effects on the morale and prospects of Taiwan, not in the belief that the island had become unviable or not worth protecting, but for important reasons of grosse politik. There is no real analogy in the case of South Korea to this. No significant pressure exists in the United States for derecognition of the Republic of Korea; at most there is a little for cross-recognition (that is, relations with both Koreas). Furthermore, the Republic of Korea enjoys diplomatic relations with a large number of countries in addition to the United States, whereas Taiwan now has them with very few, the Republic of Korea being one. The international community therefore feels a greater stake in the survival of the Republic of Korea than in that of Taiwan (or the Republic of China). This consideration, which has some psychological and political importance, contributes to making the future of South Korea, even though it is contiguous with its main adversary, appear more secure than that of Taiwan.

Another Asian country with whose political system South Korea's has sometimes been compared, especially during late 1980 when it seemed that Kim Dae Jung might suffer the same fate as Zulfikar Ali Bhutto, is Pakistan. Not only in this respect but in others, the comparison appears rather farfetched. By any reasonable standard, both the political and the economic systems of South Korea are much more dynamic and effective, and more likely to prove stable, than those of Pakistan. The political cultures of the two countries are so different that it is difficult to compare them with respect to the level of freedom; the author, who has visited both countries in the fairly recent past, considers that on balance the comparison runs in favor of South Korea, the greater efficiency of whose political controls is more than outweighed by serious internal tensions in Pakistan and the tendency of the Zia government to institute an Islamic state. The only real resemblance is the significant political role of the military in both cases.

IN CONCLUSION

In the last analysis, South Korea's political record ought to be judged on its own merits, rather than by comparison with that of other countries. Considering the difficulties imposed by Korea's political tradition and recent history, and above all by the North-South confrontation, the Fifth Republic has performed well enough to date to give grounds for cautious optimism about its future.

The military still have the ability to exert potentially decisive influence in crisis situations, but their political role in more normal times is evidently diminishing. Those military leaders who have gone into politics inevitably tend to take on something of the outlook as well as the functions of civilians. The institutions established by the constitution of the Fifth Republic, such as the National Assembly, are likely to acquire increasing vitality, at least as long as there are no more major political crises. The termination of martial law, and still more the commutation of Kim Dae Jung's sentence, seem to have been a turning point. Military leaders were evidently reluctant to see him spared, but the favorable effects of the commutation of his sentence impressed them with the wisdom of listening to other points of view on important political questions beside their own. President Chun has made it clear in various ways, including the removal of some generals from their posts, that he does not intend to allow the military to become a threat to the political system that he now heads.

The new leadership of South Korea sees its major policies and programs as falling within four main areas. It is trying to give South Korea a political system capable of evolving in the direction of greater freedom, subject to the overriding requirement for stability; to reform the country's public and social life through campaigns against official corruption (which has been a serious problem in the history of the Republic of Korea), crime, injustice, and the like; to regenerate economic momentum after a period of serious difficulties; and to expand the Republic of Korea's external relations and enhance its security. In all these fields the new leadership has made energetic efforts and begun to achieve results.

In the longer term, the crucial test of the Fifth Republic will probably be its ability to maintain the continuing viability of South Korea as the sole surviving non-Communist area on the east coast of Asia. To do this it will have to keep at a manageable level its vulnerability to the disaster that would do more harm to the welfare of the people of South Korea than would any other realistically imaginable, in addition to precipitating a major international crisis—another attack from the North.

A Western-style parliamentary democracy in the Republic of Korea, desirable though it seems to the Korean opposition and much of the outside world, appears unattainable for the foreseeable future. The obstacles are the Korean political tradition—centralizing authoritarianism overriding strong factional tendencies—the harsh legacy of Japanese colonial rule, and most of all the division of the country— for which the superpowers and not the Koreans are responsible—and the resulting confrontation with the hostile and powerful neighbor to the north. South Korea is compelled by its history and by geopolitics to live not only dangerously but also in a condition of less than complete freedom. What is surprising, under these circumstances, is that there is as much freedom as there is, to the point where organized political opposition can and does exist.

NOTES

1. *Korea Herald*, July 17, 1981.
2. Guy J. Pauker, "Southeast Asia as a Problem Area in the Next Decade," *World Politics* 11 (April 1959): 337–40.

DOCUMENTS

NOTE ON DOCUMENTS

The romanization (or spelling in the latin alphabet) of Korean words and names has never been standardized, even to the same extent as has been done in the case of Chinese. In part this is because of the nature of the sounds, as compared with those of the latin alphabet. Accordingly, no attempt has been made to standardize them here, and there are variations among documents and between the documents and the text. The confusion here accurately reflects confusion in the subject under study. It is believed, however, that the confusion will not be so great as to baffle comprehension of any important point, and anyone with sufficient interest to use the documents will probably be able to make any necessary allowances and adjustments for variations in transcription.

THE POLITICAL TRANSITION

1. GENERAL CHUN DOO HWAN, STATEMENT ON PARK ASSASSINATION, NOVEMBER 5, 1979

Prior to disclosing the facts about the slaying of the president, first let me express my sincere sympathy together with all the citizens, over the death of his excellency the late President Pak Chong-hui. Now, I will tell you the results of the investigation.

In view of the seriousness of the incident, the Joint Investigation Headquarters under the Martial Law Command has exerted every effort to uncover the facts by mobilizing all investigation forces, including the prosecutors and police. As a result, the full details of the crime of the ring led by Kim Chae-kyu, the instigator of this high treason, have been revealed and the motive and plan behind the crime, details of the incident and any other people involved are disclosed as follows:

The details of the incident: As has already been announced, the ringleader, Kim Chae-kyu, was reprimanded many times by his excellency the president for his inability to carry out his mission. His reports and suggestions to his excellency President Pak were blocked by chief bodyguard Cha. In addition, he once received a letter of reprimand from the president and, in light of the rumors of an upcoming reshuffle of key posts in connection with the recent disturbances, Kim was worried about being blamed and about his possible dismissal. Thus, he had wanton thoughts about killing the president and his chief bodyguard and seizing power, and he watched for an opportunity.

At 1600 on 26 October, upon receiving word from Cha Chi-chol, director of the Presidential Security Service, that his excellency the president would have dinner at the dining hall of the Central Intelligence Agency at Kungchong-tong, he made up his mind to carry out his plan that night. Aiming to embroil others in a revolt after slaying his excellency President Pak, Kim called the army chief of staff, Chong Sung-hwa, and the KCIA second assistant director, Kim Chong-sop, at

Source: Seoul Domestic Service broadcast, November 6, 1979.

approximately 1605 on the pretext of wanting to dine with them and invited them to dine at an annex some 50 meters from the dining hall which was used as an office by the CIA director.

Kim arrived at the site first at approximately 1700 and waited for his excellency the president to arrive. At about 1740, prior to arrival of his excellency the president, Kim Kye-won, the president's chief secretary, arrived and told Kim Chae-kyu in the dining hall garden: It is a headache that Director Cha is so arrogant and oversteps others' authority. Kim Chae-kyu replied: Right: Because of that guy, there is trouble. I will finish him off tonight. Kim Key-won nodded his agreement.

At approximately 1805, his excellency the president and Director Cha Chi-chol arrived and the dinner started soon thereafter. The participants at the dinner were his excellency the president, Cha, Chi-chol, Kim Chae-kyu, Kim Kye-won, and Song Kum-cha and Chong Hye-sun, who would serve at the dinnertable, six persons in all.

When his excellency the president reproachfully informed Kim Chae-kyu during the dinner that the Pusan situation might have resulted from the KCIA's inability to collect information, Kim Chae-kyu looked depressed. Then at about 1855 Kim Chae-kyu left the dining table for the first time to go to the lavatory. After returning, he began watching a television program while continuing to eat. At about 1900 he became agitated when he was sternly denounced by chief security officer Cha for the KCIA's inability to carry out activities in connection with the declaration of martial law on 18 October in the Pusan area.

At about 1910, Kim Chae-kyu left the dining room for the second time and went to the separate main building, where Army Chief of Staff Chong Sung-hwa and the second assistant director of the KCIA, Kim Chong-sop, who arrived there at about 1835, were dining. He told them: I am dining with his excellency; please wait until I return after dinner. Then he went to his office on the second floor of the main building, where he put his West German 32-caliber 7-shot (Walther) in his back pocket and returned to the dining area. On his way, he took the revolver out of his back pocket and put it in the right side of his trousers waistband in front of the KCIA protocol section chief, Pak Son-ho, and his secretary, Colonel Pak Hung-chu. He said to them: I will finish them off today, so you dispose of the bodyguards when you hear the gunshots in the dining room. Then he asked them: Are you ready?

When the two showed hesitation, Kim Chae-kyu encouraged them saying: The army chief of staff and the second assistant director of the KCIA are also here. Then Pak Son-ho said: We are ready. Are you going to finish off his excellency, too. There are seven bodyguards. How about waiting until the next opportunity?

Kim Chae-kyu replied: No, that is no good because information might leak out unless we do it today. Select three able people and have them support me. I will finish all of them off.

Then Pak Sun-ho replied: Then please give me 30 more minutes. Kim Chae-kyu answered: All right. I understand.

Thus he returned to the dining room, where the atmosphere had toned down. At about 1935, the chief cook, Nam Hyo-chu, told Kim Chae-kyu: The section chief wants to see you. Kim Chae-kyu then left the dining room for the third time and went to an adjacent room, where Pak Son-ho reported that the preparations had been completed.

Upon returning to the dining room and sitting down at approximately 1940, he patted Kim Kye-won, who was sitting on his right hand, and said: You should serve his excellency more intelligently.

Then Kim Chae-kyu looked at Cha Chi-chol and said: Your excellency, you are handling the affairs of state with this sort of a bug [bo-ro-chi]. How can you expect anything to go right? Then he drew his revolver from his waistband and while still seated, fired a round at chief security officer Cha, then, standing he fired a round at his excellency the president. Chief security officer Cha, who was not carrying a gun, took refuge in the lavatory with his right wrist pierced by a bullet.

His excellency President Pak was shot through the chest and began falling out of his chair to the left. Miss Chong and Miss Song, who were on hand, helped him by placing their hands on his blood-soaked chest and back to keep the blood from gushing out and said to him: "Your Excellency, are you all right?" Then his excellency the president said, "I am all right," and bent over.

At that moment, Kim Kye-won fled from the room. In the meantime, taking the gunshots in the dining room as his signal, KCIA protocol officer Pak Son-ho shot to death Chong In-hyong, chief of the Office of Presidential Security Service, and An Chae-song, deputy chief of the office, who were waiting in the reception room. Senior Secretary Colonel Pak Hung-chu, guard Yi Ki-chu and chauffer Yu Song-ok shot to death chief of the special car division of the Office of Presidential Secretary Service Kim Yong-tae and bodyguard Kim Yong-sop and wounded bodyguard Pak Sang-pom.

Meanwhile, Kim Chae-kyu again attempted to shoot at Director Cha hiding in the lavatory, but the gun did not work. Discarding the gun, Kim Chae-kyu went into the garden, where he asked Colonel Pak Hung-chu for his gun. Upon being told that all its bullets had been fired, Kim again headed toward the dining room and spotted Pak Son-ho coming out of the reception room into the corridor on the way. Kim then took Pak's .38 revolver and went into the dining room. At that movement, Director Cha was coming out of hiding in the lavatory shouting, "bodyguard! bodyguard!" and came face to face with Kim Chae-kyu. Cha then attempted to hide behind a chest in a corner of the room but Kim Chae-kyu fired one shot into his abdomen, then approached his excellency President Pak, who was bent over, and placed the pistol close to his head and fired one shot, killing him.

Meanwhile, Miss Chong and Miss Song, who had been helping the president, fled in panic to the lavatory and kitchen, respectively, just as Kim Chae-kyu was about to fire another shot into his excellency. Thus, they became witnesses to the circumstances in which his excellency died.

At that moment, Kim Won-tae [as heard], one of the culprits who was waiting nearby, came in with a M-16 rifle at the direction of protocol officer Pak Son-ho and fired one shot into An Chae-song and two shots into Chong In-hyong, who were on the floor, and two shots into Director Cha and one shot into Kim Yong-sop, who were groaning, to insure that there were no survivors.

Meanwhile, Army Chief of Staff, Chong and Kim Chong-sop, who were in a separate building, and were just meeting, exchanged greetings and talked about the current domestic situation, including the situation in Pusan and Masan. When they had almost finished dinner, they heard several gunshots. Thinking something was unusual, the chief of staff asked the assistant director, "Aren't those gunshots?" Then Kim Chong-sop left the room, instructed a guard to check with the Kungjong-dong police box nearby regarding the gunshots, returned to the table and began eating some fruit.

At approximately 1943, Kim Chae-kyu was hurriedly leaving the scene of the crime without his shoes and jacket when he met Kim Kye-won, who had previously fled the dining room, and said to him: "I did what I said I would do. Everything is finished now." Then Kim Chae-kyu hurriedly dashed toward the adjacent building, saying in a high-pitched voice "Where is the car? Come out with the guests from the room! Water, water . . ." and, sweating, entered the adjacent building in haste and drank a cup of water offered by a guard.

Then Kim Chae-kyu grabbed the arm of Chief of Staff Chong and led him toward the entrance of the building, saying "Chief of staff, chief of staff, a serious thing has happened. Hurry into the car." Chief of Staff Chong said to him, "What's up?", to which Kim Chae-kyu replied: "Let's talk about it in the car."

At the time, Army Chief of Staff Chong thought Kim Chae-kyu was fleeing from a surprise attack and took a seat in the middle of the back seat of Kim Chae-kyu's car. Kim Chae-kyu sat on Chong's right, Kim Chong-sop to his left, and Colonel Pak Hung-chu in the front seat.

In the car, Army Chief of Staff Chong emphatically asked Kim Chae-kyu, "What is the matter?" "A serious thing happened. Let's go to the Central Intelligence Agency," answered Kim Chae-kyu.

"What happened?" the army chief of staff asked again. Kim Chae-kyu did not answer but made a sign by raising his thumb, which meant his excellency, to indicate that the president had been shot. When the army chief of staff asked, "Is his excellency dead?" Kim Chae-kyu answered, "It is certain that he is dead."

Kim Chae-kyu impatiently checked several times to see whether security cars were following them. Then he repeatedly stressed, "We must keep it secret. There will be serious trouble if the enemy learns about it."

When Army Chief of Staff Chong asked: "Is it infiltration from the outside or an internal affair?" Kim Chae-kyu answered, "I myself don't know very well," and then repeatedly emphasized that it must be kept secret.

Realizing that the car was headed for the 1 March overpass, Army Chief of Staff Chong asked, "Where are we headed?" to which Kim Chae-kyu replied: "To the Central Intelligence Agency." Then, thinking that it would be easy to command in case it was necessary to carry out an operation and that they would be protected, the army chief of staff said, "Let's go to army headquarters," while Kim Chae-kyu hesitated, Colonel Pak Hung-chu in the front seat said, "Let's do so." The car then changed direction and headed for army headquarters. At that time, Kim Chae-kyu momentarily thought about threatening the army chief of staff. During the car ride, Kim Chae-kyu told Colonel Pak Hung-chu to "take off your jacket and shoes and give them to me," whereupon Colonel Pak Chung-chu gave Kim Chae-kyu a spare jacket and shoes that he had been carrying.

The car arrived at the bunker of army headquarters at around 2005, after starting off from Kungchong-dong traveling past the Naija Hotel, Kwanghwamun, the 1 March overpass, Huam-tong and the main road of the 8th U.S. Army post. Upon arriving at the bunker of army headquarters and entering the situation room, the army chief of staff had Colonel Cho, director of the situation room, to urgently connect him by phone with the minister of national defense, the chairman of the joint chiefs of staff, the chief of naval operations, the air force chief of staff and the deputy commander of the combined forces command, and personally asked them to come to the bunker. He then summoned the deputy chief of staff and assistant chiefs of staff and ordered the 1st and 3d armies into a state of emergency. Believing that an internal assault had taken place at Chong-wadae, the army chief of staff instructed the commander of the Capital Security Command to thoroughly control the troops and ordered some other army units in the capital area to prepare for mobilization. At the same time, he instructed the commanders of the necessary units in the capital area to come to the situation room of army headquarters.

Prior to that, at approximately 1955, after Kim Chae-kyu had left the scene, Kim Kye-won again entered the dining room to find that director Cha Chi-chol was still alive and moaning. But he neglected Cha and called in CIA security guards Yu Song-ok and So Yong-chun to carry the body of his excellency to the armed forces Seoul District hospital in the president's car.

After leaving the president's body at the hospital, he ordered Yu Song-ok and So Yong-chun not to show the body to anyone without his permission. Then, leaving them at the hospital, he left and arrived at the Chongwadae by taxi at around 2015. He then notified the prime minister, some ministers and senior secretaries to come to Chongwadae.

At around 2045, Kim Kye-won, after having the senior secretaries present leave the room, Kim Kye-won told the prime minister and the ministers of home affairs and justice, who had responded to his summons that his excellency had had an accident, thus concealing the full details of the incident.

He told Deputy Director of the Presidential Security Service Lieutenant General Yi Chae-chon: the director of the Presidential Security Force is unable to command. Therefore, you must thoroughly heighten vigilance, control the troops and avoid rash and thoughtless actions. He then added: a grave national incident has occurred. However, at this moment I cannot say what it is.

Meanwhile, the defense minister, the chairman of the joint chiefs of staff, the deputy commander of the combined forces, the chief of staff of the air force and the vice chief of naval operations arrived at the bunker of army headquarters at approximately 2030 hours. The chief of staff of the army then told them that his excellency had been shot.

Receiving this report, the defense minister ordered the army chief of staff to summon Kim Kye-won on the telephone.

Carrying out the order, Pak Hung-chu, who was standing next to the defense minister, called Kim Kye-won and conveyed the message ordering Kim Kye-won to come to the bunker at army headquarters. Kim Kye-won insisted that the defense minister come to the Blue House instead. At this moment, Kim Chae-kyu spoke directly to Kim Kye-won on the phone: "Brother, please come here. Why do you stay there when everything has been done? Everyone has gathered here, so please come here with the prime minister." Upon hearing this, and thinking that Kim Chae-kyu was holding the army chief of staff hostage, Kim Kye-won agreed.

When the defense minister asked Kim Chae-kyu about the shooting, Kim said that although he did not have exact knowledge of the situation, it was true that his excellency had died. He then urged that martial law be promptly declared and that absolute secrecy be ensured. While the defense minister discussed desirable measures with the chairman of the joint chiefs of staff, the army chief of staff, the air force chief of staff, the deputy commander of the combined forces and the vice chief of naval operations, Kim Chae-kyu stood up on two occasions to threaten them.

At approximately 2050 hours, the commander of the army Counter Intelligence Corps, having received an order from the defense minister to report to him, arrived at the bunker of army headquarters without having had a chance to change clothes. Reviewing the situation, and having received confirmation from the director of the Seoul District Army Hospital that his excellency was dead, and considering the importance of the situation, he set up an impromptu command headquarters at the army headquarters detachment of the Counter Intelligence Corps and summoned all executive members under his command.

At approximately 2130 hours, the prime minister, the foreign minister, the minister of home affairs, the minister of justice, Kim Kye-won and the first senior secretary for state affairs at the office of the president, Yu Hyok-in, arrived at the army headquarters bunker. Immediately upon arriving, the ministers asked Kim Chae-kyu: "What is the matter?" to which Kim Chae-kyu emphatically replied: "The president is now in trouble. This is a serious situation. Accordingly, absolute secrecy should be ensured for two or three days and martial law should be declared through the convocation of a cabinet meeting to tighten vigilance on the frontline and to prevent bloodshed throughout the country."

At approximately 2225 hours, Kim Chae-kyu stealthily took Kim Kye-won into the lavatory of the bunker and asked him to ensure absolute secrecy, saying: "We should first get control of the situation by issuing a martial law decree and lead the situation into a military revolution by changing the Martial Law Command into a revolutionary committee."

At approximately 2230 hours, the prime minister, feeling the necessity for convoking a cabinet meeting while discussing measures to remedy the situation with members of the cabinet and military leaders, issued an order to convene a cabinet meeting. The defense minister proposed holding the cabinet meeting in the conference room of the Ministry of National Defense in view of the fact that the army headquarters bunker was too small for that purpose, and thus they moved to the Ministry of National Defense to hold the cabinet meeting.

At approximately 2240 hours, the first senior secretary for state affairs, Yu Hyok-in, told the vice minister of the Ministry of Government administrations to convene a cabinet meeting. The prime minister and the minister of culture and public information, who had moved to the reception room of the Defense Ministry following the convocation of the cabinet meeting, insisted that convincing reasons be made clear to the people without delay in the event martial law should be decreed. To this, Kim Chae-kyu continued to insist that the reasons should not be made clear and that only an announcement should be issued stating that "an emergency situation" exists. He then repeatedly and emphatically stressed: "The Soviet Union did not make an announcement on the behavior of Brezhnev for a week."

Meanwhile, at approximately 2330 hours, Kim Kye-won, who was acting hesitantly in view of the resolute attitude of the cabinet members and knowing that the revolt of Kim Chae-kyu would not succeed, stealthily entered the room of the assistant to the defense minister and sent a message to the army chief of staff asking him to come to the room. When he saw the army chief of staff and the defense minister enter the room together, he informed them that Central Intelligence Agency Director Kim was a criminal.

The defense minister and the army chief of staff then decided to arrest Kim Chae-kyu.

The chief of staff promptly came down to the army headquarters bunker and ordered the movement of some units in the capital area, and at around 2340, instructed the chief of the security command and the chief of the military police to arrest Kim Chae-kyu. The chief of the security command called the military police chief at the provisional command post within army headquarters and, along with staff officers, made a plan to arrest Kim Chae-kyu.

In accordance with the plan, the military police chief and the investigator of the security command had General Cho, assistant to the defense minister, convey a fake message to Kim Chae-kyu saying that "the army chief of staff wants to see you at the bunker in army headquarters," in order to get Kim out of the minister's reception room. After getting him out of the room, they lured him to the rear gate of the Defense Ministry through the emergency exit, not through the corridor where Kim Chae-kyu's bodyguards were, and led him into a waiting car, at the same time disarming him and taking him into custody. It was then around 0040 the next day. The pistol Kim Chae-kyu was carrying was a .38 5-shot Smith and Wesson revolver with 1 bullet in it and 4 empty cartridges.

At around 2350, a cabinet session was held at the conference room of the Defense Ministry to decide why and when martial law should be decreed. With the cabinet members, including the prime minister, strongly insisting that the session could not promulgate martial law without confirming his excellency's death, the prime minister adjourned the session, deciding to take action after confirming the death of his excellency the president. Led by Kim Kye-won, the prime minister, the deputy prime minister, the defense minister, the home affairs minister and the culture and information minister arrived at the Armed Forces Seoul District Hospital at 0120 the next day and confirmed the death of his excellency the president after being briefed by the chief of the hospital.

At 0200 they returned to the Defense Ministry and after discussing how to deal with the situation, resumed the cabinet session and decided at approximately 0345 to promulgate martial law effective at 0400 the same day. At around 0410, the government spokesman announced the promulgation of martial law.

The chief of the Armed Forces Seoul District Hospital pronounced that his excellency the president was dead before being brought into the hospital at 1955. The body of the president was moved to Chongwadae by hospital ambulance at around 0300.

The criminal motives of Kim Chae-kyu: Kim Chae-kyu received written reprimand from his excellency the president regarding his involvement in matters of rights and interests, was revealed as inept due to his repeated failure to properly deal with the recent domestic situation; had been insulted by Director Cha who, despite being younger than him and junior to him in the military, had become so haughty as to meddle in all Kim's business; had been unhappy with the president at the thought that he trusted Director Cha and not him; and in particular, with the rumor of a reshuffle of major government posts circulating, had been uneasy over the fact rumor that he might be relieved of his post because of the disturbances in Pusan and Masan.

Obsessed with the absurd idea that the best man for the presidency was he himself and mistakenly believing that those in office and the military leaders were under his influence, Kim planned the killing of the president based on his belief that when he eliminated the president, and exploiting the situation in Pusan and Masan, he would be able to gain control by controlling the martial law force and by utilizing his immense power as KCIA director and the vast organizational power of the KCIA.

As for the plan to kill the president, being afraid that it might leak out, Kim Chae-kyu began planning it on his own this past June. He planned as follows: that the method of killing would be gunfire; that the place would be the KCIA dining room located at Kungjong-tong; that the time would be any time deemed appropriate; that he would kill his excellency the president and chief security officer Cha himself; and that the Chongwadae bodyguards would be disposed of by his right-hand men Pak Son-ho, Colonel Pak Hung-chu and his bodyguards.

In particular, he planned to have the army chief of staff and Kim Chong-sup, the second assistant director of the KCIA, present at the scene of the killing after-wards, thereby making it appear that they had participated in the killings and putting them under his control. He also planned to use threatening measures when he failed to persuade the army chief of staff.

Immediately after the killings, he had the vicious scheme in mind to convene a cabinet meeting and declare martial law. To consolidate his own position, he planned to keep his excellency's death a secret for three days. The KCIA would investigate and deal with the case on the pretext that the scene of the killing was inside the KCIA's own building. The fact that the killing was committed by him-self would be either disclosed or concealed according to the degree of mourning of the people. The military would perform the sole mission of national defense while the KCIA would perform the missions of putting the political situation under control and of implementing political policies. However, he would plan whether he would come into power under the existing system or run for presi-dent after amending the Constitution.

The conclusion of the investigation is that: the military or other organizations were in no way connected with the case; there was no participation or any manipulation on the part of a foreign power in the case; and that the case was a homicide for the purpose of rebellion committed by a megalomaniac whose egregious and vain dream was to become president.

Besides the seven criminals who attempted to disrupt constitutional order, including the principal culprit Kim Chae-kyu and a criminal who destroyed evi-dence, a total of 111 persons were summoned and interrogated during the course of the investigation to determine their possible involvement in the case. Among them, 33 persons were designated as witnesses and the remaining 78 persons were released after being given warnings.

2. INDICTMENT OF PARK ASSASSINS, DECEMBER 5, 1979

Defendant Kim Chae-kyu, 53, former ROK Central Intelligence Agency Chief, a native of Sonsan, Kyongsang-pukto, with address at Pomun-dong, Seoul.

Defendant Kim Kye-won, 56, ex-chief secretary to the late president, a native of Yongju, Kyongsang-pukto, with address at Nonhyon-dong, Seoul.

Defendant Pak Song-ho, 45, former chief of the KCIA Protocol Section, a native of Chongdo, Kyongsang-pukto, with address at Taebang-dong, Seoul.

Defendant Pak Hung-chu, 38, an army colonel, former secretary to codefendant Kim Chae-kyu, a native of Hwanghak-tong, Seoul, with address at Haengdang-dong, Seoul.

Defendant Yi Ki-chu, 31, former KCIA guard, a native of Puchon, Kyonggi-do, with address at Chunggok-dong, Seoul.

Defendant Yu Song-ok, 36, ex-driver of KCIA, a native of Koyang-gun, Kyonggi-do, with address at Pulgwang-dong, Seoul.

Defendant Kim Tae-won, 32, former KCIA guard, a native of Yongin, Kyonggi-do, with address at Yongsan, Seoul.

Defendant Yu Sok-sul, 31, former KCIA guard, a native of Kochang, Kyongsang-namdo, with address at Simmun-no, Seoul.

All but Yu Sok-sul are charged with murders and attempted insurrection. Articles 89, 88, 87 and 30 of the penal code are applied in presenting the charges against the seven. Yu Sok-sul is charged with hiding evidence. Article 155 of the penal code is applied.

Premeditated plot: Defendant Kim Chae-kyu, failing to cope with the country's political situation as the Central Intelligence Agency chief, felt insecure amid rumors that he might be replaced. The defendant was also discontent about President Pak Chong-hui's attitude of favoring the president's chief bodyguard Cha Chi-chol, his junior in age and military experience, although he felt that Cha was insolent and abused his power. The defendant began to plot to kill the president and take over power last April. The defendant plotted to kill the president and Cha by himself and let his confidant-aides Pak Son-ho and Pak Hung-chu eliminate Cha's accompanying aides. The defendant made the plot alone for security reasons.

Source: Korea Herald , December 5, 1979.

The defendant plotted to declare martial law on the pretext of national stability and order after the assassination. He planned to use his power and organization as KCIA chief for controlling martial law troops and coping with the post-assassination situation by force. The defendant plotted to establish a so-called revolutionary council to exercise legislative, judicial and administrative power, with himself becoming its head and by so doing securing a power base for running for the presidency. The defendant tried to use the development of demonstrations in Pusan and Masan and seize an opportunity for implementing his plot.

Preparations: At around 4 pm Oct 25, the defendant received a phone call from Cha while he was at his annex office at Pil-dong, Chung-ku, Seoul. The telephone message was that the president would meet the defendant for dinner at the KCIA restaurant at Kunjong-dong at around 6 pm.

The defendant decided to implement his plot after receiving the call. He telephoned ROK Army Chief of Staff Gen Chong Sung-hwa and Deputy Assistant KCIA Chief Kim Chong-sop, asking them to come to his office about 59 meters from the restaurant by 6:30 pm for dinner, with an intention to use them after the planned assassination.

At around 4:30 pm, he went to his bedroom on the second floor of his office near the restaurant, took out a German-made .32-caliber pistol from a safe, loaded seven bullets and checked the gun before hiding it behind books on a shelf.

At 5:50 pm the defendant met his codefendant Kim Kye-won in the garden near the front door of the restaurant. Defendant Kim Chae-kyu said to his codefendant Kim Kye-won, "I will finish them today," and asked Kim Kye-won for help. Codefendant Kim Kye-won agreed. At around 6:05 pm, the president and Cha arrived. During their dinner, defendant Kim Chae-kyu left the restaurant at 7 pm and met the army chief of staff and the deputy assistant KCIA chief who were waiting for him at his office.

Defendant Kim Chae-kyu told them that he would meet them again later and went upstairs, picked up the pistol from the bookshelf and tucked it in a trouser pocket. On his way back to the restaurant, the defendant Kim Chae-kyu met Pak Son-ho and Pak Hung-chu. He ordered them to finish the presidential bodyguards and was told that they would be ready 30 minutes later. Pak Son-ho relayed his chief's instructions to codefendant Yu Song-ok and Yi Ki-chu and said, "We will be rewarded if we do our jobs well today." Pak Son-ho told them to shoot and kill the presidential bodyguards in the kitchen when they hear the sound of shots fired by their chief in the restaurant.

Crime: Defendant Kim Chae-kyu left his seat at the dinner table for the third time at around 7:38 pm and went to his office to receive a report on preparations from Pak Son-ho. He returned to the dinner table at around 7:40 pm. When he took his seat, he nudged his codefendant Kim Kye-won and said, "Take good care of his excellency." When he said the word, he produced his pistol and fired one shot at Cha striking him in the right hand. He then rose and fired one shot at the president, who was sitting to his front across the table, striking him in the chest. He tried to shoot continuously but his gun failed. He went out of the restaurant, took a .38 revolver from Pak Song-ho and returned. He shot Cha in the abdomen and fired one bullet at the groaning president, striking him behind the ear.

Codefendant Kim Kye-won had watched all along Kim Chae-kyu's moves in and out of the restaurant, aware that the time was imminent for Kim Chae-kyu to implement his plot. When Kim Chae-kyu shot Cha and the president, he left his seat and stood near the entrance and watched the shootings of presidential bodyguards. Codefendant Pak Son-ho shot one bullet at An Chae-song, deputy section chief of the Presidential Security Office, and another at Chon In-hyon, section chief of the office.

Codefendants Pak Hung-chu, Yi Ki-song and Yu Song-ok, who were waiting in a Gemini car parked near the kitchen, fired a volley toward the president's driver, Kim Yong-tae, bodyguards Kim Yong-sop and Pak Sang-pom and kitchen hand Yi Chong-o and restaurant driver Kim Yong-nam. Codefendant Kim Tae-won came out of a waiting room with an M-16 rifle at the sound of gunshots. He was told by codefendant Pak Song-ho to kill presidential bodyguards. He was also told by codefendant Yi Ki-chu to check and finish those who had not been fatally shot.

Codefendant Kim Tae-won entered the waiting room in the restaurant, fired one shot at An and two shots at Chong and went to the room where Cha was groaning. He shot twice at Cha and went to the kitchen where he fired one bullet at Kim Yong-sop.

The president, Cha, An, Kim Young-tae and Kim Yong-sop died at around 7:50 p.m. Pak Sang-pom suffered a wound requiring three weeks' treatment.

Defendant Kim Chae-kyu went to his office at around 7:43 p.m. and met the army chief of staff and the deputy assistant KCIA chief. He said a big thing happened and asked the two to get into his car. Once in the car, the army chief of staff asked what happend. Defendant Kim Chae-kyu, hiding his crime, said the president was shot and killed. He asked them to go with him to the KCIA headquarters, emphasizing a need to take measures for public security and against possible invasion threats from communist North Korea.

The army chief of staff countered by asking that they go to the army headquarters. They arrived at the army headquarters at around 8:05 p.m. where defendant Kim Chae-kyu met the chiefs of the armed forces branches. He tried to emphasize a need to keep the president's death a secret for three days as a precautionary measure against the enemy. He tried to induce the army chief and chiefs of the other military services and Cabinet members to declare martial law.

Secretary Armed

Kim Kye-won, former presidential chief secretary, was equipped with a revolver at around 7:43 p.m. after being informed of the importance of maintaining security by Kim Chae-kyu. The ex-presidential chief secretary received the pistol from Yi Ki-chu. Kim Kye-won sent the body of President Pak to the armed forces hospital in Seoul aboard the presidental sedan at around 7:55 p.m. in order to make it appear that he tried to save President Pak's life if the situation would turn about.

When President Pak's body arrived at the hospital, he ordered Maj Song Kae-yong, an army surgeon, to make a diagnosis. He asked the army surgeon and Capt Chong Kyu-hyong to save the man's life without fail in spite of the fact that the army surgeon told him the president was dead five minutes before the diagnosis started. Kim did not tell the two army officers that the man was President Pak Chong-hui. He went to Chongwadae after ordering Yu Song-ok who was guarding the hospital not to allow anybody in the hospital to contact anyone outside the hospital. Kim told seven presidential senior secretaries, including Choe Kwang-su, the then senior protocol secretary, as well as Lt Gen Yi Chae-chon, President Pak's vice chief security officer, to hold themselves in readiness because something grave happened to the president. He also said to them, "His Excellency President Pak encountered great trouble and is being hospitalized while Cha Chi-chol, presidential chief bodyguard, cannot command his unit. So you must strengthen the guard to prevent people from committing rash acts." He gave time to Kim Chae-kyu and his killer squad by saying to the president's men that mobilization of troops belonging to the presidential security office is not necessary.

False Report

The presidential senior secretaries and the presidential vice chief bodyguard rushed to the presidential residence to attend an emergency meeting which was held at around 8:40 p.m. Kim Kye-won made a false report to Prime Minister Choe-Kyu-ha at around 8:30 p.m. when he said to Choe that the president was killed with shots fired by Kim Chae-kyu while the former KCIA chief was arguing with Cha at the dinner tonight. He said it was necessary to proclaim martial law.

When asked what happened to President Pak by Ku Cha-chun, minister of home affairs and Kim Chi-yol, minister of justice, he only replied that President Pak was injured, concealing the truth that the president was slain.

After receiving a telephone call from Kim Chae-kyu in which the ex-director of KCIA asked him to come to the army headquarters with the prime minister, Kim Kye-won went to the office of the army chief of staff in an army bunker along with the prime minister, minister of home affairs and minister of justice at around 9:30 p.m. When he arrived at the bunker, he found Kim Chae-kyu, Minister of National Defense No Chae-hyon and key army generals there, and thought the former KCIA chief had assumed the reins of the military. He said to the defense minister, "Something happened to the president. Cha's excessive toughness caused the accident," and proposed to the minister to cope with the situation under the leadership of Prime Minister Choe.

After hearing from Kim Chae-kyu the future plan of the crime, he misjudged that the insurrection attempt was successful. Responding favorably to the proposal made by Kim Chae-kyu in the office of the defense minister to the prime minister and other Cabinet members that the reason why martial law should be proclaimed is not due to the death of president but maintaining public order caused martial law to be proclaimed, he proposed to the attendants that martial law be proclaimed due to the incapacitation of the president.

Defendant Pak Son-ho ordered Kim Tae-won to finish Cha Chi-chol after checking him at around 8 p.m. and confirmed the move of the troops through the report transmitted from the KCIA branch office on Mt Namsan to the KCIA headquarters. He also ordered Yu Song-ok who carried the body of President Pak to the armed forces hospital in Seoul to maintain public security.

Pak Hung-chu, who was standing by outside the restaurant at around 9:45 p.m., went to the office of the KCIA restaurant and rode a sedan along with Kim Chae-kyu, the army chief of staff and the deputy assistant KCIA chief to an army bunker. As he stayed in the room of the army chief of staff's adjutant, he arranged telephone calls between Kim Chae-kyu and Kim Kye-won who was in Chongwadae. He closely watched the process of the crime and ordered Capt Kim In-su, a bodyguard team leader for Kim Chae-kyu, to send the former KCIA chief's security vehicle to the army headquarters and to deploy one KCIA man each in places near the Seoul railroad station and Namdaemun gate. He also ordered the army captain to immediately report to him on troop moves by radio. He accompanied Kim Chae-kyu and protected the security of the former KCIA director.

Yi Ki-chu ordered Kim Tae-won to shoot to death presidential bodyguards, including Cha Chi-chol, after checking them under Pak Son-ho's order at around 8:05 p.m. When a man from the presidential security office rushed to the restaurant to check about the gunshots, Yi told a lie that he never heard the gunshots. He continued contacts with Yu Song-ok, who carried President Pak's body to the armed forces hospital in Seoul and let Yu Sok-sul bury weapons including pistols used in the crime in order to hide the evidence at around 7 a.m. of Oct 27.

Defendant Yu Song-ok took one .38 revolver at around 7:34 p.m. from Kim Yong-sop who was fatally shot in the kitchen and from Pak Sang-pom who was seriously wounded. He left one of the guns with the restaurant boilerman Kang Mu-hong and tucked the other in his trousers at the waist.

At around 7:55 pm, he helped codefendant Kim Kye-won in sending the president to the hospital. He placed his hand over the president's eyes in an attempt to hide the fact that the patient was the president. He stopped hospital superintendent Air Force Brig Gen Kim Pyong-su from making a phone call outside and kept contact by phone with codefendant Yi Ki-chu while waiting for instructions from codefendant Kim Chae-kyu.

Defendant Kim Tae-won went to the Ewha Woman's University Hospital at Chongno 6-Ga at around 10 pm and met cook Yi Chong-o, who was receiving treatment there. He told Yi not to telephone his home. He asked Yi to say he was wounded in an accidental firing, if anyone inquired. He returned to the guards' room in the restaurant compound and was told by codefendant Pak Son-ho that things were going well at the army headquarters. He continued to stand guard waiting for instructions from codefendant Kim Chae-kyu.

At around 11:30 pm, in the defense minister's room, the prime minister, the home minister and the justice minister showed an attitude of opposing defendant Kim Chae-kyu's proposal. Codefendant Kim Kye-won thought codefendant Kim Chae-kyu was not getting through with his demand. Kim Kye-won changed his mind and went to the defense minister's annex office and called in the defense minister and the army chief of staff. He told them that "Kim Chae-kyu killed the president."

Kim Chae-kyu was subsequently held by military investigation authorities and thus an attempt to disrupt the constitutional rule failed.

Defendant Yu Sok-sul was resting in the guards' waiting room when he heard the sound of gunshots coming from the restaurant at around 7:40 pm. He was soon told by cook Kim Il-son that presidential bodyguards and a cook were shot and wounded in the kitchen. He heard at around 5 am the next day over the radio that the president, Cha and some other presidential bodyguards were shot and killed. Despite his knowledge of the shootings and murders, the defendant packed and buried one American-made .38-caliber revolver and six of its bullets, one pistol with a serial number 38 K4491 and five of its ammunition rounds and one used shell, one German-made .32 revolver with serial number 159270 and four of its bullets and a slipper in the garden, as told by codefendant Yi Ki-chu.

3. STATEMENT OF DEFENSE MINISTER, DECEMBER 12, 1979

Dear citizens: During the investigation of Kim Chae-kyu—the chief culprit in the assassination of His Excellency President Pak Chong-hui—new facts came to light which Kim Chae-kyu concealed. As a result, at 1900 hours [1000 GMT 12 Dec] yesterday evening, the army sent its military investigators to the official residence of the chief of staff of the army, Chong Sung-hwa, to ascertain the facts.

A minor conflict took place between the guards at the official residence and the military investigators. However, Chief of Staff Chong Sung-hwa is all right and is presently being arraigned and is under investigation. The army has also arrested some general officers involved in the incident and is investigating them.

I consider it regrettable to have to investigate the Chief of Staff, Chong Sung-hwa, and some other general officers on the charge of involvement in the assassination of His Excellency President Pak Chong-hui. The shooting, which took place at about 0200 hours [1700 GMT 12 Dec] this morning at the Defense Ministry building was the result of a mistaken clash between the guards already in positions and the martial law reinforcements. There were no casualties.

At present, martial law army troops in some areas of the city have been reinforced in order to strengthen the defense posture of the capital area. I therefore urge the citizens to be calm. The government has appointed General Yi Hui-song as the army chief of staff and commander of the Martial Law Command effective today. At the present time, the army has established a new command system and is completely and unwaveringly fulfilling its mission.

Dear fellow countrymen: It is highly regrettable that such an unfortunate incident has taken place at such an important time when security and social order should be maintained.

Considering the desire of the majority of the nation's people for gradual political development, the government and the army are doing their utmost to fulfill that desire. I therefore request all the nation's people to devote themselves to their assigned duties and trust in the government and army free of hesitation or doubts.

[signed]

No Chae-hyon, Minister of National Defense

Source: Seoul Domestic Service broadcast, December 12, 1979.

4. STATEMENT OF MARTIAL LAW COMMANDER, DECEMBER 18, 1979

Dear fellow countrymen: I have assumed a heavy duty as the commander of the Martial Law Command. I can only view soberly my heavy responsibilities to realize our people's wishes for development, to acknowledge the encouragement of friendly nations and to thoroughly check and smash the North Korean puppets' provocations aimed at realizing their wild dreams to communize our country by taking advantage of the current emergency situation.

In view of the gravity of the situation facing us, and in consideration of the heavy responsibilities assigned to us, we are going to perform our martial law activities calmly and resolutely, based upon the wishes and cooperation of all our people. I believe this is possible if all officers and men of the martial law forces honorably maintain law and order and support pan-national efforts so the people's wishes can be realized one by one and quiet development can continue. Since the mandate of the martial law forces as well as my own wishes can only be realized through the full understanding and cooperation of all the people, I would like to clearly announce the policies to be pursued by the Martial Law Command in the performance of its activities.

I regret the 12 December incident which caused uneasiness among our people. Even though the facts of the incident have already been disclosed by the initial announcement on the incident released by the Defense Minister, more details will be disclosed within the next several days. I would like to make clear that in dealing with the incident the armed forces are doing their best to follow lawful procedures and to observe constitutional order. In addition, they are taking quick emergency measures so the North Korean puppets cannot exploit the current situation and so the unity and combat preparedness of the armed forces are in peak condition, unaffected to even the slightest degree.

I, therefore, hope our people will not be misled by negative rumors and that they will go about their business with peace of mind and trust in the armed forces.

Dear fellow countrymen, as you know, national defense is the primary mission of the armed forces. Politics is outside the realm of the armed forces.

I, therefore, clearly express the firm principle that the armed forces should not interfere in politics and I make it clear that it is a constant wish of the armed forces that political development should be made by the patriotic politicians of good sense.

Source: Seoul Domestic Service broadcast, December 18, 1979.

The mission of members of the armed forces is to devote their lives to defending the country and nation with loyalty and a sense of justice, to establish appropriate measures for constantly grasping and analyzing the national defense situation and to maintain a posture of peak readiness by eliminating any weakness which may be exploited by the enemy.

So that the armed forces can remain within the realm of their primary mission and in order to attain the prosperity and development of the country and nation, I believe it is the task of all people to correct and eradicate, with a single act, the following negative and detrimental factors which are still deeply rooted in our society. I sincerely ask for your joint efforts.

1 The practice of borrowing terms or using stereotyped words or methods of agitation of the North Korean puppets without having an awareness of the line and plot of our enemy, the North Korean puppets, to communize South Korea, is likely to be an encouragement to the North Korean puppets, risking the danger that they will misjudge the situation and attack South Korea. Therefore, such practice should be totally rejected.

2 Toadyism which sacrifices the pride of the country and nation in order to emphasize assertions of individuals or groups should by all means be corrected.

3 The practice of some public servants whose duty it is to serve the people, to govern the people, but who associate themselves with irregularities and unlawful conduct, thus bringing about the public's denunciation of even the faithful public servants, should be duly denounced.

4 The practice of turning away from ethics in business activities which are in the interests of the public, thus harming the unity of the people, should be corrected.

5 The practice of unconditionally rejecting the thoughts and judgments of others by asserting that one's own thoughts and judgments are the only right ones should be absolutely eradicated.

6 The rationale that one can achieve his objective by using any means or methods without distinguishing between propaganda and agitation should be totally eradicated in order to bring about the construction of a righteous society.

In order to correct or eradicate these negative and detrimental factors, the concerted efforts of all the people are necessary. I would like to emphasize that the martial law forces will actively support such efforts of all people and will never tolerate conduct by individuals, organizations or groups that would jeopardize national security by violating law and order.

Dear fellow countrymen: Our martial law forces will unselfishly perform their martial law activities according to existing policies and will return to their primary mission as members of the armed forces after completing the objectives of martial law at the earliest date.

Along with all the people who wish for calm stability and quiet development, the martial law forces will continue their orderly advance in the future and will exert every possible effort to ensure that their endeavors in performing their martial law activities will stand with honor before our descendants and history.

[Signed] Yi Hui-song, General, ROK Army
Commander of the Martial Law Command. 18 December 1979

5. REPORT ON INVESTIGATION OF GENERAL
CHUNG SEUNG HWA, DECEMBER 24, 1979

[Report by Defense Ministry spokesman (Pak Chin-su) on the outcome of investigation into crimes of former Army Chief of Staff Chong Sung-hwa and others in connection with 13 December announcment by minister of national defense on their suspected involvement in slaying of the President by Kim Chae-kyu—live at the Ministry of National Defense]

Details of Their Arrest:

In the process of investigating the insurrection by the Kim Chae-kyu clique, Gen Chong Sung-hwa, the then army chief of staff, came under suspicion. So, during a period of four days from 29 October to 1 November 1979, he, who was serving at the time as a martial law commander, made an affidavit before an investigating officer of the integrated investigation team. He made the affidavit on his own volition in his office. However, he tended to display his authority as the martial law commander who was in charge of martial law administration in such a manner as finding faults with (?the investigating officer), saying that the details of the investigation were far from the truth. By so doing, he obstructed the free conduct of the investigation and made it impossible to determine the truth concerning his suspected involvement. Even in the process of making the affidavit, he made amendments several times and after it was made, he delivered notes for its revision, thus forcing changes to be made in it and concealing the truth concerning his involvement. Accordingly, this brought about an incomplete outcome of the investigation.

In investigating the 26 October slaying of the president, the integrated investigation team set as its top priority the national security and public security and order, which are the utmost national tasks, and under the policy of conducting the investigation in this context, concentrated efforts, first of all, on the investigation of the main culprit Kim Chae-kyu and others and came up with an announcement concerning the incident.

In the course of continuing the investigation, it was disclosed that former Army Chief of Staff Chong had received a large sum of money from Kim Chae-kyu and it was learned that he had made supicious moves such as holding meetings and keeping in contact with former Commander of the Third Army Yi Kon-yong and

---

Source: Seoul Domestic Service Broadcast, December 24, 1979.

former Commander of the Special Forces Command Chong Pyong-chu, thus making it incumbent to promptly probe into this.

However, it was feared that, in case the investigation was directed against the incumbent martial law commander, the government might be put in turmoil by a systematic resistance of the Kim Chae-kyu clique and its followers at a time when the people were not yet over their shock from the 26 October incident. In light of this, the investigation was unavoidably put off until the political situation was stabilized following the presidential election.

Meanwhile, the trial of the Kim Chae-kyu clique proceeded amid stubborn rumors at home and abroad that former Army Chief of Staff Chong Sung-hwa was involved in the incident. There was even the rumor that Army Chief of Staff Chong and the commander of the security command, who is the chief of the integrated investigation team, were collaborating to whitewash the incident.

(?The integrated investigation team) carefully watched his behavior, hoping that Army Chief of Staff Chong would be aware of this, would judge himself unfit, in view of his morality and public opinion, to carry out the duties as the administrator in charge of the case involving his suspected involvement and would resign from the post in accordance with his conscience.

Far from resigning, he took advantage of his powerful authority as martial law commander and administrator in charge of the trial and committed acts exceeding his jurisdiction.

The first instance of this was that Gen Yi Chae-chon, who was the deputy director general of Presidential Security Force at the time the president was slain, was told by the then chief secretary to the president, Kim Kye-won, that the president had been hospitalized due to an accident [yugo] and that Director-General of Presidential Security Force Cha Chi-chol could not carry out his duties. However, he failed to promptly take such measures as confirming the truth at the Seoul District hospital and taking proper measures, assembling and alerting all the personnel of the Presidential Security Force, issuing a notice of emergency and dispatching presidential bodyguards to the spot.

At a staff meeting of Presidential Security Forces convened, at around 2200 hours that day, he intentionally concealed the accident which had befallen the president. At around 2230, when asked by the army chief of staff whether (?the president) was all right, he replied by saying that nothing was wrong.

Likewise, he, as the man in charge of the Presidential Security Force, neglected his duties by not taking action even though he knew that the president had been hospitalized due to an accident. This became clear in the course of the investigation and, accordingly, he was arrested and indicted.

Nonetheless, on the vague grounds that he had made great contributions to the development of the armed forces, (?Chong) released him, who was charged with neglecting the important duty of providing security for the head of state. After his release, (?Chong) did not take even such a basic action as reprimanding him. Rather he was unfair enough so as to encourage him.

The second instance is that, after the 26 October incident, it was suggested to (?Chong) that he be prudent in approving overseas trips by those who are unfit for such trips as their behavior was not certain and reject their trips. However, there are instances he even neglected his duties as the martial law commander by allowing persons to take trips after he was personally requested not to do so.

As the trial of the Kim Chae-kyu clique progressed, during which unrestrained remarks professing the justness of the crime were permitted, there grew the possibility that this might mislead public opinion and, using this as an excuse, that (?Chong) as the administrator in charge of the trial, might take unfair actions such as commuting sentences handed down on the defenders involved in the crime. This led to a situation where the investigation could not be put off any further.

The integrated investigation team, which is in a position to present indisputable investigation results to the people, judged the stability of the political situation as having settled gradually following the presidential election and that the time was right to start up the investigation.

Accordingly, in order to prevent the investigation plan from being detected in advance, to prevent the investigation from being hampered by the exercise of his power as martial law commander and in case of the rejection of the investigation, and to prevent a disturbance from being triggered by his followers, the integrated investigation team, with the approval of his excellency the president, tried to calmly arrest him at his official residence soon after the close of working hours when it would be impossible for the suspect to promptly exercise his rights to issue orders as the army chief of staff, and thereby to confirm the crimes of which he was suspected.

At 1900 hours on 12 December, 1979, the investigators arrived at the official residence of the army chief of staff and asked him to voluntarily present himself at the investigation headquarters and cooperate in the investigation. However, as was feared, former Army Chief of Staff Chong refused to be escorted and yelled in protest. Thereupon, the guards at the official residence immediately opened fire and the investigators shot back at them, thus a commotion occurred, which, regretfully, resulted in casualties.

Meanwhile, when the investigation was about to be conducted against the above mentioned Yi Kon-yong, Chong Pyong-chu and others, who were later rounded up as they were also suspected of being involved in Kim Chae-kyu's crime, they learned that the former army chief of staff—the central figure of their group— had been arrested. Under the pretext that the arrest of former Army Chief of Staff Chong, a just action in the investigation, was an abduction, they, taking advantage of the organizations under their command, assembled sympathizers and impudently mobilized troops. Thus they refused to comply with the investigation through the mobilization of military vehicles including tanks.

Fearing that this situation, if it developed further, might not just pose as a simple act of resistance but even lead to a situation in which the nation's security and order were disrupted, the martial law troops were reinforced and additional troops deployed, thus putting them under arrest and subjecting them to the investigation.

Details of the Crimes of Those Who Are Under Investigation.

Chong Sung-hwa, former army chief of staff: First, detection of an emergency at the proximity. At around 1640 hours on 26 October 1979, (?Chong) was told by Kim Chae-kyu over the telephone to come to Kungchong-dong [location of KCIA dining hall] in civilian attire for supper at 1830 hours. He accepted the offer and arrived at the Kungchong-dong KCIA dining compound at about 1835 hours, where he met for the first time with Kim Chong-sop, second assistant director of the KCIA, and was told by him that Kim Chae-kyu was dining with the president. At around 1910 hours, Kim Chae-kyu appeared and said to (?Chong) that he would return as soon as the dinner with his excellency was over and asked him to wait for him, dining with Assistant Director Kim. So, he dined with Kim Chong-sop, talking about topics ranging from the Pusan and Masan situation, to public opinion trends, and housing projects for the noncommissioned officers.

At around 1940 hours he heard gun shots which he believed originated from the direction of Chahamun [area near Kungchong-dong] and said to Kim Chong-sop: "Aren't those gunshots?" Then Kim Chong-sop promptly went out and came back. About 3 or 4 minutes later, Kim Chae-kyu suddenly appeared with no jacket on and said to (?Chong), frightened and out of breath: "Chief of staff, there is a big trouble [kunil natsumnida]." Then Chong Sung-hwa said several times: "What's the matter?" However, Kim pulled on the sleeve of Chong Sung-hwa, saying: "Let's talk about it in the car." Thus, Chong Sung-hwa could have instinctively known that an emergency involving his excellency had just occurred not far away.

Second, learning of Kim's possible involvement.

At around 1950 hours (?Chong) left Kungchong-dong in a car with Kim Chae-kyu, Kim Chong-sop and Pak Hung-chu and as the car proceeded from there by the Naeja Hotel, through Kwanghamun to the Samil elevated highway, Kim Chae-kyu said: "Let's go to Namsan [where the KCIA offices are located]." Then Chong Sung-hwa asked several times: "What is the matter?" To which Kim Chae-kyu replied by pointing his thumb down to express that his excellency the president was dead and stressed the need for the maintenance of security and the declaration of martial law, saying that it is certain that the president was dead. He said to (?Chong): "What units could be mobilized in case martial law is declared?" and "The future of the nation rests upon the shoulders of Chief of Staff Chong."

At this moment, former Chief of Staff Chong asked himself: "In a situation in which the president was killed, how could Kim Chae-kyu escape unscathed?"

and suspected that Kim Chae-kyu may have done the deed [irul chojiruda] in view of the fact that Kim was trying not to talk about who the killer was and what had happened and because Kim was pressing for the declaration of martial law, by encouraging him saying that the future of the nation is up to him [Chong Sung-Hwa]. In view of his suspicion, (?Chong) directed the car to the army headquarters judging that he should go there to command the armed forces.

Third, Kim Chae-kyu strongly suspected as the killer.

Arriving at the army headquarters bunker at around 2005, former Chief of Staff Chong ordered the duty officer to usher Kim Chae-kyu, Kim Chong-sop and Pak Hung-chu into his office and summoned the minister of national defense, the chairman of the joint chiefs of staff, the chief of naval operations, the air force chief of staff and the deputy commander of the ROK-U.S. Combined Forces Command.

After that, at around 2010 hours, he first called the commander of the Capital Garrison Command who told him that the situation was calm. Chong then told him not to respond to any orders from anyone but the army chief of staff. Thus he confirmed that the Capital Garrison Command was not involved. Then, the thought occurred to him that it might have been carried out by the director of the Presidential Security Force, Cha Chi-chol. However, in view of the fact that the Capital Garrison Command, which is under the authority of the director of the Presidential Security Force, was not involved, the suspicion that Kim Chae-kyu was the killer became stronger.

Fourth, a wild opportunistic desire.

At this time, the former Army Chief of Staff Chong was overcome with a strange desire.

Reviewing the relations between the two: In 1962 former Chief of Staff Chong had become friendly with Kim Chae-kyu, then president of the Naju Fertilizer Company, while the former was the chief of the army counterintelligence corps. From that time on he had frequent contacts with Kim Chae-kyu—until 1974 when Kim Chae-kyu retired from the army—while the two were serving as division commanders and also on various occasions such as the Seoul gatherings of generals whose native home was north Kyongsang Province and on the occasions of the change of command of the Third ROK Army Corps. Thus the friendly relations between the two were further fostered. Around December 1977, right after assuming the post of commanding general of the First ROK Army, he called on Kim Chae-kyu at the latter's KCIA office in Kungchong-dong.

After assuming the post of chief of staff of the ROK Army in January 1979, with Kim Chae-kyu's strong recommendation, he paid a visit to Kim on 3 February 1979 to thank him for his recommendation. Since March 1979, the two attended parties with their wives and held banquets and played golf on several occasions. Thus their relations were of an especially close nature. At banquets, they called each other brother [hohyong hojae].

In October of 1979 he received a huge amount of money from Kim Chae-kyu, without any justifiable reason, which was given to elicit his sympathy and obtain his favor in the event that Kim Chae-kyu were to launch his deed. Thus, inseparably close ties have been created between the two.

Moreover, he felt that opportunistic behavior was the only wise way to protect his own interests and believed that Kim Chae-kyu, as director of the KCIA, had a huge organization and power and, therefore, great forces behind the screen must be involved in the incident.

Fifth, mobilizing the military forces in accordance with Kim Chae-kyu's wish and keeping in step with Kim Chae-kyu.

Subsequently, he directed that the vice chief of staff, deputy chief of staff for intelligence, deputy chief of staff for operations, headquarters commandant, provost marshal and commander of Capital Garrison Command be summoned and to mobilize the "00" [unnamed] division and "0" [unnamed] airborne brigade and issued an emergency alert to commanding generals of the First and the Third ROK armies.

After that, he explained to Kim Chae-kyu his action concerning the mobilization of military forces and asked him which objectives to occupy first when the martial law forces are mobilized. He took down every word of Kim Chae-kyu's answer that broadcasting stations, power plants and banks should first be occupied, thus letting Kim Chae-kyu know that he was mobilizing and deploying the martial law forces in accordance with his wishes and in consultation with him. Thus he tacitly acted in concert with Kim Chae-kyu.

Sixth, aiding and abetting Kim Chae-kyu's crime.

On the arrival of the commander of the Capital Garrison Command at about 2040, he guided the commander into his office and issued an order to encircle the Chongwadae [the ROK presidential mansion], keeping a long distance from the objective, thus blocking the mobilization of the Chongwadae security forces. At about 2100, he telephoned Yi Chae-chon, deputy chief of the Chongwadae security forces, and confirmed that there was nothing unusual at the Chongwadae, that no security forces were involved in the incident and that the place of the incident was not the Chongwadae. Thus he could have had a firm belief that Kim Chae-kyu was the culprit. Nevertheless, in order to make it easier for Kim Chae-kyu to commit the criminal act, he blocked the mobilization of the Chongwadae security forces by issuing an order that the security forces should be placed under the complete control of Yi Chae-chon and action should be taken not to give rise to any conflict by maintaining cooperation with the commander of the Capital Garrison Command.

After this, he directed the vice deputy chief of staff to cancel the order to mobilize the "00" division and "0" airborne brigade judging that, on the contrary, mobilization of these units would constitute an obstacle. At about 2130, the prime minister, home and justice ministers, and Kim Kye-won arrived at the headquarters of the ROK Army and Kim Chae-kyu insisted that emergency martial law be proclaimed but the death of his excellency be kept secret. However, the cabinet members insisted that the death of his excellency be made public because keeping it secret was impossible.

At about 2330, former Army Chief of Staff Chong headed for the office of the defense minister in order to learn of the developments at the cabinet meeting. On his way to the defense minister's office, at the office of the assistant to the defense minister, along with former defense minister No Chae-hyon, he was told by Kim Kye-won—who realized that the situation would not develop as originally planned—that Kim Chae-kyu was the culprit. Then he directed the commander of the army security command and the provost marshal to keep Kim Chae-kyu in custody. In directing this, he told the provost marshal that he should keep Kim Chae-kyu in custody in cooperation with the commander of the army security command and that the commander of the army security command should move Kim Chae-kyu someplace downtown and treat him courteously. Thus he aided and abetted Kim Chae-kyu's criminal act by acting opportunistically to the end.

Around 0040 on 27 October 1979, personnel of the army security command, who provided Kim Chae-kyu with safe protection as directed, had recognized him as the culprit and reported the fact immediately. After receiving the report, the commander of the army security command at about 0100 reported to former Army chief of Staff Chong that Kim Chae-kyu was, without doubt, the culprit and he should be investigated. It was not until this time that he [Chong] directed an investigation be started.

Yi Kon-yong, former commander of the Third Army.

He came to know Kim Chae-kyu in 1961 when he was an instructor at the army college and Kim was the deputy Superintendent at the college. In December 1976 when Kim was appointed director of the KCIA, he picked Yi as the first assistant director and concurrently as the second deputy director—the second man in charge of overall KCIA affairs. Thus a relationship started in which Yi became Kim's righthand man.

Since October 1978 Yi was promoted, with Kim's help, to become deputy army chief of staff and, later, commander of the Third Army, a field commander's post commanding combat troops. Serving in that post, Yi twice received great sums of money from Kim Chae-kyu who sought to buy his favor with the intent to make him a sympathizer in case he carried out the deed. Yi received great sums of money from Kim once more in October 1979 just before Kim carried out the deed.

When an investigation of his suspected connection with Kim Chae-kyu was considered, he, at the time of 12 December incident, contacted the commander of the Capital Garrison Command and others and tried to mount a systematic resistance by mobilizing troops.

Chong Pyong-chu, former commander of the Special Forces Command.

Chong was from the Andong agricultural school, the school from which Kim Chae-kyu graduated earlier. When Kim served as a division commander, Chong served under him as his chief of staff and as a regimental commander. Thus, the two had developed an intimate relationship since the days they were in the service. Even when Kim was minister of construction and deputy director of the KCIA, Chong contacted him frequently.

Since 1975 he received money which Kim offered regularly every month to further cement the relationship between them. Around September 1978, ostensibly to purchase intelligence equipment for his unit, Kim illegally provided him some 50 million won, thus consolidating a relationship in which he became Kim's follower. In October 1979 he received a great sum of money which Kim offered with the intent to seek his sympathy and participation in case of emergency. Thus he became Kim's follower and an investigation into his connection and suspected relations with Kim was being considered.

At the time of the 12 December incident, he was in close contact with the former commander of the Capital Garrison Command Chang Tae-wan, and former director of the joint chiefs of staff [Hapcham Ponbujang] Mun Hong-ku and others and sought to mount a resistance by systematically mobilizing the troops.

Mun Hong-ku, former director of the joint chiefs of staff.

Since he was picked by Kim Chae-kyu to be chief of staff in November 1968, when Kim was the commander of the security command, the two became close to each other. In November 1969, with Kim's influence, he was appointed commander of the first division. Thus the two maintained a relationship in which he became one of Kim's followers. From then on, he frequently received money from Kim.

At the time of the 12 December incident, he moved to the Capital Garrison Command and acting in collaboration with the commander of the Capital Garrison Command, Chang Tae-wan, inspired Kim's followers, such as Chong Pyong-chu, commander of the Special Force Command, to unity and resistance.

Chang Tae-wan, former commander of the Capital Garrison Command.

Since he served as chief of staff under Chong Sung-hwa when Chong was the chief inspector of the First Army headquarters in 1970, he maintained a close relationship with Chong even when Chong served as the commander of the 26th division from 1975 to 1978. While serving as the deputy chief of staff for training at army headquarters in September 1979 he was praised by Chong as an excellent general. After the assassination in November 1979 he was picked to be commander of the Capital Garrison Command, thus resolving to remain loyal to Army Chief of Staff Chong. He served Army Chief of Staff Chong by altering the chain of command of the Capital Garrison Command which, in case of an emergency, is supposed to be under the command of the director of the Presidential Security Force, to come under the command of the army chief of staff.

At the time of 12 December incident, he mobilized armored units and troops under the pretext of rescuing former Army Chief of Staff Chong and issued an order to fire while asking the commander of the Third Army, Yi Kon-yong, to assist him with two divisions. Thus he mounted a systematic resistance.

In accordance with the aforementioned details of the criminal acts and circumstances turned up as a result of the investigation, former Army Chief of Staff Chong Sung-hwa will be indicted for aiding and abetting the crime of insurrection committed by Kim Chae-kyu and Chong's followers, Yi Kon-yong, Mun Hong-ku, Chong Pyong-chu and Chang Tae-wan will face justice in accordance with their crimes.

Report on the Casualties That Day

Due to the clashes at the official residence of the army chief of staff and at the Ministry of National Defense, a total of 23 persons were either killed or wounded; there were 3 killed, 4 seriously wounded and 16 slightly wounded. Among those who were hospitalized four have already been released from the hospital and the remaining individuals will soon be out of the hospital. The following were killed: Major Kim of the Special Forces Command, military policeman Cpl Pal of the integrated investigation team and Sgt Chong of the Ministry of National Defense.

Words of Request [Tangbuui Mal]

In view of the fact that there had been widespread suspicions and speculations among the people at home and abroad whether former Army Chief of Staff Chong Sung-hwa was involved in the crime committed by Kim Chae-kyu and at a time when some impure elements are taking advantage of this in their vicious maneuvers to disrupt national consensus and disturb social order, it is first of all fortunate that we have rapidly achieved stability and unity in the armed forces and thus have further consolidated the state of national security by thoroughly probing into the crimes of those who were involved in the slayings and by eliminating their followers—subversive elements within the armed forces.

It is regrettable that there were disturbances which made the people uneasy and which resulted in casualties.

The political development plan of the new government, which is set out on the basis of national consensus, should proceed steadfastly and the expected economic difficulties of the nation should be overcome through the protection and promotion of business activities for the nation's continuous economic development. It is hoped that each of us will remain faithful to one's own task and will demonstrate the Korean people's characteristic spirit of overcoming the numerous difficulties encountered in the course of history.

6. PROCLAMATION OF EXTRAORDINARY MARTIAL LAW, MAY 17, 1980

At 0000 hours this morning the Martial Law Command announced Martial Law Decree No. 10. The contents of the decree are as follows:

1. As the emergency martial law proclaimed on 27 October 1979 has extended the area of its enforcement to all areas of the Republic of Korea effective at 0000 hours this morning in accordance with Article 8 of the law on the martial law, the martial law decree which is in effect has been changed as follows:

2. For the security of the state and for the maintenance of public peace and order:

A. All political activities will be banned and indoor and outdoor assemblies for political purposes and demonstrations will also be banned. Indoor and outdoor assemblies with no political purpose will be reported. However, ceremonial occasions and religious functions which have no political purpose are excepted.

B. Press, publications, reportage and radio reports will be subjected to advance censorship in advance.

C. All universities, including junior colleges, will be closed for the time being.

D. The desertion from jobs without pertinent reasons, sabotage and strike activities will be banned.

E. The spreading of groundless rumors will be prohibited. In addition, the act of slandering the former and present heads of state and the use of declarations and language in the same vein as used by the North Korean puppets and any other agitating remarks and acts corrupting public order at public meetings will not be permitted.

3. The people's daily life and their regular economic activities will be guaranteed.

4. The entrance into and departure from the country by foreigners and their travel in the country will be guaranteed to the maximum.

Those who violate the above decrees will be arrested, detained and searched without warrant and will be sternly punished.

[Signed] 17 May 1980. Army General Yi Hui-song, commander of the Martial Law Command

---

Source: Seoul Radio broadcast, May 17, 1980.

7. DECREE ESTABLISHING SPECIAL COMMITTEE FOR NATIONAL SECURITY MEASURES, MAY 27, 1980

Article 1 (*Establishment*): The Special Committee for National Security Measures (*hereinafter called Special Committee*) is hereby established to assist and advise the President in the direction and supervision of matters related to Martial Law and in deliberation on matters of state affairs, in accordance with Articles 9 and 11 of the Martial Law Act under Extraordinary Martial Law.

Article 2 (*Composition*): The Special Committee shall be composed of the Prime Minister, Deputy Prime Minister-Economic Planning Minister, Minister of Foreign Affairs, Minister of Home Affairs, Minister of Justice, Minister of National Defense, Minister of Education, Minister of Culture and Information, Director of the Central Intelligence Agency, Chief Secretary to the President, the Martial Law Commander, Chairman of the Joint Chiefs of Staff, Chiefs of Staff of the Army, Navy and Air Force, Commander of the Defense Security Command, and no more than ten additional members appointed by the President.

Article 3 (*Convening of Meetings*): The President shall chair the Special Committee, determine the agenda, and convene and preside over each meeting.

Article 4 (*Establishment of the Standing Committee*): The Standing Committee for National Security Measures (*hereinafter called Standing Committee*) shall be established upon the mandate of the Special Committee in order to plan such matters as are provided in Article 1 and to coordinate and supervise their implementation.

Article 5 (*Composition of the Standing Committee*): The Standing Committee shall be composed of the chairman and no more than 30 members. The chairman of the Standing Committee shall be appointed by the President from among the members of the Special Committee, and members of the Standing Committee shall be appointed or nominated by the President.

Article 6 (*Establishment of Subcommittees*): Clause 1—Subcommittees can be established within the Standing Committee in order to define and dispose of the affairs of the Standing Committee. Clause 2—The number, kind and definition of proper business of the subcommittees shall be determined by the Standing Committee after obtaining Presidential approval.

Source: The Special Committee for National Security Measures: Background and Necessity, Seoul: Korean Overseas Information Service, 1980.

Article 7 (*Operational Bylaws*): Matters concerning operation of the Special Committee not defined and referred to herein and other necessary matters shall be determined by the Special Committee.

Addendum (*Date of Enforcement*): This Presidential Decree shall take effect from the day of its promulgation.

8. REPORT ON THE INVESTIGATION OF KIM DAE JUNG, JULY 1980

I PRELIMINARY REMARKS

Results of Investigation

The Martial Law Command completed on July 4 an investigation of the attempted insurrection involving Kim Dae-jung and his followers. The Command will refer Kim Dae-jung and 36 of his followers to General Court Martial prosecution on charges of attempted insurrection and violating the National Security Law, Anti-Communist Law, Foreign Exchange Control Law and Martial Law decrees.

The Command decided to take no action against and freed with a warning or admonition those who surrendered during the investigation, those who repented of their wrongdoings and actively cooperated in the investigation, and those who followed blindly in the commission of minor offenses. This decision provides them an opportunity to start afresh and contribute to national harmony. They include Lee Yong-hee, Chang Eul-pyong, Song Chang-dal, Kim Chae-wui, Lee Hyun-pae, Kim Seung-hun, Hahm Se-wung, Kim Dong-kil and Lee Young-hui.

Since the results of an interim investigation of Kim Dae-jung were made public last May 22, the Joint Investigation authorities have intensively probed the suspected attempt at insurrection. As a result, it has been determined that Kim Dae-jung and a group of his followers conspired to overthrow the incumbent Government by violence and set up an interim regime headed by Kim Dae-jung. They formed a vast network of private organizations fronted by the People's Alliance and, using reinstated students as activists, incited campus disturbances with demagoguery in an attempt to cause a bloody revolutionary state by leading the student disturbances into violent and simultaneous popular uprisings across the country.

In addition, Kim Dae-jung was found to have engaged in such anti-state activities as supporting the policy directions of the North Korean Communists

Source: Report on the Investigation of Kim Dae Jung, Seoul: Korean Overseas Information Service, 1980.

during his stay abroad organizing Hanmingtong (the National Congress for the Restoration of Democracy and Promotion of the Unification of Korea), an anti-state organization in the U.S. and Japan; to have illegally possessed and used unlawfully introduced foreign currencies; and to have openly and deliberately violated Martial Law decrees.

Background of Investigation

The authorities, while observing the escalating student disturbances, noted that they were well organized and meticulously planned. The countrywide coordination of slogans, tactics and timing led them to suspect the presence of a central, controlling figure. After closely investigating a number of possibilities, it was discovered that Kim Dae-jung, by organizing reinstated students and student body presidents, had been covertly manipulating the disturbances.

Confident that the sudden demise of President Park Chung Hee was a golden opportunity to push his way into power, Kim Dae-jung promoted both illegal and legal schemes to that end. He mounted a legal struggle to return to and control the New Democratic Party, while pusuing illegal demagoguery via his private organizations.

When it became apparent by March 27 that it was impossible for Kim to seize power through the New Democratic Party due to strong opposition from the party's main faction, he concluded it was likewise impossible for him to gain power through any legal means. Kim therefore decided that only civil uprisings or bloody, violent revolution could achieve his goal, and devised a strategy based on nationwide student disturbances.

Kim schemed to set up an interim regime he himself would head, once the present Government had been overthrown in the midst of turmoil. As the student disturbances grew in intensity after May 13, massive student demonstrations were staged in the streets of major cities, gravely endangering national security.

Judging that the decisive moment was approaching as he had planned, Kim gave instructions for civil uprisings in all major cities at noon on May 22 to overthrow the Government. Changchung Park was chosen as the site in Seoul. Kim's illegal attempt to seize power threatened the disruption of constitutional government and the very survival of 37 million people. The Government was thus compelled to declare Nationwide Martial Law and launch a thorough investigation of Kim Dae-jung and his followers.

II PHASED INSURRECTION CONSPIRACY

Kim Dae-jung's insurrection conspiracy can be divided into four stages—the restoration of civil rights, an attempt to control the New Democratic Party, a plot to overthrow the Government and plans for an interim government.

Restoration of Civil Rights

Knowing that all else depended on having his civil rights restored, Kim Dae-jung ordered Park Yong-rok, Cho Yun-hyung and Lee Yong-hee, all loyal supporters in the New Democratic Party, to organize a Committee for the Restoration of Civil Rights within the party to arouse public opinion and apply pressure on the Government. Subsequently the party issued a statement demanding that the Government restore the civil rights at an early date of all decree violators who had been released.

On February 16, Kim also met illegally in the home of Yun Po-sun with his close right-hand men, including Ye Chun-ho, Suh Nam-dong, Mun Ik-hwan, Lee Mun-yong, Ko Un-tae, Shim Jae-kwon, a reinstated Seoul National University student, and Suh Kyong-sok of the Urban Industrial Mission. At this meeting, they adopted a resolution vowing to work for the restoration of Kim's civil rights. Furthermore, Kim prepared to enlist the support of expelled professors and students during the upcoming new semester (the Korean school semester begins in March) with a view to expanding his organizational network.

Attempt to Control the New Democratic Party

As soon as his civil rights were restored on February 29, Kim Dae-jung began a vigorous effort to control the New Democratic Party which had gained much support by claiming that it would be the next government party. Kim had his supporters within the party—Ye Chun-ho, Song Won-young, Noh Seung-hwan, Chung Dae-chol, Lee Yong-hee, and Cho Se-hyung—work to enlist the support of provincial chapter chairmen, while concentrating on gaining the support of other key party members.

Having secured the support of 27 National Assemblymen and about 60 percent of local chapter chairmen, Kim Dae-jung hoped that he would be able to seize control of the party and on that basis gain control of the Government. Contrary to his initial expectations, however, Kim was not able to convince a majority to support his cause despite the fact that he gave Ye Chung-ho 10 million won to recruit local chapter chairmen.

At this point, Kim Dae-jung called the 27 National Assemblymen who supported him and key members of his staff to his home on March 27 to discuss future strategy. After he was told that even if he did rejoin the party, his chances of controlling it were very slim, Kim decided to abandon his efforts and instead promote his bid to power through his private organizational network. Still, to protect his interests in the party, he had his supporters within the National Assembly organize themselves into the Situation Review Forum of NDP Assemblymen.

Plot to Overthrow the Government

1. Organization

a. Network of Private Organizations

Even before he gave up his attempt to control the New Democratic Party, Kim began to expand his network of private organizations in order to prepare to overthrow the Government and seize power. These efforts began immediately after he was released from house arrest on December 8, 1979.

Immediately after the restoration of his civil rights, Kim formed an office of security and a secretariat to train and control the people and organizations under him. It was the job of these offices to act as liaison, relay instructions, confirm work completed, carry out surveillance and collect information. Furthermore, they controlled who would see Kim and kept a supply of medals with his portrait, autographed ball-point pens and photographs to hand out to visitors. Pak Sa-do, residing in Seoul, was convinced to make 5,000 medals with Kim's portrait, valued at 1,750,000 won, on the promise that he would be a candidate for the Seoul City Council election.

Ye Chun-ho was chief secretary, Kim Chae-wui and Pak Chong-yul, deputy chief secretaries, Kim Hyong-guk, political affairs secretary, Han Hwa-gab, policy secretary, Kim Ok-tu, general affairs secretary, Yu Hun-gun, protocol secretary and Lee Hyop, press secretary. Pak Song-chol, a retired Marine Corps major general who had stood security for the release of Kim in 1949 when he was arrested for involvement in the South Korean Workers' Party, was made chief bodyguard. There were about 30 bodyguards under him, including his younger brother and sons. In addition, there was a spokesman, and an Office of Policy Study, directed by Lee Mun-yong. This office acted as the brains of the organizational network, evaluating the situation, inventing slogans for student demonstrations and preparing speeches and propaganda booklets.

Between December 7 last year and early April this year, Kim Hong-il, his eldest son, organized the Fraternal Federation of Democratic Youth comprised of former and incumbent student body presidents and students who had been expelled from school and/or released from prison. This activist organization, totalling no fewer than 400 students, was to infiltrate various campuses and control the organizers of student demonstrations. Kim Hong-il was chairman, Song Chang-dal, president and Kwon Hyok-chung, organizational chief. Other Kim supporters also acted as advisors, steering committee members, executive department members and campus and provincial chapter chiefs. Thus the reinstated students were named the Federation chapter chiefs in Kukmin University, Chungang University and Sogang University as well as in such provinces as Kyonggido, Chungchongdo, Kyonsangdo, Chollado and Pusan.

From late January through March 10, 1980, Kim Chong-wan, one of Kim's right-hand men, organized the Democratic Fraternity for Constitutional Politics, the membership of which reached 20,000 across the country including former legislators, former officials, professors and lawyers. Ye Chun-ho, Kim Chong-wan, and Kim Yun-shik were the leaders with Kim Sang-hyon, Kye Hun-je, Lee Yong-sop and Yang Song-u on a leadership committee. There were also provincial chapters led by other Kim supporters

In mid-March, Kim Sang-hyon organized the Korea Politico-Cultural Institute to train Kim Dae-jung's followers by recruiting young political aspirants in their twenties to forties. Kim Sang-hyun became president and Pak Chong-hun and Kim Chang-hwan, vice-presidents. The organization also included advisors, a chairman, vice-chairman, planning committee, secretariat, planning office, policy study office, information office and public relations office. The institute had a membership of about 5,000 scattered throughout the country.

Following his decision not to join the party, Kim determined to gain complete control of the People's Alliance that was at the time under a troika system. On April 10, 1980, he met at 5 p.m. in the home of Yun Po-sun with such leading members of this organization as Mun Ik-hwan, Ye Chun-ho, Lee Mun-yong, Shim Jae-kwon, Ko Un-tae, Kim Chong-wan, Kye Hun-je, Kim Yun-shik, Pak Hyong-gyu, Yi U-jong, So Kyong-sok and Kim Pyong-gol and explained to them his motive in deciding not to join the New Democratic Party.

At this meeting, he said that the outlook for political development was not good in light of Prime Minister Shin Hyon-hwack's remarks on the Yushin system in an interview with the *Sankei Shimbun* newspaper of Japan on March 11 and newspaper reports on March 15 that political power would be divided between the president and the prime minister under the new constitution. He then stressed that before anything else, they must fight to have Martial Law lifted, the remnants of the Yushin system eliminated, the Government's Constitutional Amendment Deliberation Committee discontinued, the schedule for political development shortened, those dissidents still in jail released and civil rights restored to all those released prisoners who had not had them already restored. In spite of this urgent need to fight, he said, president Kim Young-sam of the New Democratic Party held an easy-going and optimistic view of the political situation.

Kim Dae-jung told the meeting that he feared a continued confrontation with the party mainstreamers might give the people the impression that he was trying to become the party's presidential candidate. As he did not want to give this impression, he had decided not to join the party and would instead continue to fight within the People's Alliance to restore democracy. Thus he camouflaged his true intention of seizing power.

Following this meeting, Kim Dae-jung on April 10 called his supporters within the People's Alliance to Room 501 of the Park Hotel and held a press conference to announce his decision not to join the New Democratic Party but to continue his fight in the above organization.

Subsequently he reorganized the People's Alliance to strengthen his personal control. Among the changes he made was to shift the leadership from a

troika (three chairmen) system to a central committee, place the steering committee under the central committee and rename the sub-committees as standing
committees. He then placed his supporters in key positions. The chairmanship of
the central standing committee went to Mun Ik-hwan and the vice-chairmanships
to Ye Chun-ho, Lee Mun-yong, Ko Un-tae, Hahm Se-ung, Kim Seung-hun and
Kye Hun-je. The central committee was filled with 30 of his supporters including
Han Sung-hon, Kim Yun-shik, Han Wan-sang, Kim Chong-wan and Yi Hae-dong.
At the same time, three reinstated students Chang Ki-pyo, Shim Jae-kwon and
Lee Hyon-bae were made organization chief, public information chief and
secretary-general respectively. Central Committee member Cho Song-u was made
planning chief and Lee Shin-bom (who is the vice-chairman of the Fraternal Federation of Democratic Youths), chief of covert operations. Thus Kim Dae-jung
took control of the People's Alliance in spite of the strong objection of Yun Po-
sun and Ham Sok-hon, co-chairmen, that it was a purely national movement and
must not and could not be exploited for the political ambitions of any specific
person.

Thus controlling the People's Alliance, Kim Dae-jung established a chain of
command from the central standing committee chairman, Mun Ik-hwan, to such
field activists as Cho Song-u and Lee Shin-bom, and through these activists to
the associations of reinstated students in universities and colleges throughout the
country. Again, through these associations of reinstated students, he was able to
control the student governments and thus to manipulate campus disturbances
and violent student demonstrations from behind the scenes. In close cooperation
with his other organizations, the People's Alliance was the command post to plot
and manipulate campus disturbances and rebellions.

Having expanded a private network of organizations throughout the country,
Kim Dae-jung embarked on a series of activities which can only be described as
demagoguery. It began with a speech at the YWCA on March 26 and was followed by lectures at Hankook Seminary on April 16 and Tongkuk University
on April 18. For these speeches, he planted his own supporters to increase the
size of the audience and induce applause. He tried to whip up his audiences'
emotions against the Government by chanting "the tree of democracy grows on
human blood," using a typical technique of demagogues throughout history by
taking a well-known quote and distorting it and using it to his own purposes.

In a period between February 12, even before the restoration of his civil
rights, and April 28, Kim Dae-jung met about 450 presidents of students groups
and leaders of reinstated students from various colleges, including Shim Chae-
chol of Seoul National University, Chung Tong-nyon of Chonnam University,
Lee Sung-jong of Hankook Seminary and Cho Tae-won of Pusan National University, in his home in Tongkyodong. Kim encouraged them against the Government and urged them to rise up and overthrow the Government in support of
him, personally, He then gave them operating funds plus various mementos such
as a medal incribed with his portrait, ballpoint pens bearing his name, his pic-
tures and propaganda papers carrying his signature.

b. Raising and Distribution of Funds

Kim Dae-jung collected the huge amount of 1.2 billion won from numerous politicians, businessmen and political hopefuls with the promise that when he seized power he would give them business favors, various central or provincial government appointments, and national or provincial assembly candidacies.

Kim used about 300 million won of this fund to manipulate the violent student disturbances, by handing out money to his followers and reinstated students of various colleges in amounts varying from 300,000 won to five million won. Among those who received money were:

Ye Chun-ho to win support of National Assemblymen and organize them,
Lee Yong-hee to win support of non-Assembly politicians and organize them,
Lee Mun-yong to operate Kim's Office of Policy Study,
Han Sung-hon to produce propaganda materials,
Kim Hong-il to finance Kim's private organizations,
Kim Chong-wan and No Kyong-gyu to organize the Democratic Fraternity for Constitutional Politics,
Chung Tong-nyon for demonstrations at Chonnam National University,
Shim Chae-chol and Shim Jae-kwon for demonstrations at Seoul National University,
Song Ki-won and Lee Sok-pyo for demonstrations at Chungang University,
Yun Yo-ryon for demonstrations at Sungjon University,
Pak Song-hyok and Kim Taek-chun for demonstrations at Sogang University,
Lee Sung-jong for demonstrations at Hankook Seminary,
Pak Kye-dong, Shin Kye-ryun and Pak Il-nam for demonstrations at Korea University,
Pae Ki-son for demonstrations at Kukmin University,
Yun Yong-gun for demonstrations at Hankook University of Foreign Studies,
Choe Man-jin for demonstrations at Myongji University,
An Suk for demonstrations at Ewha Women's University,
Cho Tae-won for demonstrations at Pusan National University, and
Kim Pong-u for demonstrations at Kyonghi University.

It has also been confirmed that Kim used part of the political donations he received for personal purposes. He purchased Hanshin Kongyong Apartment 216-201 in Seoul for 30 million won and rented Hyeson Apartment 1039 for nine million won for his eldest son, Kim Hong-il. He also bought Sujong Apartment C-1401 for 30 million won for his second son, Kim Hong-up.

Besides this money raised in Korea, Kim also received a total of 47.4 million yen from some members of the Hanmintong under the influence of the Chochongryon, a pro-Pyongyang Korean organization in Japan during his stay in the United States and Japan between October 11, 1972 and August 8, 1973. He had full knowledge that the money was tainted, coming from the Chochongryon. The total broke down into: 15 million yen from Kim Chong-chung, five million yen and US$3,000 from Pae Dong-ho; and 25.3 million yen raised by Kwak Dong-ui, Kim Chae-hwa and Cho Hwal-jun.

Of the total, Kim Dae-jung spent nine million yen and 18.4 million yen to found the American and Japanese headquarters of the Hanmintong.

In August 1979, Kim received 200,000 yen from Tokuma Utsonomiya, who amounts to the North Korean spokesman in Japan, through Rep. Kim Nok-young of the Unification Party. Again in April 1980, he received US$10,000 from his brother-in-law living in Maryland, U.S., through an American traveller. Kim did not convert these foreign currencies into won as required by law. He gave US$2,700 to an overseas Korean traveller and kept the remainder illegally in his home, thus violating the Foreign Exchange Control Law.

c. Spread of Propaganda

The Korean Politico-Cultural Institute was a center for the publication and dissemination of propaganda leaflets and speeches of Kim Dae-jung. President Kim Sang-hyon was given 6 million won by Kim Dae-jung to win over young political aspirants. He also sponsored a meeting of reinstated professors, under the guise of a political science seminar to camouflage the training of Kim Dae-jung supporters. The institute distributed some 6,000 copies of Kim Dae-jung's propaganda material through its nationwide network. It also produced tapes of Kim Dae-jung's speeches at the YWCA, Hankook Seminary and Tongguk University for nationwide distribution, thus playing a leading role in winning support for Kim's political goal.

The Office of Policy Study also produced propaganda material. This office published all the public speeches of Kim Dae-jung, as well as propaganda leaflets. Especially, it closely analyzed the student demonstrations to supply new catchwords and methods to escalate the disturbances.

Han Sun-hon, legal advisor to Kim Dae-jung, established a printing shop with 12 million won received from Kim and registered it in the name of Han's wife, Kim Song-ja, to exclusively print Kim Dae-jung propaganda.

Furthermore, Kim Dae-jung had Lee Ho-chol, a novelist, Song Kon-ho, a former journalist, and Yu In-ho, a college professor, establish the Council of Intellectuals with 134 members. Then on May 15, he had the council issue a statement, signed by all the members, demanding the lifting of Martial Law and more rapid political development. In this way, they encouraged the intensification of the student demonstrations.

Kim especially tried to persuade novelists, poets and other men and women who visited him to follow his way of mass agitation, saying that they should actively commit themselves to political activities in the example of André Malraux who joined the cabinet of the French Fifth Republic.

d. Penetration of the Media

In February 1980, Kim Dae-jung ordered journalist-turned-Assemblyman Cho Se-hyong and Professor of journalism Lee Young-hui to win as many journalists as possible to his cause. Cho met leftist-oriented So Tong-gu, chief of the research department of the *Kyonghyang Shinmun* newspaper and several other newsmen and introduced them to Kim who promised to establish a newspaper company for them when he took over power.

After this meeting, So Tong-gu approached Yi Kyong-il, foreign news editor of the *Kyonghyang Shinmun* newspaper, No Song-dae, deputy chief of the news department of the Munhwa Broadcasting Station, and six other reporters to stage an illegal boycott to create press turmoil and spread false rumors. In addition, *Tong-a Ilbo* newspaper reporter Sim Song-mu and Tong-a Radio announcer Pak Chong-yol, following Kim Dae-jung's lead, engaged in political activities sympathetic to North Korea and for this were arrested.

Finally, Kim Dae-jung approached the Association of Korean Journalists to convince all reporters in the country to stage a nationwide press strike on May 20th, around the time of his planned mass uprising, but he failed to gain the support of the press.

2. Instigation of Student Disturbances

The purpose of the Fraternal Federation of Democratic Youth was to act for Kim Dae-jung on campuses and to systematically encourage demonstrations in the first instance and instigate violence in the second. At the same time, they spread propaganda for Kim on campuses as well as in the streets of major cities and mobilized audiences for student meetings. They also incited citizens to join the student demonstrations by misleading public opinion, while reporting to Kim the progress of student demonstrations and relaying Kim's instructions to student leaders.

The Federation was also a channel of funds from Kim Dae-jung to the students. In early March Kim gave two reinstated Korea University students, Pak Kye-dong and Pak Il-nam, 150,000 won and instructions about the demonstrations. Pak Il-nam then convinced the president of the Korea University student government to play a leading role in the street demonstrations of Korea University students. Between mid-April and early May, Kim gave Tun Yo-ryon, president of the Sungjon University student government, a total of 500,000 won on three different occasions while encouraging him to continue to lead student demonstrations. On May 11, Kim also gave Shim Chae-chol, president of Seoul National University student government, 500,000 won and a promise that he would receive an important job in the Education Ministry when Kim took over power. Shim was also given one million won in an election fund for president of the student body. Thus he was convinced to take part in violent student demonstrations.

The Federation also spread 2,000 copies of *The Way to Save a Democratic Nation*, 17,000 copies of *With National Spirit*, 5,000 copies of *A Collection of Kim Dae-jung's Speeches* and 5,000 copies of *Korea's Coordinates on the World Map in the 1980s*.

The Democratic Fraternity for Constitutional Politics was also active on campuses in the winter and spring. No Kyong-gyu, chief of the Kyongsangnamdo chapter, received a total of 300,000 won on three occasions between December 1979 and early May 1980 with instructions to expand his chapter, influence the course of student demonstrations in Pusan and lay a bridge for reinstated Pusan National University student, Cho Tae-won, to contact Kim Dae-jung to receive funds and instructions. In mid-December 1979, No took eight students from Pusan University, including Cho Tae-won, to visit Kim at his home. Kim encouraged the students, saying that the October 26 incident should be understood in the context of the heroic student demonstrations in Pusan and Masan.

On April 24th, the Fraternity produced 100,000 copies of Kim's declaration of secession from the New Democratic Party and on May 7th, 50,000 copies of a national manifesto to expedite democratization issued in the name of the People's Alliance and distributed them to campuses across the country.

Having completed an organizational network and realizing the impossibility of seizing power through legitimate political activities, Kim turned to the students as the only means to seize power. The atmosphere on campuses was already in mid-March becoming tense as student rallies in support of increased campus autonomy and against military drill spread to Sungkyunkwan University, Sogang University, Yonsei University and Seoul National University. Kim was determined to guide the demonstrations into anti-government riots to be used as a tool to overthrow the Government.

Visiting Toksan in Chungchongnamdo to attend a memorial service for independence fighter Yun Pong-kil on April 29, Kim emphasized that for the sake of the restoration of democracy, Martial Law should be repealed, the Government should abandon its work on the constitutional amendment, the Government's schedule for political development should be shortened, and a transfer of government power should be realized before the end of this year. He stated that to this end, he would launch a national movement to expedite democratization.

To buttress this pronouncement, Kim Dae-jung called a meeting of his right-hand men in his home on May 1 to discuss the student demonstrations. He advised those at the meeting that the demonstrations and sit-ins on the issues of pro-government professors and nepotism on campus should be led to include such political demands as complete elimination of the Yushin system, the lifting of Martial Law and a shortening of the political development schedule. Then when students took to the streets, citizens would be induced to join with them and the demonstration would spread across the country. When this happened, the Government would give in, he said. He told the meeting that efforts should be made to organize a mass uprising in the middle of May when the National Assembly would convene a special session.

Those attending the meeting were Mun Ik-hwan, chairman of the People's Alliance central committee; Lee Mun-yong, Ko Un-tae, Ye Chun-ho and Han Wan-sang, standing committee members; Lee Hyun-pae, Chung Ki-pyo and Shim Jae-kwon, all reinstated Seoul National University students; and Cho Sung-woo, a reinstated Korea University student.

Kim also formed the Research Institute of Democratic Systems, a quasi interim government, so as to prepare for the seizure of power when the Government fell. Furthermore, by having Cho Sung-woo and Shim Jae-kwon take charge of influencing and controlling student disturbances, Kim saw to it that the reinstated student societies and student bodies of various universities would stage violent demonstrations simultaneously, coordinated through the Fraternal Federation of Democratic Youth.

At 7 p.m. on May 3, Kim again called a meeting of the central standing committee of the People's Alliance in his home to discuss a national manifesto to expedite democratization to be issued in the name of the People's Alliance and to include the same demands made at Toksan on April 29. The committee met again at 3 p.m. on May 6 to make the final decision to issue the manifesto on the following day as a means to intensify the student demonstrations.

According to this decision, Kim held a press conference to announce the manifesto at 8 a.m. on May 7 in the Christian Hall in downtown Seoul, inviting some 30 domestic and foreign reporters. At the same time, he had Kim Chong-wan, one of his enthusiastic supporters, produce some 50,000 copies of the manifesto for distribution to universities and colleges and to many people in all walks of life throughout the country to gain support for a mass uprising in violation of the constitutional order of society. These copies were disseminated through his private organizational network across the country in a day, and major points of the manifesto appeared as catchwords and demands in the student demonstrations on the following day.

In the meantime, Ko Un-tae, a member of the central standing committee of the People's Alliance met Song Ki-won, a reinstated Chungang University student, at his home on March 20 and again on May 5, and handed him a demonstration fund of 500,000 won he had received from Kim Dae-jung, telling him that "our seizure of power is now around the corner." He said that the students should take the lead in overthrowing the Government and promised that if and when Kim Dae-jung came to power, they would make Song an inspection officer in the Ministry of Education.

At about the same time, Kim Sang-hyon of the Korea Politico-Cultural Institute arranged for Chong Tong-nyon of Chonnam University to visit Kim Dae-Jung on both May 5 and 8. Kim Dae-jung gave him 5 million won to organize mass rallies—the very demonstrations that led to the Kwangju turmoil.

At noon on May 8, reinstated student Cho Sung-woo called a meeting of reinstated student representatives of various colleges, including Lee Shin-pom and Mun Kuk-ju, both of Seous National University, at the Aechon restaurant near the Kangnam Express Bus Terminal. At this meeting, it was agreed that the students must intensify the demonstrations into a violent riot in order to make Kim Dae-jung president on the strength of the People's Alliance. They reasoned that if the students attacked and seized government offices with sticks, Molotov cocktails and other weapons, the embattled police would withdraw, making bloody clashes with the military unavoidable. When the people were roused and joined the disturbance at this stage, the military, too, would be rendered powerless, making it easy to overthrow the Government. The participants agreed that various colleges should stage violent demonstrations under their responsibility. When they reported the results of this meeting to Kim Dae-jung in Room 501 of the Park Hotel on May 12, he encouraged them to carry out their plan as discussed.

At 5 p.m. on May 12, Kim Dae-jung held a meeting of his close associates, including Mun Ik-hwan, Ye Chun-ho and Lee Mun-yong, in Room 521 of the Park Hotel to receive reports from his field activists, Chang-Ki-pyo and Shim Jae-kwon, on the progress of the student demonstrations. At this meeting, he was told that 45 student leaders from 26 universities around the country had held an all-night meeting in the Student Hall of Seoul National University the night before and had come to the following decisions:

1) to intensify the student struggle if the Government closes the campuses,
2) to demand the lifting of Martial Law and an announcement of a clear schedule of political development, and
3) to demand a meeting with the Prime Minister to discuss a solution to campus issues.

Kim was also informed of another meeting of student leaders slated for May 16 at Ewha Women's University to discuss new strategy. After receiving these reports, he ordered his staff to observe the student demonstrations of Seoul National University, Yonsei University and Korea University closely so as to lead them into a mass uprising when the opportune time came.

Fueled by this series of back-stage manipulations, the campus disturbances intensified all across the country, culminating in extremely violent demonstrations in downtown Seoul on May 14 and 15, a development which endangered national security and caused a loss of human life, equipment and property.

Kim Dae-jung continuously sent his most trusted associates to encourage the demonstrators and report back the progress. Based on an evaluation of each new development, he handed out new slogans and instructions, thereby carefully directing the street demonstrations to violence. He entertained the wild fancy that if the violent demonstrations were to be linked to a popular uprising, he would be able to seize power.

Kim Dae-jung managed to place the splinter Unification Party under his influence. Thus, on May 14, acting President of the Unification Party Kim Nok-yong and Policy Study Chief Chon Tae-yol issued a statement, on Kim Dae-jung's instructions, saying that the cry of the students is the cry of the nation. On the following day, the party again issued a statement demanding the organization of an Extraordinary Measures Committee for Solution of the Situation. It threatened to launch a national campaign against the Government if their demands were refused, instigating a rebellion to overthrow the Government. The party thus played a major role in escalating campus disturbances into a violent mass uprising.

Kim Dae-jung called in his closest staff including Ye Chun-ho, Mun Ik-hwan and Lee Mun-yong on May 15 to prepare a final plan for insurrection. They decided to stage a simultaneous uprising at noon on May 20 unless the demands embodied in the national manifesto to expedite democratization including the repeal of Martial Law and the resignation of specific officials were met by May 19. Kim Dae-jung, however, put off 'D-day' until May 22 in order to take advantage of such factors as the confirmation of the verdict against Kim Chae-kyu (the assassin of President Park), the opening of a special National Assembly session and the added time to direct the student demonstration to violence.

Through Shim Jae-kwon, Kim Dae-jung informed the presidents of the student bodies who were meeting at Ewha Women's University on May 16–17 that 'D-day' had been changed. He instructed the student leaders to carry out the campus demonstrations according to his plan.

Kim Dae-jung thus schemed to stage nationwide rallies on noon, May 22, with the demonstrations in Seoul to be at Changchung Park and elsewhere at city hall plazas. Citizens were to wear black ribbons on their chests and members of the central standing committee of the People's Alliance, prison garb. They expected to lead the demonstrations into a popular uprising and in this way Kim Dae-jung conspired to paralyze the Government and seize power.

Plans for Interim Government

As campus disturbances became increasingly violent, Kim Dae-jung decided the time was ripe for a mass uprising. He therefore established the Research Institute of Democratic Systems at a meeting with his immediate staff members, including Mun Ik-hwan, Lee Mun-yong and Ye Chun-ho, at his home on May 1.

This institute was to provide the framework of an interim government to take power once the incumbent Government was overthrown. He appointed the ministers of this shadow cabinet from among his supporters, under Ye Chun-ho as the institute's chairman and Lee Mun-yong as its president. In addition, he named 26 standing directors and 14 research committee members.

Kim Dae-jung's shadow cabinet members were:

National Revival—Pak Hyong-gyu
History and Culture—Paek Nak-chong
Religion and Education—So Nam-dong
Press and Social Affairs—Song Kon-ho
Women's Affairs—Yi Hyo-jae
Democratic Politics—Chang Ul-byong
Labor Affairs—Tak Hui-jun
Agricultural Policy—Yu In-ho
Economy—Im Chae-gyong
National Security and Diplomacy—Yang Ho-min
National Unification—Mun Ik-hwan
Political Morals—An Pyong-mu
Education—Han Wan-sang
Administration—Lee Mun-yong

Kim Dae-jung received a written agreement from each appointee to ensure their allegiance.

Yi Taek-ton, one of Kim Dae-jung's supporters in the National Assembly, visited Kim's home on May 5 and urged him to formally propose a national council for the solution of social and political unrest due to student demonstrations, with Kim Dae-jung and five others serving as advisors and Mun Ik-hwan and two others as executive committee members.

Kim Dae-jung agreed and instructed Yi to devise a plan for demanding the reorganization of President Choi Kyu-hah's Government to pave the way for the nullification of the existing Constitution. Kim thus took another step toward realizing his scheme of setting up an interim government. Yi Taek-ton subsequently met Lee Shin-pom in Seoul on May 16 to discuss the details of the council's organization.

III KWANGJU TURMOIL

Origin of Kwangju Turmoil

The investigation also determined that Kim Dae-jung engineered the origins of the Kwangju turmoil, an unprecedented national tragedy. Kim's direct and indirect assistance to radical student demonstrations in the Honam area, his birthplace, exceeded that delivered to any other area, in the expectation that popular uprisings could most easily be achieved within his main political base.

Chung Tong-nyon, a reinstated Chonnam University student, visited Kim's home on April 12. Kim Dae-jung discussed student demonstrations in the Kwangju area with Chung, and gave him a personalized memento while encouraging him to continue struggling. Chung came again on May 5, accompanied by Kim Sang-hyon, director of the Korea Politico-Culture Institute, and requested an operating fund of five million won. Kim initially gave him three million won, and provided the remaining two million won on May 8.

Kim also gave Chung a "list of criminals involved in the kidnapping of Kim Dae-jung," as well as books, propaganda brochures and other seditious publications for distribution at Chonnam and Chosun Universities in Kwangju. Kim also urged Chung to stage anti-government activities to press demands for the repeal of Martial Law and the shortening of the schedule for political development. He instructed Chung to oppose any constitutional amendment featuring a division of power between the president and prime minister.

Upon his return to Kwangju, Chung Tong-nyon followed Kim Dae-jung's instructions by passing 2.7 million won on May 6 to Park Kwan-hyun, president of the Chonnam University student body; and 1.7 million won on May 10 to Yun Han-pong, a reinstated Chonnam University student in charge of demonstrations by Chosun University students. These funds were to be used to support demonstrations.

Kim had thus engineered the very street demonstration by Chonnam University students on May 18 that was the origin of the Kwangju turmoil. Chosun University students later joined the Chonnam University demonstration, making it the detonator of the entire Kwangu disturbance.

As the Kwangju disturbance worsened after May 18, some 40 street-thug supporters of Kim Dae-jung rushed to Kwangju from Seoul. Once in Kwangju they formed three- to four-man teams and armed themselves with kitchen knives, hoes, and iron pipes before joining the massive demonstrations to break police cordon lines, burn or otherwise destroy public buildings—broadcasting stations, city hall and police stations. They also commandeered motor vehicles and attacked armories; in short, they played key roles in the Kwangju turmoil. The leaders of this group of thugs were Choi Chang-shi (head of the 'OB' faction), Chu Kyu-myon (owner of the San Paulo Salon in Seoul), Choi Tong-sop (head of the Tong-sop Martial Arts Association), and Kim Sung-hwan (a martial arts instructor).

In the meantime, Kim Pong-su, an ex-convict and member of Kim Dae-jung's private organization in Kwangju, along with Kim Yu-kon and some ten others, participated in the turmoil as masked rioters and drove a commandeered truck carrying a placard that read "Free Kim Dae-jung!", further aggravating the turmoil. Alerted to the Martial Law forces' advance into Kwangju, they cached carbines and ammunition at the foot of Mt. Taebond near Kwangju and fled on May 28. Upon reaching Seoul, seven of them went into hiding at an unlicensed inn near Mapo and plotted ways to touch off a Kwangju-like turmoil in Seoul, but were arrested soon after their arrival. Kim Yu-kon stated that he took part in the turmoil with Kim Dae-jung's promise to make him a provincial post office director when he seized power.

Choi Tok-kil, another member of Kim Dae-jung's private organization in Kwangju, mobilized some ten other members living in Kwangju to move through the crowd and spread wild rumors designed to aggravate regional sentiments, such as: "Kyongsangdo Province soldiers came here to exterminate Chollado Province people," "They stabbed women's breasts," and "Martial Law troops killed 200 to 300 demonstrators." Thus they used citizens' outrage over groundless rumors to provoke them into joining the disturbances, playing a decisive role in further aggravating the situation.

Hong Nam-soon, a lawyer in charge of the Chollanamdo chapter of Kim's Fraternity of Democratic Politics, had recruited approximately 300 new members for the Fraternity after being personally urged by Kim Dae-jung on five occasions from February 29 to early May to expand the organization in the Chollanamdo area and provided with 300,000 won as encouragement. Hong performed such behind-the-scenes tasks as directing Kim Wun-ki, a reinstated Chonnam University sophomore, to scatter seditious printed material including the "list of criminals involved in the kidnapping of Kim Dae-jung."

Moreover, when the Kwangju turmoil intensified with the rioters seizing the provincial government building, Hong often visited the seized offices from May 23–26 cloaked as a "citizens' crisis settlement committee" member. During those visits, he presented 1 million won to the rioters and encouraged them "not to turn in weapons under any circumstances and carry on the fight."

All of this evidence is eloquent proof that the unprecedentedly tragic Kwangju turmoil was largely due to advance manipulation by Kim Dae-jung.

Post-Kwangju Turmoil Schemes

A group of about 10 reinstated students—including Cho Sung-woo, concurrently Democratic Youth Association chairman and People's Alliance central committee member, Lee Shin-pom, a reinstated Seoul National University Law College senior, and Lee Hae-chan of Seoul National University—plotted to ignite a Kwangju-like turmoil in Seoul. They had gone underground when their plan to stage a countrywide popular uprising on May 22 was thwarted by the May 17 extension of Martial Law.

In some 16 secret meetings between May 19 and June 12, they prepared and distributed printed material in an attempt to create a Kwangju-like turmoil in Seoul. Carrying Molotov cocktails and poison bamboo needles, they recruited other reinstated students and first tried to stage a violent demonstration in the Kuro Industrial Area on June 12 by forming a commando team to agitate and mobilize workers.

Their plan called for mounting another violent demonstration near the Hwashin Department Store the following day. The signal was to be a Molotov cocktail thrown at 6 p.m. According to their scenario, the demonstration would worsen following clashes with Martial Law forces, facilitating the paralysis and overthrow of the Government.

All were arrested just prior to the planned disturbances.

IV CONCLUSION

The investigation results detailed above show that Kim Dae-jung, as part of his attempted insurrection, established four phases in his struggle for power, and to fulfill them mounted both legitimate and illegal campaigns.

First, he succeeded in having his civil rights restored, thus preparing the way for legal political struggles. He then sought to seize control of the New Democratic Party.

However, when the New Democratic Party mainstreamers refused to yield to Kim, and when his obsessive pursuit of personal political ambition was clearly no longer to be tolerated, Kim Dae-jung relinquished his grasping for control of the party and concentrated on illegal struggles for power through his private organizations and demagoguery. He restructed an assortment of private organizations, including the People's Alliance, to facilitate their more effective use in agitating popular uprisings.

Convinced that transforming student demonstrations into violent riots to create a state of anarchy was the only way to spark a popular uprising, Kim Dae-jung set up various private organizations, chiefly among reinstated professors and students. He then infiltrated his followers onto the campuses, covertly engineered student disturbances and induced violent street demonstrations. He also tried to stir public distrust of the legitimacy of the incumbent Government and its schedule for political development with wild rumors and outrageous demagoguery.

In particular, Kim Dae-jung orchestrated student demonstrations and slogans with the phases of his struggle for power. He fabricated and spread assorted rumors in a bid to estrange the people from the military, the last bulwark of national security and political and social stability. He also ensured that student slogans were designed to achieve the same result.

The campus disturbances worsened as Kim Dae-jung schemed. Despite Martial Law, students began taking to the streets in force on May 13. On May 14 and 15, students staged extremely violent demonstrations in Seoul and other major cities, paralyzing the cities and challenging the authority of the Republic.

In the course of struggling to overthrow the Government and seize power, Kim Dae-jung went so far as to conceive the idea of an interim regime formed around his private organizations. The investigation found Kim completely prepared to seize power promptly once the incumbent Government was overthrown.

Moreover, by assigning some persons to several organizations and putting them in charge of different would-be recruits and covert action channels, Kim sought to represent his network of organizations as vast and broadly supported, while boosting his followers' sense of participation and pride by distributing many "high posts."

To sum up, despite the fact that the Government took the people's aspirations into full account and made public pledges to implement the political schedule announced immediately after the October 26 assassination of President Park, and has been doing its utmost to honor those pledges, Kim Dae-jung and a group of his followers conspired to overthrow the incumbent Government by violence and set up an interim regime headed by Kim himself. The Government was thus compelled to declare Nationwide Martial Law on May 17 and launched a thorough investigation of Kim and his followers.

To achieve stable and steady political development, there must be a political climate in which all politicians can work in concert to overcome crises by transcending partisan interests and tactics.

In spite of the results of the investigation of Kim Dae-jung and his supporters, the previously announced political timetable—with a constitutional referendum by the end of October this year and a new administration by June next year—will be implemented as originally planned.

9. STATEMENT ON COMMUTATION OF SENTENCES OF KIM DAE JUNG AND OTHERS, JANUARY 23, 1981

The government Friday commuted the capital sentence for Kim Dae-Jung after it was upheld by the Supreme Court earlier in the day.

The government also reduced prison terms for eleven others involved in the case by two to five years.

In an announcement, Minister of Culture and Information Lee Kwang-Pyo, government spokesman, said the state council (cabinet) decided on the commutation at the instructions of President Chun Doo Hwan.

It said President Chun asked the government to study the question of commuting the death sentence imposed on Kim Dae-Jung in consideration of various circumstances.

The Supreme Court found Kim Dae-Jung guilty of violating the national security and anti-communist laws and conspiring for insurrection.

The following is the full text of the announcement by Minister of Culture and Information Lee Kwang-Pyo:

The government was instructed by President Chun Doo Hwan to study the question of commuting the death sentence imposed on Kim Dae-Jung and upheld today by the Supreme Court after he was found guilty of violating the national security law and the anti-communist law and of conspiring for insurrection, as well as the sentences of the others convicted in this case. Accordingly, the state council was called into session to discuss the matter . . . the state council was asked to pay attention to the following considerations.

The fact that those convicted, including Kim Dae-Jung, endangered national security by violating the laws of this country, especially by forming an anti-state organization and conspiring for insurrection, has been clearly proved by thorough examinations and trial proceedings at the initial, appellate and supreme court trials . . . additional factors were also taken into account:

First, the time has come to usher in a new historical era by ending the confrontation-dominated political situation of the 1970s and the national chaos following the October 26, 1979 incident. The affair of Kim Dae-Jung and the others is a sad political legacy from the old era. Thus there is no need to besmirch the opening chapter of the Fifth Republic with a nightmare of the past.

Source: Korean Information Service, Washington, D.C., January 23, 1981.

Second, friendly nations and persons at home and abroad have appealed for clemency from a humanitarian standpoint.

Third, Kim Dae-Jung himself has submitted a petition in which he expresses repentance for endangering national security, apologizes to the people and appeals for magnanimity and generous consideration in favor of himself and the others. The basic policy of the government is to treat magnanimously anyone who repents of his wrongdoings, regardless of the gravity of the crime or his previous ideology.

In consideration of the above points, the state council has concluded that it is appropriate from the standpoint of national reconciliation to grant commutations to Kim Dae-Jung and the others convicted in this case. The council therefore resolves that the sentences be commuted as shown below:

Convicted	Confirmed Sentence	Commuted Sentence
1) Kim Dae-Jung	Death	Life Imprisonment
2) Lee Mun-Yong	20 Years	15 Years
3) Mun Ik-Hwan	15 Years	10 Years
4) Koh Eun-Tae	15 Years	10 Years
5) Cho Sung-Woo	15 Years	10 Years
6) Yeh Chun-Ho	12 Years	8 Years
7) Lee Shin-Pom	12 Years	9 Years
8) Kim San-Hyun	10 Years	7 Years
9) Lee Hae-Chan	10 Years	7 Years
10) Sol Hoon	10 Years	7 Years
11) Song Ki-Won	10 Years	7 Years
12) Lee Suk-Pyo	7 Years	5 Years

10. STATEMENT BY PRESIDENT CHUN DOO HWAN ON LIFTING OF MARTIAL LAW, JANUARY 24, 1981

Dear fellow countrymen: The government has decided to totally lift the emergency martial law, which has been in force nationwide with the exception of Cheju Island, effective 0000 on 25 January 1981.

This decision is made on the basis of the judgment that the state of the national crisis, sustained since the 26 October incident, has now been wisely overcome through your cooperation and unity and that overall stability in our society is now fully restored.

This measure is also aimed at ensuring a fair, just and free atmosphere for the upcoming elections, including the presidential election, thereby consolidating the foundation of the new fifth republic.

I sincerely would like to thank all of the people for their active cooperation in martial law affairs, enduring many inconveniences for a long time. I would like to extend my thanks to the officers and men of the ROK Army for their faithful service in martial law affairs.

My fellow countrymen, I think you all clearly recall the situation of extreme confrontation, sedition, disorder and lawlessness which was rampaging in our society following the 26 October emergency status.

Through our experience, we became keenly aware of how the absence of stability can harm the nation. In a word, stability is the basis of all national development. Just as a structure cannot be properly built if the foundation is not solid, implementation of democratic politics, economic prosperity, promotion of a firm defense capability and of our national culture cannot be achieved unless stability is guaranteed. In a state of disorder and unrest there would be only retrogression instead of progress, distrust instead of trust and confrontation instead of reconciliation.

The martial law status over the last 15 months was aimed at maintaining stability. Stability has a real value when it is achieved through active participation by the people. It is not desirable to have stability secured by physical measures.

Martial law is being lifted today not because there is no need for stability or the need for it has been reduced. The true significance in lifting martial law lies in the fact that the maintenance of stability should not be attained by the government but by the people, not by physical strength but by the will of the people.

Source: Seoul Domestic Service broadcast, January 24, 1981.

My fellow countrymen, we are taking a vigorous step forward to build a new era, a new history and a new republic. At this point, I think the spirit of the new era should be fully displayed in maintaining the nation's stability. We should never again have to secure our stability, which is vital to the firm existence of the nation and to the people's peaceful life, through physical means. We should no longer waste the valuable energy and time of our people by harming and later restoring our stability.

Fellow countrymen, let us all strive to promote stability on a firm and solid base. I am convinced that our efforts will be met by fruitful results because there are people who want and are resolved to maintain stability and there is a government determined and able to safeguard our security.

Signed, President Chon Tu-hwan; 24 January 1981.

CONSTITUTIONAL DOCUMENTS

11. THE YUSHIN CONSTITUTION, DECEMBER 1972

PREAMBLE

We, the people of Korea, possessing a glorious tradition and history from time immemorial, imbued with the sublime spirit of independence as manifested in the March 1st Movement, and with the ideals of the April 19th Righteous Uprising and the May 16th Revolution, now being engaged in the establishment of a new democratic Republic which consolidates further the basic, free, democratic order on the foundation of the historic mission of the peaceful unification of the fatherland, determined:

To afford equal opportunities to every person;

To provide for the fullest development of the capacity of each individual in all fields of political, economic, social and cultural life;

To help each person discharge his duties and responsibilities;

To promote the welfare of the people domestically, and to strive to maintain permanent world peace internationally, and thereby to ensure the security, liberty and happiness of ourselves and our posterity eternally;

Do hereby amend, through national referendum, the Constitution, ordained and established on the Twelfth Day of July in the year of Nineteen Hundred and Forty Eight A.D., and amended on the Twenty Sixth Day of December in the year of Nineteen Hundred and Sixty Two A.D.

CHAPTER I: GENERAL PROVISIONS

Article 1. (1) The Republic of Korea shall be a democratic Republic.

(2) The sovereignty of the Republic of Korea shall reside in the people, and the people shall exercise sovereignty either through their representatives or by means of national referendum.

Source: Korea Annual 1973.

Article 2. The conditions necessary for being a Korean national shall be determined by law.

Article 3. The territory of the Republic of Korea shall consist of the Korean Peninsula and its adjacent islands.

Article 4. The Republic of Korea shall endeavor to maintain international peace and renounce all aggressive wars.

Article 5. (1) Treaties duly ratified and promulgated in accordance with this Constitution and the generally recognized rules of international law shall have the same effect as domestic laws of the Republic of Korea.

(2) The status of aliens shall be guaranteed in accordance with international law and treaties.

Article 6. (1) All public officials shall be servants of the entire people, and shall be responsible to the people.

(2) The status and political impartiality of public officials shall be guaranteed in accordance with the provisions of law.

Article 7. (1) The establishment of political parties shall be free, and the plural party system shall be guaranteed.

(2) Organization and activities of political parties shall embody necessary organizational arrangements to enable the people to participate in the formation of political will.

(3) Political parties shall enjoy the protection of the State in accordance with the provisions of law. However, if the purposes or activities of a political party are contrary to the basic democratic order, or endanger the existence of the State, the Government shall bring action against it in the Constitution Committee for its dissolution, and the political party shall be dissolved in accordance with the decision of the Constitution Committee.

CHAPTER II: RIGHT AND DUTIES OF CITIZENS

Article 8. All citizens shall be assured dignity and value as human beings, and it shall be the duty of the State to guarantee such fundamental rights of the people to the utmost.

Article 9. (1) All citizens shall be equal before the law, and there shall be no discrimination in political, economic, social, or cultural life on account of sex, religion or social status.

(2) No privileged castes shall be recognized, nor ever be established in any form.

(3) The awarding of decorations or distinctions of honor in any form shall be effective only for recipients, and no privileged status shall be created thereby.

Article 10. (1) All citizens shall enjoy personal liberty. No person shall be arrested, detained, seized, searched, interrogated, punished, subjected to involuntary labor, or branded as security risk except as provided by law.

(2) No citizen shall be subject to torture of any kind, nor be compelled to testify against himself in criminal cases.

(3) Warrants issued by a judge upon request of a prosecutor must be presented in case of arrest, detention, search or seizure. However, in case the

criminal is apprehended flagrante delicto, or in the case where there is danger that a criminal who has committed a crime may escape or destroy evidence, the investigating authorities may request an ex post facto warrant.

(4) All persons who are arrested or detained shall have the right to prompt assistance of counsel. When a criminal defendant is unable to secure the same by his own efforts, the State shall assign a counsel for the use of the defendant as provided by law.

Article 11. (1) No person shall be prosecuted for a criminal offense unless such act constitutes a crime prescribed by law at the time it was committed, nor shall be placed in double jeopardy.

(2) No restrictions shall be imposed upon the political rights of any citizen, nor shall any person be deprived of property rights by means of retroactive legislation.

Article 12. No citizen shall be subject to restriction of freedom of residence or the change thereof, except as provided by law.

Article 13. No citizen shall be subject to restriction of freedom of choice of occupation, except as provided by law.

Article 14. No citizen shall be subject to violation of freedom of residence except as provided by law. In case of search or seizure in the residence, a warrant issued by a judge upon request from a prosecutor shall be presented.

Article 15. No citizen shall be subject to violation of privacy of correspondence except as provided by law.

Article 16. (1) All citizens shall enjoy freedom of religion.

(2) No State religion shall be recognized, and religion and politics shall be separated.

Article 17. All citizens shall enjoy freedom of conscience.

Article 18. No citizen shall be subject to restriction of freedom of speech and press, or freedom of assembly and association, except as provided by law.

Article 19. (1) All citizens shall have freedom to participate in the sciences and arts.

(2) The rights of authors, inventors and artists shall be protected by law.

Article 20. (1) The right of property of all citizens shall be guaranteed. Content thereof and limitations shall be determined by law.

(2) The exercise of property rights shall conform to public welfare.

(3) In case of expropriation, use or restriction of private property for public purposes, the standard and method of compensation shall be determined by law.

Article 21. All citizens who have attained the age of twenty shall have right to vote in accordance with the provisions of law.

Article 22. All citizens shall have the right to hold public office in accordance with the provisions of law.

Article 23. All citizens shall have the right to submit written petitions to any State authority in accordance with the provisions of law.

(2) The State authority shall be obliged to examine such petitions.

Article 24. (1) All citizens shall have the right to be tried in conformity with the law by competent judges as qualified by the Constitution and law.

(2) Citizens who are not on active service or employees of the military forces shall not be tried by courts-martial except in case of espionage in military affairs or in case of crimes in regard to sentinel, sentry-posts, provision of harmful food, and prisoners of war as defined by law; and except when an extraordinary state of siege has been declared, or except when the President has taken an emergency measure concerning the judicial power of the Courts.

(3) All citizens shall have the right to prompt trial. A criminal defendant shall have the right to public trial without delay in the absence of justifiable reason.

Article 25. In case a criminal defendant under detention is found innocent, he shall be entitled to a claim against the State for compensation in accordance with the provisions of law.

Article 26. (1) In case a person has suffered damages by unlawful acts of public officials done in the exercise of their official duties, he may request redress from the State or public entity in accordance with the provisions of law; however, the public officials concerned shall not be immune from liabilities.

(2) In case a person on active military service, or an employee of the military forces, a public official of the police, and others as defined by law, suffers damages in connection with the execution of official duties such as combat action and training, he shall not be entitled to a claim against the State or public entity for compensation on grounds of unlawful acts of public official duties, except for compensation as determined by law.

Article 27. (1) All citizens shall have the right to receive an equal education corresponding to their abilities.

(2) All citizens who have children under their protection shall be responsible for at least their elementary education and other education as required by law.

(3) Such compulsory education shall be free.

(4) Independence and political impartiality of education shall be guaranteed.

(5) Fundamental matters pertaining to the educational system and its operation shall be determined by law.

Article 28. (1) All citizens shall have the right to work. The States shall endeavor to promote the employment of workers through social and economic means.

(2) All citizens shall have the duty to work. The contents and conditions of the duty to work shall be determined by law in confirmity with democratic principles.

(3) Standards of working conditions shall be determined by law.

(4) Special protection shall be accorded to working women and children.

Article 29. (1) The right to association, collective bargaining and collective action of workers shall be guaranteed within the scope defined by law.

(2) The right to association, collective bargaining, and collective action shall not be accorded to workers who are public officials, except for those authorized by the provisions of law.

(3) The right to collective action may be either restricted or may not be recognized in accordance with the provisions of law for public officials and

workers engaged in State, local autonomous governments, state-run enterprises, public utility businesses, and enterprises which have serious influence on the national economy.

Article 30. (1) All citizens shall be entitled to a decent human life.

(2) The State shall endeavor to promote social security.

(3) Citizens who are incapable of making a living shall be protected by the State in accordance with the provisions of law.

Article 31. All citizens shall be protected by the State for purity of marriage and health.

Article 32. (1) Liberties and rights of citizens shall not be ignored for the reason that they are not enumerated in the Constitution.

(2) Laws which restrict liberties and rights of citizens shall be enacted only when necessary for the maintenance of national security, order and public welfare.

Article 33. All citizens shall have the duty to pay taxes levied in accordance with the provisions of law.

Article 34. All citizens shall have the duty to defend the national territory in accordance with the provisions of law.

CHAPTER III: NATIONAL CONFERENCE FOR UNIFICATION

Article 35. The National Conference for Unification, being a national organization based on the collective will of the people as a whole to pursue peaceful unification of the fatherland, shall be the depository of the national sovereignty, entrusted with the sacred mission of the unification of the fatherland.

Article 36. (1) The delegates of the National Conference for Unification shall be composed of delegates elected through direct popular elections.

(2) The number of delegates of the National Conference for Unification shall be determined by law within the range of no less than two thousand and no more than five thousand persons.

(3) The President shall be the Chairman of the National Conference for Unification.

(4) Matters pertaining to the election of the delegates of the National Conference for Unification shall be determined by law.

Article 37. (1) Any person who is capable of faithfully carrying out the sovereign will of the people for the sake of peaceful unification of the fatherland from among those who are qualified to be elected to the National Assembly and who have attained the age of thirty years or more as of the election date, shall be eligible to be elected as a delegate of the National Conference for Unification.

(2) Matters pertaining to qualifications of persons eligible for election as delegates of the National Conference for Unification shall be determined by law.

(3) No delegate of the National Conference for Unification may affiliate himself with a political party, or concurrently hold membership in the National Assembly or other public positions as determined by law.

(4) The terms of office of the delegates of the National Conference for Unification shall be six years.

Article 38. (1) The President in determining or changing important unification policies may refer them for deliberation to the National Conference for Unification when deemed necessary for attaining consensus of the people.

(2) A unification policy obtaining the concurrence of more than one half of the delegates duly elected and seated at the National Conference for Unification under the provisions of Paragraph (1) shall be regarded as the collective will of the people as a whole.

Article 39. (1) The National Conference for Unification shall elect the President through secret ballot, without conducting debate.

(2) The election of the President shall require the concurrence of more than one half of the delegates duly elected and seated in the National Conference for Unification.

(3) In case no person receives the required number of votes as prescribed in Paragraph (2), a second balloting shall be conducted to elect the President. In case no person receives the required number of votes as prescribed in Paragraph (2) on the second balloting, the final balloting shall be conducted with the candidates limited to those two persons receiving the largest and second largest number of votes if not two persons have received the same number of votes; and to all those persons receiving the largest number of votes if two or more persons have received the same number of votes; and the person receiving the largest number of votes thereupon shall be elected President.

Article 40. (1) The National Conference for Unification shall elect National Assembly members, the number of which corresponds to one-third of the total number of the National Assembly members.

(2) The President shall recommend in a group the candidates for the National Assembly members as prescribed in Paragraph (1). Concurrence or objection to the election of the whole slate of candidates shall be put to a vote and their election shall be determined with the attendance of more than one half of the delegates to the National Conference for Unification duly elected and seated, and concurrence of more than one half of the delegates present.

(3) In case no concurrence is obtained as prescribed in Paragraph (2), the President shall again prepare a list of candidates with all or part of the candidates changed and submit the same to the National Conference for Unification, requesting their election, until a slate of candidates is decided upon.

(4) The president, in case he recommends candidates as prescribed in Paragraph (2), shall submit a reserve list of candidates with the order fixed within the range of one-fifth of the total number of the National Assembly members to be elected by the National Conference for Unification. The reserve candidates, if they receive the approval prescribed in Paragraph (2), shall take over the vacated memberships in the National Assembly in the order of names entered in the List.

Article 41. (1) The National Conference for Unification shall make the final confirmation on any draft amendments to the Constitution proposed and decided upon by the National Assembly.

(2) The onfirmation prescribed in Paragraph (1) shall require the concurrence of more than one half of the delegates duly elected and seated.

Article 42. Organization, operation and other matters pertaining to the National Conference for Unification shall be determined by law.

CHAPTER IV: THE PRESIDENT

Article 43. (1) The President shall be the head of the State, and represent the State vis-a-vis foreign states.

(2) The President shall have the duty to safeguard the independence, territorial integrity and continuity of the State as well as the Constitution.

(3) The President shall have the duty to pursue sincerely the peaceful unification of the fatherland.

(4) The Executive power shall be vested in an Executive Branch headed by the President.

Article 44. Citizens who are qualified to be elected to the National Assembly and who, on the date of the Presidential election, shall have resided continuously within the country for five years or more and have attained the age of forty years or more, shall be eligible to be elected to the Presidency. In this case, the period during which a person is dispatched overseas on official duty shall be considered as a period of domestic residence.

Article 45. (1) When the term of office of the President ends, the National Conference for Unification shall elect a successor at latest within thirty days before the term of the incumbent President expires.

(2) In case of vacancy in the office of the President, the National Conference for Unification shall elect a successor within three months. However, if the remaining term of office of the President is less than one year, a successor shall not be elected.

(3) In case of vacancy in the office of the President, the term of a successor shall be the remaining term of his predecessor.

Article 46. Before the President assumes his office, he shall take the following oath: "I do solumnly swear before the people that, by observing the Constitution, defending the State, endeavoring to promote freedom and welfare of the people and pursuing the peaceful unification of the fatherland, I shall faithfully execute the duties of the office of the President."

Article 47. The term of office of the Parident shall be six years.

Article 48. In case of vacancy in the office of the President or of his inability to perform his duties, the Prime Minister and the members of the State Council in consecutive order as determined by law shall act as the President . . .

Article 49. The President may submit important policies of State to national referendum in case he deems it necessary.

Article 50. The President shall conclude and ratify treaties, accredit, receive or dispatch diplomatic envoys, declare war and conclude peace.

Article 51. (1) The President shall exercise supreme command of the National Armed Forces in accordance with the provisions of the Constitution and law.

(2) The organization and formation of the National Armed Forces shall be determined by law.

Article 52. The President may issue Presidential ordinances concerning matters which are within the scope specifically delegated by law and which are required for the enforcement of law.

Article 53. (1) When in time of natural calamity or a grave financial or economic crisis, and in case the national security or the public safety and order is seriously threatened or anticipated to be threatened, making it necessary to take speedy measures, the President shall have power to take necessary emergency measures in the whole range of the State affairs, including internal affairs, foreign affairs, national defense, economic, financial and judicial affairs.

(2) In case of Paragraph (1), when the President deems it necessary, he shall have the power to take emergency measures which temporarily suspend the freedom and rights of the people as defined in the present Constitution, and to enforce emergency measures with regard to the rights and powers of the Executive and the Judiciary.

(3) The President shall notify the National Assembly without delay of such emergency measure as set forth in Paragraphs (1) and (2).

(4) The emergency measures set forth in Paragraphs (1) and (2) shall not be subject to judicial deliberations there-on.

(5) When the reason for such emergency measures ceases, the President shall terminate these measures without delay.

(6) The National Assembly may recommend to the President to lift the emergency measures with the approval of more than one half of the members of the National Assembly duly elected and seated, and the President shall comply with this unless there are any special circumstances and reasons.

Article 54. (1) The President shall, in time of war, armed conflict, or similar national emergency when there is a military necessity, or when it is required to maintain the public safety and order by mobilization of the military forces, proclaim a state of martial law in accordance with the provisions of law.

(2) The state of martial law shall be subdivided into an extraordinary state and a precautionary state.

(3) Under the extraordinary state of martial law, special measures may be taken, as provided by law, with regard to the warrant system, freedom of speech, press, assembly and association, or with regard to the rights and the powers of the Executive or the Judiciary.

(4) The President shall immediately notify the National Assembly of the proclamation of a state of martial law.

(5) When the National Assembly so requests, with the approval of more than one half of the members of the National Assembly duly elected and seated, the President shall lift the proclaimed state of martial law.

Article 55. The President shall appoint public officials in accordance with the provisions of the Constitution and law.

Article 56. (1) The President may grant amnesty, commutation and rehabilitation in accordance with the provisions of law.

(2) In granting general amnesty, the President shall receive the consent of the National Assembly.

(3) Matters pertaining to amnesty, commutation, and rehabilitation shall be determined by law.

Article 57. The President shall award decorations and other honors in accordance with the provisions of law.

Article 58. The President may attend and address the National Assembly or express thereto his views by written message.

Article 59. (1) The President may dissolve the National Assembly.

(2) In case the National Assembly is dissolved, a general election for members of the National Assembly shall be conducted within thirty to sixty days after the date of dissolution.

Article 60. The acts of the President in accordance with law shall be executed by written document, and all such documents shall be counter-signed by the Prime Minister and the members of the State Council concerned. The same shall apply to military affairs.

Article 61. The President shall not hold concurrently the offices of Prime Minister, State Council member, the head of any Executive Ministry, or other official or private positions as determined by law.

Article 62. The President shall not be charged with criminal offense during his tenure of office except for insurrection or treason.

CHAPTER V: THE EXECUTIVE

Section 1. The Prime Minister and the Members of the State Council

Article 63. (1) The Prime Minister shall be appointed by the President with the approval of the National Assembly.

(2) The Prime Minister shall assist the President and shall supervise, under order of the President, the Executive Ministries in their administration.

(3) No military personnel shall be appointed as Prime Minister unless he has retired from active service.

Article 64. (1) The members of the State Council shall be appointed by the President upon recommendation by the Prime Minister.

(2) The members of the State Council shall assist the President with regard to State affairs, and as members of the State Council, shall deliberate on State affairs.

(3) The Prime Minister may recommend to the President the removal of a member of the State Council from office.

(4) No military personnel shall be appointed as member of the State Council unless he has retired from active service.

Section 2. The State Council

Article 65. (1) The State Council shall deliberate on important policies that fall within the power of the Executive.

(2) The State Council shall be composed of the President, the Prime Minister, and members of the State Council, whose number shall be no more than twenty-five and no less than fifteen.

(3) The President shall be the chairman of the State Council, and the Prime Minister shall be the vice-chairman.

Article 66. The following matters shall be referred to the State Council for deliberation:

1) Basic plans on State affairs, and general policies of the Executive;

2) Declaration of war, conclusion of peace and other important matters pertaining to foreign policy;

3) Draft amendments to the Constitution, proposals for national referendum, proposed treaties, legislative bills, proposed ordinances of the President;

4) Proposed budgets, closing of accounts, basic plan on disposal of State properties, conclusion of contracts creating financial obligation for the State, and other important financial matters;

5) Emergency measures of the President, proclamation and termination of a state of martial law;

6) Important military affairs;

7) Dissolution of the National Assembly;

8) Matters pertaining to requests for convening extraordinary sessions of the National Assembly;

9) Awarding of honors;

10) Granting of amnesty, commutation and rehabilitation;

11) Matters regarding the determination of jurisdiction between Executive Ministries;

12) Basic plans concerning delegation or allocation of powers within the executive;

13) Evaluation and analysis of the administration of State affairs;

14) Formulation and coordination of important policies of each Executive Ministry;

15) Action for the dissolution of a political party;

16) Examination of petitions pertaining to executive policies submitted or referred to the Executive;

17) Appointment of the Prosecutor General, the presidents of the National Universities, Ambassadors, the Chief of Staff of each armed service, Marine Corps Commandant and such other public officials and the managers of important State-operated enterprises as designated by law;

18) Other matters presented by the President, the Prime Minister or a State Council member.

Article 67. (1) The National Security Council shall be established to advise the President on the formulation of foreign, military and domestic policies related to the national security prior to their deliberation by the State Council.

Article 67. (1) The National Security Council shall be established to advise the President on the formulation of foreign, military and domestic policies related to the national security prior to their deliberation by the State Council.

(2) The meetings of the National Security Council shall be presided over by the President.

(3) The organization, scope of function, and other matters pertaining to National Security Council shall be determined by law.

Section 3. The Executive Ministries

Article 68. Heads of Executive Ministries shall be appointed by the President from among the State Council members upon recommendation by the Prime Minister.

Article 69. The Prime Minister or the head of each Executive Ministry may, under the delegation of powers by law or Presidential ordinances, or ex officio, issue ordinances of the Prime Minister or the Executive Ministry concerning matters that are within their jurisdiction.

Article 70. The establishment, organization and the scope of functions of each Ministry shall be determined by law.

Section 4. The Board of Audit and Inspection

Article 71. The Board of Audit and Inspection shall be established under the President to inspect the closing of accounts of revenues and expenditures, the accounts of the State and other organizations as determined by law, and to inspect the administrative functions of the executive agencies and public officials.

Article 72. (1) The Board of Audit and Inspection shall be composed of no less than five and no more than eleven members, including the Chairman.

(2) The Chairman of the Board shall be appointed by the President with the approval of the National Assembly. The term of tenure of the Chairman shall be four years.

(3) In case of vacancy in the office of the Chairman, the tenure of a successor shall be the remaining period of the predecessor.

(4) The members of the Board shall be appointed by the President upon recommendation by the Chairman for a period of four years.

Article 73. The Board of Audit and Inspection shall inspect the closing of accounts of revenues and expenditures every year, and report the results to the President and the National Assembly in the following year.

Article 74. The organization of the Board, the scope of its function, the qualifications of the members of the Board, the range of the public officials subject to inspection and other necessary matters shall be determined by law.

CHAPTER VI: THE NATIONAL ASSEMBLY

Article 75. The Legislative power shall be exercised by the National Assembly.

Article 76. (1) The National Assembly shall be composed of members elected by universal, equal, direct and secret elections by the citizens and of members elected by the National Conference for Unification.

(2) The number of members of the National Assembly shall be determined by law.

(3) Matters pertaining to the election of members of the National Assembly shall be determined by law.

Article 77. The term of office of the members of the National Assembly shall be six years. However, the term of office of the members of the National Assembly elected by the National Conference for Unification shall be three years.

Article 78. No member of the National Assembly shall concurrently hold other public or private positions as determined by law.

Article 79. (1) During the sessions of the National Assembly, no member of the National Assembly shall be arrested or detained without the consent of the National Assembly except in case of flagrante delicto.

(2) In case of apprehension or detention of a member prior to the opening of the session, such member shall be released during the session upon the request of the National Assembly except in case of flagrante delicto.

Article 80. Members of the National Assembly shall not be held responsible outside the National Assembly for opinions expressed or vote cast within the Assembly.

Article 81. The members of the National Assembly shall not abuse their positions and privileges.

Article 82. (1) A regular session of the National Assembly shall be convened once every year in accordance with the provisions of law, and extraordinary sessions of the National Assembly shall be convened upon the request of the President or one-third or more of the members duly elected and seated.

(2) The period of regular session shall not exceed ninety days and an extraordinary session, thirty days.

(3) The National Assembly shall not convene for more than 150 days annually, including regular and extraordinary sessions. However, the days of any extraordinary session convened upon request of the President shall not be included in this count.

(4) If the President requests the convening of an extraordinary session, the period of the session and the reasons for the request shall be clearly specified.

(5) During an extraordinary session of the National Assembly convened at the request of the President, only bills submitted by Executive shall be discussed and disposed, and the National Assembly shall hold its sessions only within the length of the period requested by the President.

Article 83. The National Assembly shall elect one Speaker and two Vice Speakers.

Article 84. Unless otherwise provided for in the Constitution or in law, the attendance of more than one half of the members duly elected and seated, and concurrence of more than one half of the members present, shall be necessary for decisions of the National Assembly. In case of a tie vote, the matter shall be considered to be rejected by the National Assembly.

Article 85. (1) The sessions of the National Assembly shall be open to the public. However, they may not be open when so decided with the concurrence of more than one half of the members present, or when the Speaker deems it necessary to so decide for the sake of national security.

(2) Contents of sessions which are not open to the public shall not be publicized.

Article 86. Bills and other subjects submitted to the National Assembly for deliberation shall not be abandoned for the reason that they are not acted upon during the session. However, it shall be otherwise in case the tenure of the members of the National Assembly not elected by the National Conference for Unification has expired, or in case the National Assembly is dissolved.

Article 87. Bills may be introduced by members of the National Assembly or by the Executive.

Article 88. (1) Each bill passed by the National Assembly shall be sent to the Executive and the President shall promulgate it within fifteen days.

(2) In case of objection to the bill, the President may, within the period referred to in the preceding paragraph, return it to the National Assembly with the written explanation of his objection, and may request its reconsideration. The President may do the same during adjournment of the National Assembly.

(3) The President may not request the National Assembly to reconsider the bill in part, or with proposed amendments.

(4) In case there is a request for reconsideration of a bill, the National Assembly shall reconsider it, and if the National Assembly repasses the bill in the original form with the attendance of more than one half of the members duly elected and seated, and with concurrence of two-thirds or more of the members present, the bill shall become law.

(5) If the President does not promulgate the bill, or does not request the National Assembly to reconsider it within the period referred to in Paragraph (1), the bill shall become law.

(6) The President shall without delay promulgate the law as determined in accordance with foregoing Paragraphs (4) and (5). If the President does not promulgate a law within five days after it has been determined under the foregoing paragraphs, or after it has been returned to the Executive under Paragraph (4), the Speaker shall promulgate it.

(7) A law shall become effective twenty days after the date of promulgation unless otherwise stipulated.

Article 89. (1) The National Assembly shall deliberate and decide upon the national budget.

(2) The Executive shall formulate the budget for each fiscal year and submit it to the National Assembly within ninety days before the beginning of a fiscal

year. The National Assembly shall decide upon the budget within thirty days before the beginning of the fiscal year.

(3) If the budget is not adopted within the period referred [to] in the foregoing paragraph, the Executive may, within the limit of revenues and in conformity with the budget for the previous fiscal year, disburse the following expenditures until the adoption of the budget by the National Assembly:

1. The emoluments of public officials and basic expenditures for the conduct of administration.

2. Maintenance costs for agencies and institutions established by the Constitution or law and the obligatory expenditures provided by law.

3. Expenditures for continuing projects already provided for in the budget.

Article 90. (1) In case it shall be necessary to make continuing disbursements for a period of more than one fiscal year, the Executive shall determine the length of the period for such continuing disbursements. The continuing disbursements shall be approved by the National Assembly.

(2) The establishment of a reserve fund for unforeseen expenditures not provided for in the budget, or by any disbursement in excess of the budget, shall be approved by the National Assembly in advance. The disbursement of the reserve fund shall be approved by a subsequent session of the National Assembly.

Article 91. When it is necessary to amend the budget because of circumstances arising after the adoption of the budget, the Executive may formulate a supplementary or revised budget and submit it to the National Assembly.

Article 92. The National Assembly shall, without the consent of the Executive, neither increase the sum of any item of expenditure nor create any new items of expenditure in the budget submitted by the Executive.

Article 93. When the Executive plans to issue national bonds or to conclude contracts which may create financial obligation for the State outside the budget, this shall have the prior decision of the National Assembly.

Article 94. The items and rates of all taxes shall be determined by law.

Article 95. (1) The National Assembly shall have the right of concurrence to the ratification of treaties pertaining to mutual assistance or mutual security, treaties concerning international organizations, treaties of commerce, fishery, peace, treaties which cause a financial obligation for the State or people, treaties concerning the status of alien forces in the territory, or treaties related to legislative matters.

(2) The National Assembly shall also have the right of concurrence in the declaration of war, the dispatch of the armed forces to foreign states, or the stationing of alien forces in the territory of the Republic of Korea.

Article 96. (1) The Prime Minister, the State Council members and Representatives of the Executive may attend meetings of the National Assembly or its committee to report on the state of administration or to give opinions and answer questions.

(2) When requested by the National Assembly or its committees, the Prime Minister, the State Council members and Representatives of the Executive

shall appear at any meeting of the National Assembly and answer questions. If the Prime Minister or State Council members are requested to appear and answer questions, the Prime Minister or State Council members may have State Council members or Representatives of the Executive appear in any meeting of the National Assembly and answer questions.

Article 97. (1) The National Assembly may pass a motion for the removal of the Prime Minister or a State Council member individually from office.

(2) A motion for removal set forth in Paragraph (1) shall be introduced by one-third or more of the members of the National Assembly duly elected and seated, and shall be passed with the concurrence of more than one half of the members of the National Assembly duly elected and seated.

(3) When a motion referred to in Paragraph (2) is adopted, the President shall remove the Prime Minister or the relevant State Council member from office. However, when the motion for the removal of the Prime Minister is adopted, the President shall remove en masse the Prime Minister and all members of the State Council from office.

Article 98. (1) The National Assembly may establish rules concerning its agenda and internal regulations, provided they are not at variance with law.

(2) The National Assembly may review the qualifications of its members and take disciplinary action against its members.

(3) The concurrence of two-thirds or more of the members of the National Assembly duly elected and seated shall be required for the expulsion of any member.

(4) No action shall be brought to court with regard to the disposition under Paragraphs (2) and (3).

Article 99. (1) In case the President, the Prime Minister, Cabinet members, Heads of Executive Ministers, members of the Constitutional Committee, Judges, members of the Central Election Management Committee, members of the Board of Audit and Inspection and other public officials designated by law have violated the Constitution or other laws in the exercise of their duties, the National Assembly shall have power to pass motions for their impeachment.

(2) A motion for impeachment, pursuant to the preceding paragraph, shall be proposed by one-third or more of the members of the National Assembly duly elected and seated shall be necessary to institute impeachment, provided that the motion of an impeachment against the President shall be proposed by more than one half of the members of the National Assembly duly elected and seated, and the concurrence of two-thirds or more of the members of the National Assembly duly elected and seated shall be required for impeachment of the President.

(3) Any person against whom impeachment has been instituted shall be suspended from exercising his power until the impeachment has been tried.

(4) The decision on impeachment shall not cause other than dismissal from public position. However, it shall not exempt the impeached person from civil or criminal liability.

CHAPTER VII: THE COURTS

Article 100. (1) The judicial power shall be vested in courts composed of judges.

(2) The courts shall be composed of the Supreme Court, which is the highest court of the State, and other courts at specified levels.

(3) The qualifications for judges shall be determined by law.

Article 101. (1) Departments may be established within the Supreme Court.

(2) The number of judges on the Supreme Court shall be sixteen or less.

(3) The organization of the Supreme Court and lower courts shall be determined by law.

Article 102. The judges shall judge independently according to their conscience and in conformity with the Constitution and law.

Article 103. (1) The Chief Justice of the Supreme Court shall be appointed by the President with consent of the National Assembly.

(2) Justice of the Supreme Court shall be appointed by the President upon the proposal of the Chief Justice.

(3) The tenure of the Chief Justice shall be six years.

(4) The tenure of judges shall be ten years.

(5) Judges may be reappointed in accordance with the provisions of law.

(6) Judges shall retire from office when they reach the age as determined by law.

Article 104. (1) No judge shall be dismissed from office, nor shall he be suspended from office or his salary reduced, or suffer from other unfavorable measures except by impeachment or criminal punishment, or through disciplinary action.

(2) In the event a judge is unable to discharge his duty because of mental or physical deficiencies, he may be removed from office in accordance with the provisions of law.

Article 105. (1) When the constitutionality of a law is involved in a trial, the Court shall request of the Constitution Committee a decision, and shall judge according to the decision thereof.

(2) The Supreme Court shall have the power to make final review of the constitutionality or legality of administrative orders, regulations or dispositions, when their constitutionality or legality is involved in a trial.

Article 106. The Supreme Court may establish, within the scope of law, procedures pertaining to judicial proceedings and internal rules and regulations on routine administrative matters of the courts.

Article 107. Trials and decisions of the courts shall be open to the public; however, trials may be closed to the public by court decision when there is a possibility that such trials may disturb the national security and public safety and order, or be harmful to decent customs.

Article 108. (1) Courts-martial may be established as special courts to exercise jurisdiction over military trials.

(2) The Supreme Court shall have the final appellate jurisdiction over the courts-martial.

(3) Military trials under an extraordinary state of martial law may be limited to the original jurisdiction only in case of crimes of soldiers and civilian employees of the armed forces, in case of espionage in military affairs, and crimes as defined by law in regard to sentinels, sentry-post, provision of harmful food and prisoners of war.

CHAPTER VIII: THE CONSTITUTION COMMITTEE

Article 109. (1) The Constitution Committee shall judge the following matters:

1. The constitutionality of a law at the request of the Court.

2. Impeachment.

3. Dissolution of a political party.

(2) The Constitution Committee shall be composed of nine members, who are appointed by the President.

(3) Among the members referred to in Paragraph (2), three shall be appointed from persons selected by the National Assembly, and three persons nominated by the Chief Justice shall be appointed.

Article 110. (1) The tenure of the members of the Constitution Committee shall be six years.

(2) The members of the Constitution Committee shall not join any political party, nor shall they participate in political activities.

(3) No member of the Constitution Committee shall be dismissed except by impeachment or criminal punishment.

(4) The qualifications for the members of the Constitution Committee shall be determined by law.

Article 111. (1) When the Constitution Committee makes a decision in the case of a constitutional violation, impeachment or dissolution of the political party, the approval of more than six members shall be required.

(2) The organization, operation and other necessary matters of the Constitution Committee shall be determined by law.

CHAPTER IX: ELECTION MANAGEMENT

Article 112. (1) Election Management Committees shall be established for the purpose of fair management of elections and national referendum, and to deal with affairs concerning political parties.

(2) The Central Election Management Committee shall be composed of nine members, who are appointed by the President.

(3) Among the members referred to in Paragraph (2), three shall be appointed from among persons selected by the National Assembly, and three persons nominated by the Chief Justice shall be appointed.

(4) The Chairman of the Committee shall be appointed by the President from among its members.

(5) The tenure of the members of the Committee shall be five years.

(6) The members of the Committee shall not join political parties, nor shall they participate in political activities.

(7) No members of the Committee shall be dismissed except through impeachment or upon criminal punishment.

(8) The Central Election Management Committee may, within the limit of laws and ordinances, establish regulations pertaining to the management of elections and national referendums, or regulation concerning political parties.

(9) The organization, the scope of function and other necessary matters of the Election Management Committees of each level shall be determined by law.

Article 113. (1) Election campaigns shall be conducted under the management of the Election Management Committees of each level within the limit determined by law. Equal opportunity shall be guaranteed.

(2) The expenditures incident to the elections shall not be borne by political parties or candidates except where otherwise provided for in the law.

CHAPTER X: LOCAL SELF-GOVERNMENT

Article 114. (1) Local self-government bodies shall deal with matters pertaining to the welfare of local residents, manage properties, and may establish, within the limit of laws and ordinances, rules and regulations regarding local self-government.

(2) The kinds of local self-government bodies shall be determined by law.

Article 115. (1) A local self-government body shall have a local assembly.

(2) The organization, powers and election of the members of the local councils, the methods of election for the heads of local self-government bodies, and other matters pertaining to the organization and operation of such bodies shall be determined by law.

CHAPTER XI: THE ECONOMY

Article 116. (1) The economic order of the Republic of Korea shall be based on the principle of respect for freedom and creative ideas of the individual in economic affairs.

(2) The State shall regulate and coordinate economic affairs within the limits necessary for the realization of social justice and for the development of a balanced national economy to fulfill the basic living requirements of all citizens.

Article 117. (1) License to exploit, develop or utilize mines and all other important underground resources, marine resources, water power, and natural powers available for economic use may be granted for limited periods in accordance with the provisions of law.

(2) The land and resources shall be protected by the State, and the State shall establish a plan for their balanced development and utilization.

Article 118. Agricultural tenancy shall be prohibited in accordance with the provisions of law.

Article 119. The State may impose restriction of obligations necessary for the efficient utilization, development and preservation of farm, forest and other land in accordance with the provisions of law.

Article 120. (1) The State shall establish a plan for the development of the farming and fisheries areas on the basis of self-help of the farmers and fishermen, and shall strive for the balanced development of regional communities.

(2) Organizations founded on the spirit of self-help among farmers, and small and medium businessmen shall be encouraged.

Article 121. The State shall encourage foreign trade, and shall regulate and coordinate it.

Article 122. Private enterprises shall not be transferred to State or public ownership, nor shall their management be controlled or administered by the State except in cases determined by law to meet urgent necessities of national defense or national economy.

Article 123. (1) The development of the national economy and science and technology necessary for such development shall be promoted and enhanced.

(2) The President may establish an advisory organization for the purpose of promoting and enhancing economic skills and scientific technology.

CHAPTER XII: AMENDMENTS TO CONSTITUTION

Article 124. (1) A motion to amend the Constitution shall be introduced either by the President or more than one half of the members of the National Assembly duly elected and seated.

(2) The amendments to the Constitution proposed by the President shall be established by national referendum, and proposed amendments to the Constitution presented by members of the National Assembly shall be established by vote of the National Conference for Unification, after being adopted by the National Assembly.

(3) When an amendment to the Constitution has been established, the President shall promulgate the amendment immediately.

Article 125. (1) Proposed amendments to the Constitution introduced in the National Assembly shall be announced to the public for more than twenty days, and the National Assembly shall decide upon the proposed amendments to the Constitution within sixty days of its public announcement.

(2) Decision on the proposed amendment to the Constitution by the National Assembly shall require the concurrence of two-thirds or more of the members of the National Assembly duly elected and seated.

(3) When the proposed amendment to the Constitution has received the affirmative action referred to in Paragraph (2), it shall be referred to the National

Conference for Unification without delay; and through its vote, the amendment to the Constitution referred to the National Conference for Unification shall be voted on within twenty days of its referral.

Article 126. (1) A proposed amendment to the Constitution by the President shall be announced to the public for a period of more than twenty days, and shall be submitted to a national referendum within sixty days of its public announcement.

(2) The amendment to the Constitution submitted to a national referendum shall be established by more than one half of all votes cast by more than one half of voters eligible to vote for election of members of the National Assembly.

SUPPLEMENTARY RULES

Article 1. The present Constitution shall come into force on the date of its promulgation. However, legislation of laws necessary for the enforcement of the present Constitution, election of the President, delegates to the National Conference for Unification, and members of the National Assembly under the Constitution and other preparations pertaining to the enforcement of the Constitution may be made prior to the promulgation of the Constitution.

Article 2. (1) The term of office of the first President elected by the National Conference for Unification under the present Constitution shall start from the promulgation date of the Constitution.

(2) The terms of office of the delegates to the National Conference for Unification elected for the first time under the present Constitution shall start from the date of its initial convening and shall expire on June 30, 1978.

Article 3. The first election of members of the National Assembly under the present Constitution shall be conducted within six months from the date of its promulgation.

Article 4. The authority of the National Assembly exercised by the Extraordinary State Council from October 17, 1972 to the date of the first convening of the National Assembly under the present Constitution shall be regarded as having been exercised in accordance with the Constituion at the time of promulgating the present Constitution, and by the National Assembly formed under the present Constitution.

Article 5. The public officials and directorial officers of enterprises appointed by the government at the time of promulgating the present Constitution shall be regarded as having been appointed under the present Constitution. However, those public officials whose appointment methods and whose appointing authorities are changed under the present Constitution shall perform their duties until their successors are appointed. In this case, the terms of office of predecessors shall be until the day before the appointment date of their successors.

Article 6. (1) Laws, decrees and treaties in force at the time of the promulgation of the present Constitution shall retain their validity unless they contradict the provisions of the Constitution.

(2) Presidential decrees, state council decrees, and cabinet decrees in force at the time of the promulgation of the present Constitution shall be regarded as presidential decrees promulgated under the present Constitution.

Article 7. Laws and decrees legislated by the Extraordinary State Council, trials and budgetary measures and other actions taken thereunder, shall retain their validity, and neither court actions nor objections may be raised against them by reason of the present Constitution or otherwise.

Article 8. Agencies performing duties belonging to the authorities of agencies to be newly established under the present Constitution at the time of the promulgation of the present Constitution shall continue to fulfill these duties until new agencies are set up as prescribed under the present Constitution.

Article 9. Neither court actions nor objections may be raised against the Special Declaration issued by the President and the extraordinary measures taken thereunder from October 17, 1972 to the promulgation date of the present Constitution.

Article 10. Local assemblies under the present Constitution shall not be formed until the unification of the fatherland has been achieved.

Article 11. (1) The Extraordinary Law Concerning the Punishment of Specific Crimes, the Law Concerning the Punishment of Persons Involved in Illicit Elections, the Political Activities Purification Law and the Law Concerning the Disposition of Illicit Fortunes and laws related thereto shall retain their validity, and no legal objections may be raised against them.

(2) The Political Activities Purification Law and the Law Concerning the Punishment of Makers of Illicit Fortunes may neither be amended nor abrogated.

12. THE 1980 CONSTITUTION, SEPTEMBER 1980

PREAMBLE

We, the people of Korea, proud of a glorious history, a brilliant culture and a tradition of cherishing peace from time immemorial, imbued with the sublime spirit of independence as manifested in the March First Movement, upon the birth of the democratic Fifth Republic charged with the historic mission of the peaceful unification of the homeland and national renaissance, having determined:

To consolidate national unity with justice, humanitarianism and brotherly love;

To destroy all social vices and injustice;

To afford equal opportunities to every person and provide for the fullest development of the capabilities of each individual in all fields, including political, economic, civic and cultural life by further strengthening the basic free and democratic order;

To help each person discharge those duties and responsibilities concomitant to freedoms and rights; and

To promote the welfare of the people, strive for a lasting world peace, promote international prosperity and, thereby to create a new era in our history ensuring security, liberty and happiness for ourselves and our descendants forever,

Do hereby amend, through referendum, the Constitution, ordained and established on the Twelfth Day of July in the year of Nineteen Hundred and Forty-eight A.D., and amended on the Fifteenth Day of June in the year Nineteen Hundred and Sixty A.D., the Twenty-sixth Day of December in the year of Nineteen Hundred and Sixty-two A.D., and the Twenty-seventh Day of December in the year of Nineteen Hundred and Seventy-two A.D.

Day of October in the year of
Nineteen Hundred and Eighty A.D.

Source: Proposed Amendments to the Constitution of the Republic of Korea, Seoul: Korean Overseas Information Service, 1980.

CHAPTER I: GENERAL PROVISIONS

Article 1.

(1) The Republic of Korea is a democratic Republic.

(2) The sovereignty of the Republic of Korea shall reside in the people, and all state authority shall emanate from the people.

Article 2.

(1) Citizenship in the Republic of Korea shall be determined by law.

(2) Citizens residing abroad shall be protected by the State.

Article 3.

The territory of the Republic of Korea shall consist of the Korean peninsula and its adjacent islands.

Article 4.

(1) The Republic of Korea shall endeavor to maintain international peace and shall renounce all aggressive wars.

(2) The Armed Forces shall be charged with the sacred mission of national security and the defense of the land.

Article 5.

(1) Treaties duly concluded and promulgated in accordance with the Constitution and the generally recognized rules of international law shall have the same effect as the domestic laws of the Republic of Korea.

(2) The status of aliens shall be guaranteed in accordance with international law and treaties.

Article 6.

(1) All public officials shall be servants of the entire people and shall be responsible to the people.

(2) The office and political impartiality of public officials shall be guaranteed in accordance with the provisions of law.

Article 7.

(1) The establishment of political parties shall be free and the plural party system shall be guaranteed.

(2) Political parties shall be democratic in their organization and activities, and shall have the necessary organizational arrangements for the people to participate in the formation of the political will.

(3) Political parties shall enjoy the protection of the State and may be provided with operational funds by the State in accordance with the provisions of law.

(4) If the purposes or activities of a political party are contrary to the basic democratic order, the Government may bring action against it in the Constitution

Committee for its dissolution, and the political party shall be dissolved in accordance with the decision of the Constitution Committee.

Article 8.
The State shall strive to sustain and develop the cultural heritage and to enhance national culture.

CHAPTER II: RIGHTS AND DUTIES OF CITIZENS

Article 9.
All citizens shall be assured of human worth and dignity and have the right to pursue happiness. It shall be the duty of the State to confirm and guarantee the fundamental and inviolable human rights of individuals.

Article 10.
(1) All citizens shall be equal before the law, and there shall be no discrimination in political, economic, civic or cultural life on account of sex, religion or social status.
(2) No privileged caste shall be recognized or ever established in any form.
(3) The awarding of decorations or distinctions of honor in any form shall be effective only for recipients, and no privileged status shall be created thereby.

Article 11.
(1) All citizens shall enjoy personal liberty. No person shall be arrested, detained, searched, seized, interrogated, punished or placed under probationary supervision except as provided by law, or be subject to involuntary labor except by a criminal sentence.
(2) No citizen shall be tortured or be compelled to testify against himself in criminal cases.
(3) Warrants issued by a judge upon the request of a prosecutor shall be presented in case of arrest, detention, seizure or search. However, in case a criminal suspect is apprehended *flagrante delicto*, or where there is danger that a person suspected of committing a crime punishable by imprisonment of three years or more may escape or destroy evidence, investigative authorities may request an *ex post facto* warrant.
(4) All persons who are arrested or detained shall have the right to prompt assistance of counsel. When a criminal defendant is unable to secure counsel by his own efforts, the State shall assign counsel for the defendant as provided by law.
(5) All persons who are arrested or detained shall have the right to request the court to review the legality of the arrest or detention.
(6) In case a confession is determined to have been made against a defendant's will by means of torture, violence, intimidation, unduly prolonged arrest, deceit or etc., or in case a confession is the only evidence against a defendant,

such a confession shall not be admitted as evidence toward a conviction nor shall punishment be meted out on the basis of such a confession.

Article 12.

(1) No citizen shall be prosecuted for an act which does not constitute a crime under the law effective at the time it was committed, nor shall he be placed in double jeopardy.

(2) No restrictions shall be imposed upon the political rights of any citizen, nor shall any person be deprived of property rights by means of retroactive legislation.

(3) No citizen shall suffer unfavorable treatment on account of an act not of his own doing but committed by a relative.

Article 13.

All citizens shall enjoy freedom of residence and the right to move at will.

Article 14.

All citizens shall enjoy freedom of occupation.

Article 15.

All citizens shall be free from intrusion into their place of residence. In case of search or seizure in a residence, a warrant issued by a judge upon request of a prosecutor shall be presented.

Article 16.

No citizen shall be subject to violation of privacy.

Article 17.

The privacy of correspondence of all citizens shall not be violated.

Article 18.

All citizens shall enjoy freedom of conscience.

Article 19.

(1) All citizens shall enjoy freedom of religion.

(2) No State religion shall be recognized, and religion and politics shall be separated.

Article 20.

(1) All citizens shall enjoy freedom of speech and the press, and freedom of assembly and association.

(2) Neither speech nor the press shall violate the honor or rights of other persons nor undermine public morals or social ethics. Should speech or the press violate the honor or rights of other persons, claims may be made for the damage resulting therefrom.

Article 21.

(1) All citizens shall enjoy freedom of learning and the arts.

(2) The rights of authors, inventors and artists shall be protected by law.

Article 22.

(1) The right of property of all citizens shall be guaranteed. The contents and limitations thereof shall be determined by law.

(2) The exercise of property rights shall conform to the public welfare.

(3) Expropriation, use or restriction of private property for public necessity may be made by law, but compensation thereof shall be paid. Compensation shall be determined by law in fair assessment of the common benefit and of the interests of persons involved.

Article 23.

All citizens who have attained to the age of twenty shall have the right to vote in accordance with the provisions of law.

Article 24.

All citizens shall have the right to hold public office in accordance with the provisions of law.

Article 25.

(1) All citizens shall have the right to petition in writing to any State agency in accordance with the provisions of law.

(2) State agencies shall be obligated to examine all such petitions.

Article 26.

(1) All citizens shall have the right to be tried in conformity with the law by judges qualified under the Constitution and the law.

(2) Citizens who are not on active military service or employees of the military forces shall not be tried by a court martial except in case of crimes involving important classified military information, sentinels, sentry-posts, the supply of harmful food, prisoners of war and military articles and facilities as defined by law; and except when extraordinary martial law has been declared, or when the President has taken an emergency measure concerning the power of the Courts.

(3) All citizens shall have the right to a speedy trial. An accused shall have the right to a public trial without delay in the absence of justifiable reasons to the contrary.

(4) The accused shall be presumed innocent until a determination of guilt has been confirmed.

Article 27.

In case the accused under detention is acquitted, he shall be entitled to a claim against the State for just compensation in accordance with the provisions of law.

Article 28.

(1) In case a person has sustained damages by unlawful acts committed by public officials in the course of their official duties, he may make a claim against the State or public agency for just compensation in accordance with the provisions of law; however, the public officials concerned shall not be immune from liabilities.

(2) In case a person on active military service or an employee of the military forces, a police official or others as defined by law sustains damages in connection with the performance of official duties such as combat action, drill and so forth, he shall not be entitled to a claim against the State or public agency on the grounds of unlawful acts committed by public officials in the course of official duties, but shall be compensated as provided by law.

Article 29.

(1) All citizens shall have the right to receive an equal education corresponding to their abilities.

(2) All citizens who have children to support shall be responsible at least for their elementary education and other education as provided by law.

(3) Compulsory education shall be free.

(4) Independence, professionalism and political impartiality of education shall be guaranteed in accordance with the provisions of law.

(5) The State shall promote lifelong education.

(6) Fundamental matters pertaining to the educational system, including in-school and lifelong education, administration, finance, and the status of teachers shall be determined by law.

Article 30.

(1) All citizens shall have the right to work. The State shall endeavor to promote the employment of workers and to guarantee optimum wages through social and economic means.

(2) All citizens shall have the duty to work. The State shall determine the contents and conditions of the duty to work by law in conformity with democratic principles.

(3) Standards of working conditions shall be determined by law in such a way as to guarantee human dignity.

(4) Special protection shall be accorded to working women and children.

(5) The opportunity to work shall be accorded preferentially to those who have given distinguished service to the State, wounded veterans and policemen, and members of the bereaved families of military servicemen and policemen killed in action in accordance with the provisions of law.

Article 31.

(1) To enhance working conditions, workers shall have the right to independent association, collective bargaining and collective action. However, the right to collective action shall be exercised in accordance with the provisions of law.

(2) The right to association, collective bargaining and collective action shall not be granted to public officials, except for those authorized by the provisions of law.

(3) The right to collective action of workers employed by the central government, local governments, state-run enterprises, defense industries, public utilities or enterprises which have a serious impact on the national economy may be either restricted or denied in accordance with the provisions of law.

Article 32.

(1) All citizens shall be entitled to a life worthy of human beings.

(2) The State shall endeavor to promote social security and welfare.

(3) Citizens who are incapable of earning a livelihood shall be protected by the State in accordance with the provisions of law.

Article 33.

All citizens shall be entitled to live in a clean environment. The State and all citizens shall have the duty to protect the environment.

Article 34.

(1) Marriage and family life shall be entered into and sustained on the basis of individual dignity and equality of the sexes.

(2) The health of all citizens shall be protected by the State.

Article 35.

(1) Freedoms and rights of citizens shall not be neglected on the grounds that they are not enumerated in the Constitution.

(2) The freedoms and rights of citizens may be restricted by law only when necessary for national security, the maintenance of law and order or for public welfare. Even when such restriction is imposed, no essential aspect of the freedom or right shall be violated.

Article 36.

All citizens shall have the duty to pay taxes in accordance with the provisions of law.

Article 37.

(1) All citizens shall have the duty of national defense in accordance with the provisions of law.

(2) No citizen shall be discriminated against on account of the fulfillment of his obligation of military service.

CHAPTER III: THE EXECUTIVE

Part 1. The President

Article 38.

(1) The President shall be the Head of State and represent the State *vis-a-vis* foreign states.

(2) The President shall have the responsibility and duty to safeguard the independence, territorial integrity and continuity of the State and the Constitution.

(3) The President shall have the duty to pursue sincerely the peaceful unification of the homeland.

(4) Executive power shall be vested in the Executive Branch headed by the President.

Article 39.

(1) The President shall be elected by the presidential electoral college through a secret ballot.

(2) Any person desiring to become a presidential candidate shall be registered at the recommendation of a political party or of a number of members of the presidential electoral college as determined by law.

(3) The election of the President shall be by the concurrence of the majority of the total members of the presidential electoral college.

(4) In case no person receives the required number of votes as prescribed in Paragraph (3), a second ballot shall be conducted. In case no person receives the required number of votes as prescribed in Paragraph (3) on the second ballot, a final ballot shall be conducted between the two persons receiving the largest and second largest number of votes if no two persons have received the same largest number of votes; or between all persons receiving the largest number of votes if two or more persons have received the same largest number of votes; and the person receiving the largest number of votes thereupon shall be elected the President.

(5) Matters pertaining to presidential elections shall be determined by law.

Article 40.

(1) The presidential electoral college shall be composed of presidential electors elected by universal, equal, direct and secret ballot by citizens.

(2) The number of presidential electors shall be determined by law, but shall be more than 5,000.

(3) Matters pertaining to the election of presidential electors shall be determined by law.

Article 41.

(1) Any person who is eligible to run for the National Assembly and who has reached the age of thirty or over as of the date of the election shall be eligible

to be elected as a presidential elector. However, members of the National Assembly and public officials shall not become presidential electors.

(2) No presidential elector shall be arrested or detained except in case of *flagrante delicto*.

(3) Presidential electors may affiliate themselves with political parties.

(4) No presidential elector shall be elected a member of the National Assembly through the first National Assembly election following his election as an elector.

(5) The presidential electoral college shall dissolve on the day the term of office of the President elected by the electoral college commences.

Article 42.

Citizens who are eligible for election to the National Assembly and who, on the date of the presidential election, shall have resided continuously within the country for five years or more and have reached the age of forty years or more, shall be eligible to be elected to the presidency. The period during which a person is dispatched overseas on official duty shall be considered as a period of domestic residence.

Article 43.

(1) The presidential electoral college shall elect a successor at least thirty days before the term of office of the incumbent President expires.

(2) In case a vacancy occurs in the office of the President, a presidential electoral college shall be newly formed and a successor shall be elected within three months.

Article 44.

The President, at the time of his inauguration, shall take the following oath: "I do solemnly swear before the people that, by observing the Constitution, defending the State, endeavoring to develop national culture, promoting the freedom and welfare of the people, and pursuing the peaceful unification of the homeland, I will faithfully execute the duties of the President."

Article 45.

The term of office of the President shall be seven years, and the President shall not be reelected.

Article 46.

In case of a vacancy in the office of the President, or the inability of the President to discharge the powers and duties of the presidency, the Prime Minister or the members of the State Council in the order of priority as determined by law shall act as the President.

Article 47.

The President may submit important policies relating to diplomacy, national defense, unification and other matters relating to the national destiny to a national referendum if he deems it necessary.

Article 48.

The President shall conclude and ratify treaties; accredit, receive or dispatch diplomatic envoys; and declare war and conclude peace.

Article 49.

(1) The President shall be Commander-in-Chief of the Armed Forces in accordance with the provisions of the Constitution and law.

(2) The organization and formation of the Armed Forces shall be provided by law.

Article 50.

The President may issue presidential decrees concerning matters delegated by law within the scope defined by law which are deemed necessary to enforce the law.

Article 51.

(1) In time of natural calamity or a grave financial or economic crisis, or of hostilities or similar grave extraordinary circumstances threatening the security of the State, thereby making it necessary to take speedy measures in order to safeguard the State, the President shall have the power to take necessary emergency measures covering the whole range of State affairs, including internal affairs, foreign affairs, national defense and economic, financial and judicial affairs.

(2) In case of Paragraph (1), the President, when he deems it necessary, may temporarily suspend the freedoms and rights of the people prescribed in the Constitution, and may take special measures with respect to the powers of the Executive and the Judiciary.

(3) In case the measures in Paragraphs (1) and (2) are taken, the President shall notify the National Assembly thereof without delay and shall obtain the concurrence of the National Assembly. In case no concurrence is obtained, the measures shall lose effect forthwith.

(4) The emergency measures prescribed in Paragraphs (1) and (2) shall be restricted to the shortest necessary period for the attainment of their objective. When the cause for the emergency measures ceases to exist, the President shall terminate the measures without delay.

(5) The President shall lift the emergency measures when the National Assembly so requests with the concurrence of a majority of the total members of the National Assembly.

Article 52.

(1) When there is a military necessity or a necessity to maintain the public safety and order by mobilization of the military forces in time of war, armed

conflict or similar national emergency, the President may declare martial law in accordance with the provisions of law.

(2) Martial law shall be of two types, extraordinary martial law and precautionary martial law.

(3) Under extraordinary martial law, special measures may be taken, as provided by law, with respect to the necessity for warrants, freedom of speech, the press, assembly and association, or with respect to the powers of the Executive and the Judiciary.

(4) When martial law is declared, the President shall notify the National Assembly thereof without delay.

(5) The President shall lift martial law when the National Assembly so requests with the concurrence of a majority of the members of the National Assembly.

Article 53.

The President shall appoint public officials in accordance with the provisions of the Constitution and law.

Article 54.

(1) The President may grant amnesty, commutation and restoration of rights in accordance with the provisions of law.

(2) The President shall receive the consent of the National Assembly in granting a general amnesty.

(3) Matters pertaining to amnesty, commutation and restoration of rights shall be determined by law.

Article 55.

The President shall award decorations and other honors in accordance with the provisions of law.

Article 56.

The President may attend and address the National Assembly or express his views by written message.

Article 57.

(1) The President may, after consultation with the National Assembly Speaker and deliberation at the State Council, dissolve the National Assembly with specific reason when there is substantial cause to believe that such a dissolution is necessary for the security of the State and the interests of all the people. However, the National Assembly shall not be dissolved within one year of its formation.

(2) The President shall not dissolve the National Assembly twice for the same reason.

(3) If the National Assembly is dissolved a general election for members of the National Assembly shall be conducted within thirty to sixty days from the date of dissolution.

Article 58.

The acts of the President under law shall be executed by written document, and such documents shall be countersigned by the Prime Minister and the members of the State Council concerned. The same shall apply to military affairs.

Article 59.

The President shall not concurrently hold the office of Prime Minister, a member of the State Council, be head of any Executive Ministry, nor other public or private posts prescribed by law.

Article 60.

The President shall not be charged with a criminal offense during his tenure of office except for insurrection or treason.

Article 61.

Matters pertaining to the status and courteous treatment of former Presidents shall be determined by law.

Part 2. The Executive Branch

Section 1. The Prime Minister and Members of the State Council

Article 62.

(1) The Prime Minister shall be appointed by the President with the consent of the National Assembly.

(2) The Prime Minister shall assist the President and shall supervise, under order of the President, the administration of the Executive Ministries.

(3) No member of the military shall be appointed Prime Minister unless he is retired from active duty.

Article 63.

(1) The members of the State Council shall be appointed by the President on the recommendation of the Prime Minister.

(2) The members of the State Council shall assist the President in the conduct of State affairs and, as constituents of the State Council, shall deliberate on State affairs.

(3) The Prime Minister may recommend to the President the removal of a member of the State Council from office.

(4) No member of the military shall be appointed a member of the State Council unless he is retired from active duty.

Section 2. The State Council

Article 64.

(1) The State Council shall deliberate on important policies that fall within the power of the Executive.

(2) The State Council shall be composed of the President, the Prime Minister, and other members whose number shall be no more than 30 and no less than fifteen.

(3) The President shall be the Chairman of the State Council, and the Prime Minister shall be the vice-chairman.

Article 65.

The following matters shall be referred to the State Council for deliberation:

1. Basic plans for State affairs, and general policies of the Executive;

2. Declaration of war, conclusion of peace and other important matters pertaining to foreign policy;

3. Draft amendments to the Constitution, proposals for national referendums, proposed treaties, legislative bills, and proposed presidential decrees;

4. Budgets, closing of accounts, basic plan for disposal of State properties, contracts incurring financial obligation on the State, and other important financial matters;

5. Emergency measures by the President, and declaration and termination of martial law;

6. Important military affairs;

7. Dissolution of the National Assembly;

8. Requests for convening an extraordinary session of the National Assembly;

9. Awarding of honors;

10. Granting of amnesty, commutation and restoration of rights.

11. Matters pertaining to the determination of jurisdiction between Executive Ministries;

12. Basic plans concerning delegation or allocation of powers within the Executive;

13. Evaluation and analysis of the administration of State affairs;

14. Formulation and coordination of important policies of each Executive Ministry;

15. Action for the dissolution of a political party;

16. Examination of petitions pertaining to executive policies submitted or referred to the Executive;

17. Appointment of the Chairman of the Joints Chiefs of Staff, the Chief of Staff of each armed service, the Prosecutor General, the presidents of national universities, ambassadors, and such other public officials and managers of important state-run enterprises as designated by law; and

18. Other matters presented by the President, the Prime Minister or a member of the State Council.

Article 66.

(1) An Advisory Council on State Affairs, composed of elder statesmen, may be established to advise the President on important affairs of State.

(2) The immediate former President shall become the Chairman of the Advisory Council on State Affairs. In the absence of an immediate former President, the President shall appoint the Chairman.

(3) The organization, function and other necessary matters pertaining to the Advisory Council on State Affairs shall be determined by law.

Article 67.

(1) A National Security Council shall be established to advise the President on the formulation of foreign, military and domestic policies related to national security prior to their deliberation by the State Council.

(2) The meetings of the National Security Council shall be presided over by the President.

(3) The organization, function and other necessary matters pertaining to the National Security Council shall be determined by law.

Article 68.

(1) An Advisory Council on Peaceful Unification Policy may be established to advise the President on the formulation of peaceful unification policy.

(2) The organization, function and other necessary matters pertaining to the Advisory Council on Peaceful Unification Policy shall be determined by law.

Section 3. The Executive Ministries

Article 69.

Heads of Executive Ministries shall be appointed by the President from among members of the State Council on the recommendation of the Prime Minister.

Article 70.

The Prime Minister or the head of each Executive Ministry may, under the powers delegated by law or presidential decree, or *ex officio*, issue ordinances of the Prime Minister or the Executive Ministry concerning matters that are within their jurisdiction.

Article 71.

The establishment, organization and function of each Executive Ministry shall be determined by law.

Section 4. The Board of Audit and Inspection

Article 72.

The Board of Audit and Inspection shall be established under the President to inspect the closing of accounts of revenues and expenditures, the accounts of the State and other organizations as prescribed by law, and to inspect the administrative functions of the executive agencies and public officials.

Article 73.

(1) The Board of Audit and Inspection shall be composed of no less than five and no more than eleven members, including the Chairman.

(2) The Chairman of the Board shall be appointed by the President with the consent of the National Assembly. The term of office of the Chairman shall be four years, and he may be reappointed only once.

(3) In case of a vacancy in the office of the Chairman, the term of a successor shall be the remaining period of the term of the predecessor.

(4) The members of the Board shall be appointed by the President on the recommendation of the Chairman. The term of office of the members shall be four years, and they may be reappointed only once.

Article 74.

The Board of Audit and Inspection shall inspect the closing of accounts of revenues and expenditures every year, and report the results to the President and the National Assembly in the following year.

Article 75.

The organization of the Board, its functions, the qualifications of the members of the Board, the range of the public officials subject to inspection and other necessary matters shall be determined by law.

CHAPTER IV: THE NATIONAL ASSEMBLY

Article 76.

Legislative power shall be vested in the National Assembly.

Article 77.

(1) The National Assembly shall be composed of members elected by universal, equal, direct and secret ballot by the citizens.

(2) The number of members of the National Assembly shall be determined by law, but the number shall be more than 200.

(3) The constituencies of members of the National Assembly, proportional representation and other matters pertaining to National Assembly elections shall be determined by law.

Article 78.

The term of office of members of the National Assembly shall be four years.

Article 79.

Members of the National Assembly shall not concurrently hold any other office prescribed by law.

Article 80.

(1) During the sessions of the National Assembly, no member of the National Assembly shall be arrested or detained without the consent of the National Assembly except in case of *flagrante delicto*.

(2) In case of apprehension or detention of a member of the National Assembly prior to the opening of a session, such member shall be released during the session upon the request of the National Assembly, except in case of *flagrante delicto*.

Article 81.

No member of the National Assembly shall be held responsible outside the National Assembly for opinions officially expressed or votes cast in the Assembly.

Article 82.

(1) Members of the National Assembly shall maintain high standards of integrity.

(2) Members of the National Assembly shall give preference to national interests and shall perform their duties in accordance with conscience.

(3) Members of the National Assembly shall not, through abuse of their positions, acquire rights and interests in property or position, or cause other persons to acquire the same, by means of contracts with or dispositions by the State, public agencies or industries.

Article 83.

(1) A regular session of the National Assembly shall be convened once every year in accordance with the provisions of law, and extraordinary sessions of the National Assembly shall be convened upon the request of the President or one-third or more of the total members.

(2) The period of regular sessions shall not exceed ninety days and of extra-ordinary sessions thirty days.

(3) The National Assembly shall not convene for more than one hundred and fifty days annually, including regular and extraordinary sessions. However, any extraordinary session convened upon the request of the President shall not be included in this count.

(4) If the President requests the convening of an extraordinary session, the period of the session and the reasons for the request shall be clearly specified.

(5) During an extraordinary session of the National Assembly convened upon the request of the President, only those bills submitted by the Executive shall be acted on, and such a session shall be held only within the length of time requested by the President.

Article 84.

The National Assembly shall elect one Speaker and two Vice-Speakers.

Article 85.

Unless otherwise provided for in the Constitution or in law, the attendance of a majority of the total members, and the concurrence of a majority of the members present, shall be necessary for decisions of the National Assembly. In case of a tie vote, the matter shall be regarded as rejected.

Article 86.

(1) Sessions of the National Assembly shall be open to the public. However, they may be closed to the public when so decided by a majority of the members present, or when the Speaker deems it necessary to do so for the sake of national security.

(2) Proceedings of sessions which are not open to the public shall not be publicized.

Article 87.

Bills and other matters submitted to the National Assembly for deliberation shall not be abandoned on the ground that they were not acted upon during the session in which they were introduced. However, it shall be otherwise in case the terms of the members of the National Assembly has expired, or in case the National Assembly is dissolved.

Article 88.

Bills may be introduced by members of the National Assembly or by the Executive.

Article 89.

(1) Each bill passed by the National Assembly shall be sent to the Executive and the President shall promulgate it within fifteen days.

(2) In case of objection to the bill, the President may, within the period referred to in Paragraph (1), return it to the National Assembly with written explanation of his objection, and request it be reconsidered. The President may do the same during adjournment of the National Assembly.

(3) The President shall not request the National Assembly to reconsider the bill in part, or with proposed amendments.

(4) In case there is a request for reconsideration of a bill, the National Assembly shall reconsider it, and if the National Assembly repasses the bill in the original form with the attendance of more than one-half of the total members, and with concurrence of two-thirds or more of the members present, it shall become law.

(5) If the President does not promulgate the bill, or does not request the National Assembly to reconsider it within the period referred to in Paragraph (1), it shall become law.

(6) The President shall without delay promulgate the law as prescribed in accordance with the foregoing Paragraphs (4) and (5). If the President does not promulgate a law within five days after it has become law under Paragraph (5),

or after it has been returned to the Executive under Paragraph (4), the Speaker shall promulgate it.

(7) A law shall take effect twenty days after the date of promulgation unless otherwise provided.

Article 90.

(1) The National Assembly shall deliberate and decide upon the national budget bill.

(2) The Executive shall formulate the budget bill for each fiscal year and submit it to the National Assembly within ninety days before the beginning of a fiscal year. The National Assembly shall decide upon it within thirty days before the beginning of the fiscal year.

(3) If the budget bill is not passed by the beginning of the fiscal year, the Executive may, in conformity with the budget of the previous fiscal year, disburse funds for the following purposes until the budget bill is passed by the National Assembly:

1. The maintenance and operation of agencies and institutions established by the Constitution or law;

2. Execution of the obligatory expenditures provided by law; and

3. Continuation of projects previously approved in the budget.

Article 91.

(1) In case it shall be necessary to make continuing disbursements for a period longer than one fiscal year, the Executive shall obtain the approval of the National Assembly for a specified period of time.

(2) A reserve fund shall be approved by the National Assembly in total. The disbursement of the reserve fund shall be approved during the next session of the National Assembly.

Article 92.

When it is necessary to amend the budget, the Executive may formulate a supplementary revised budget bill and submit it to the National Assembly.

Article 93.

The National Assembly shall, without the consent of the Executive, neither increase the sum of any item of expenditure nor create any new items in the budget submitted by the Executive.

Article 94.

When the Executive plans to issue national bonds or to conclude contracts which may incur financial obligations on the State outside the budget, it shall have the prior concurrence of the National Assembly.

Article 95.

Types and rates of taxes shall be determined by law.

Article 96.

(1) The National Assembly shall have the right to consent to the conclusion and ratification of treaties pertaining to mutual assistance or mutual security; treaties concerning important international organizations; treaties of friendship, trade and navigation; treaties pertaining to any restriction in sovereignty; peace treaties; treaties which will burden the State or people with an important financial obligation; or treaties related to legislative matters.

(2) The National Assembly shall also have the right to consent to the declaration of war, the dispatch of armed forces to foreign states, or the stationing of alien forces in the territory of the Republic of Korea.

Article 97.

The National Assembly may inspect specific matters of State affairs, and may demand the production of documents directly related thereto, the appearance of a witness in person and the furnishing of testimony or opinions. However, the National Assembly shall not interfere with a judicial trial, or a criminal investigation in process or prosecution.

Article 98.

(1) The Prime Minister, members of the State Council or government delegates may attend meetings of the National Assembly or its committees and report on the state of administration or deliver opinions and answer questions.

(2) When requested by the National Assembly or its committees, the Prime Minister, members of the State Council or government delegates shall attend any meeting of the National Assembly and answer questions. If the Prime Minister or State Council members are requested to attend, the Prime Minister or State Council members may have State Council members or government delegates attend any meeting of the National Assembly and answer questions.

Article 99.

(1) The National Assembly may pass a motion for the removal of the Prime Minister or a State Council member from office. However, no motion shall be passed for the removal of the Prime Minister within one year from the date of the consent of the National Assembly to his appointment.

(2) A motion for removal prescribed in Paragraph (1) may be introduced by one-third or more of the total members of the National Assembly, and shall be passed with the concurrence of a majority of the total members of the National Assembly.

(3) When a motion referred to in Paragraph (2) is passed, the President shall remove the Prime Minister or the State Council member concerned from office. However, when a motion for removal of the Prime Minister is passed, the President shall remove the Prime Minister and all members of the State Council from office.

Article 100.

(1) The National Assembly may establish the rules of its proceedings and internal regulations, provided that they are not in conflict with law.

(2) The National Assembly may review the qualifications of its members and may take disciplinary actions against its members.

(3) The concurrence of two-thirds or more of the total members of the National Assembly shall be required for the expulsion of any member.

(4) No action shall be brought to court with regard to decisions taken under Paragraphs (2) and (3).

Article 101.

(1) In case the President, the Prime Minister, members of the State Council, Heads of Executive Ministries, members of the Constitution Committee, judges, members of the Central Election Management Committee, members of the Board of Audit and Inspection, and other public officials designated by law have violated the Constitution or other laws in the performance of official duties, the National Assembly may pass motions for their impeachment.

(2) A motion for impeachment prescribed in Paragraph (1) shall be proposed by one-third or more of the total members of the National Assembly, and shall require concurrence of a majority of the total members of the National Assembly for passage. However, a motion for the impeachment of the President shall be proposed by a majority of the total members of the National Assembly, and shall require the concurrence of two-thirds or more of the total members of the National Assembly.

(3) Any person against whom a motion for impeachment has been passed shall be suspended from exercising his power until the impeachment has been decided.

(4) A decision on impeachment shall not extend further than removal from office. However, it shall not exempt the person impeached from civil or criminal liability.

CHAPTER V: THE COURTS

Article 102.

(1) Judicial power shall be vested in courts composed of judges.

(2) The courts shall be composed of the Supreme Court, which is the highest court of the State, and other courts at specified levels.

(3) Qualifications for judges shall be determined by law.

Article 103.

(1) Departments may be established in the Supreme Court.

(2) Departments exclusively in charge of public administration, tax, labor, military, etc., may be established in the Supreme Court.

(3) There shall be Supreme Court Justices at the Supreme Court. However, judges other than Supreme Court Justices may be assigned to the Supreme Court in accordance with the provisions of law.

(4) The organization of the Supreme Court and lower courts shall be determined by law.

Article 104.

Judges shall rule independently according to their conscience and in conformity with the Constitution and law.

Article 105.

(1) The Chief Justice of the Supreme Court shall be appointed by the President with the consent of the National Assembly.

(2) The Supreme Court Justices shall be appointed by the President on the recommendation of the Chief Justice.

(3) Judges other than the Chief Justice and the Supreme Court Justices shall be appointed by the Chief Justice.

Article 106.

(1) The term of office of the Chief Justice shall be six years and he shall not be reappointed.

(2) The term of office of the Justices of the Supreme Court shall be five years and they may be reappointed in accordance with the provisions of law.

(3) The term of office of judges other than the Chief Justice and Justices of the Supreme Court shall be ten years and they may be reappointed in accordance with the provisions of law.

(4) The retirement age of judges shall be determined by law.

Article 107.

(1) No judge shall be removed from office except by impeachment or criminal punishment, nor shall he be suspended from office, have his salary reduced or suffer any other unfavorable treatment except by disciplinary action.

(2) In the event a judge is unable to discharge his official duties because of mental or physical impairment he may be removed from office in accordance with provisions of law.

Article 108.

(1) When the constitutionality of a law is a prerequisite to a trial, the court, if it construes that the law at issue runs counter to the Constitution, shall request a decision of the Constitution Committee, and shall judge according to the decision thereof.

(2) The Supreme Court shall have the power to make a final review of the constitutionality or legality of administrative decrees, regulations or dispositions, when their constitutionality or legality is a prerequisite to a trial.

(3) Administrative adjudication may be established as a procedure prior to a judicial trial. The procedure of administrative adjudication shall be determined by law and shall be in conformity with the principles of judicial procedures.

Article 109.

The Supreme Court may establish, within the scope of law, regulations pertaining to judicial proceedings and internal rules and regulations on administrative matters of the court.

Article 110.

Trials and decisions of the courts shall be open to the public. However, trials may be closed to the public by court decision when there is a danger that such trials may undermine the national security or disturb public safety and order, or be harmful to public morals.

Article 111.

(1) Courts-martial may be established as special courts to exercise jurisdiction over military trials.

(2) The Supreme Court shall have the final appellate jurisdiction over courts-martial.

(3) The organization and authority of courts-martial, and the qualifications of their judges shall be determined by law.

(4) Military trials under an extraordinary martial law may not be appealed in case of crimes of soldiers and employees of the military; military espionage; and crimes as defined by law in regard to sentinels, sentry-posts, supply of harmful food, and prisoners of war.

CHAPTER VI: THE CONSTITUTION COMMITTEE

Article 112.

(1) The Constitution Committee shall judge the following matters:

1. The constitutionality of a law upon the request of the courts;

2. Impeachment; and

3. Dissolution of a political party.

(2) The Constitution Committee shall be composed of nine members appointed by the President.

(3) Among the members referred to in Paragraph (2), three shall be appointed from persons selected by the National Assembly, and three appointed from persons nominated by the Chief Justice.

(4) The Chairman of the Constitution Committee shall be appointed by the President from among the members.

Article 113.

(1) The term of office of the members of the Constitution Committee shall

be six years and they may be reappointed in accordance with the provisions of law.

(2) The members of the Constitution Committee shall not join any political party, nor shall they participate in political activities.

(3) No member of the Constitution Committee shall be expelled from office except by impeachment or criminal punishment.

(4) The qualifications of the members of the Constitution Committee shall be determined by law.

Article 114.

(1) When the Constitution Committee makes a decision on the unconstitutionality of a law, impeachment or dissolution of a political party, the concurrence of six members or more shall be required.

(2) The organization, operation and other necessary matters of the Constitution Committee shall be determined by law.

CHAPTER VII: ELECTION MANAGEMENT

Article 115.

(1) Election Management Committees shall be established for the purpose of fair management of elections and national referendums, and dealing with affairs concerning political parties.

(2) The Central Election Management Committee shall be composed of three members appointed by the President, three members selected by the National Assembly, and three members nominated by the Chief Justice of the Supreme Court. The Chairman of the Committee shall be elected from among the members.

(3) The term of office of the members of the Committee shall be five years.

(4) The members of the Committee shall not join political parties, nor shall they participate in political activities.

(5) No member of the Committee shall be expelled from office except by impeachment or criminal punishment.

(6) The Central Election Management Committee may, within the limit of laws and decrees, establish regulations pertaining to the management of elections, national referendums, and matters concerning political parties.

(7) The organization, function and other necessary matters of the Election Management Committees at each level shall be determined by law.

Article 116.

(1) Election Management Committees at each level may issue necessary instructions to administrative agencies concerned with respect to matters pertaining to elections such as the preparation of the rosters of voters.

(2) Administrative agencies concerned, upon receipt of such instructions, shall comply.

Article 117.

(1) Election campaigns shall be conducted under the management of the Election Management Committees at each level within the limit set by law. Equal opportunity shall be guaranteed.

(2) Expenditures for elections shall not be borne by political parties or candidates, except as otherwise provided by law.

CHAPTER VIII: LOCAL AUTONOMY

Article 118.

(1) Local governments shall deal with matters pertaining to the welfare of local residents, manage properties, and may establish, within the limit of laws and decrees, rules and regulations regarding local autonomy.

(2) The types of local governments shall be determined by law.

Article 119.

(1) A local government shall have a council.

(2) The organization and powers of local councils, and the election of members; election procedures for heads of local government bodies; and other matters pertaining to the organization and operation of local government bodies shall be determined by law.

CHAPTER IX: THE ECONOMY

Article 120.

(1) The economic order of the Republic of Korea shall be based on the principle whereby freedom and creative ideas of the individual in economic affairs are respected.

(2) The State shall regulate and coordinate economic affairs within the limit necessary for the realization of social justice and for the balanced development of the national economy to fulfill the basic living requirements of all citizens.

(3) Monopolistic and oligopolistic practices shall be properly regulated and coordinated.

Article 121.

(1) Licenses to exploit, develop or utilize mines and all other important underground resources, marine resources, water power, and natural powers available for economic use may be granted for limited periods of time in accordance with the provisions of law.

(2) The land and natural resources shall be protected by the State, and the State shall establish a plan necessary for their balanced development and utilization.

Article 122.

Tenant farming shall be prohibited in accordance with the provisions of law. However, the leasing of farmland and the management of farmland on consignment to increase agricultural productivity and to ensure the rational utilization of farmland, shall be recognized in accordance with the provisions of law.

Article 123.

The State may impose restrictions or obligations necessary for the efficient and balanced utilization, development and preservation of farmland, mountains and other land in accordance with the provisions of law.

Article 124.

(1) The State shall establish a plan for the development of farming and fishing villages on the basis of the self-help of farmers and fishermen, and shall strive for the balanced development of regional communities.

(2) The State shall protect and foster the business activities of small and medium industries.

(3) The State shall foster organizations founded on the spirit of self-help among farmers, fishermen and businessmen engaged in small and medium industry and shall guarantee their political impartiality.

Article 125.

The State shall, in accordance with the provisions of law, guarantee the consumer protection movement intended to encourage sound consumption activities and improvement in the quality of products.

Article 126.

The State shall foster foreign trade, and may regulate and coordinate it.

Article 127.

Private enterprises shall not be nationalized or transferred to public ownership, nor shall their management be controlled or administered by the State, except in cases determined by law to meet urgent necessities of national defense or national economy.

Article 128.

(1) The State shall strive to develop the national economy, and shall promote and enhance science and technology.

(2) The State shall establish a national standard.

(3) The President may establish an advisory body for the purpose referred to in Paragraph (1).

CHAPTER X: AMENDMENTS TO THE CONSTITUTION

Article 129.

(1) A proposal to amend the Constitution shall be introduced either by the President or by a majority of the total members of the National Assembly.

(2) Amendments to the Constitution for the extension of the term of office of the President or for a change allowing for the reelection of the President shall not be effective for the President in office at the time of the proposal for such amendments to the Constitution.

Article 130.

Proposed amendments to the Constitution shall be put before the public by the President for twenty days or more.

Article 131.

(1) The National Assembly shall decide upon the proposed amendments within sixty days of the public announcement, and passage by the National Assembly shall require the concurrence of two-thirds or more of the total members of the National Assembly.

(2) The proposed amendments to the Constitution shall be submitted to a national referendum not later than thirty days after passage by the National Assembly, and shall be determined by more than one-half of all votes cast by more than one-half of voters eligible to vote in elections for members of the National Assembly.

(3) When the proposed amendments to the Constitution receive the concurrence prescribed in Paragraph (2), the amendments to the Constitution shall be finalized, and the President shall promulgate it without delay.

SUPPLEMENTARY PROVISIONS

Article 1.

This Constitution shall enter into force as of the date of its promulgation.

Article 2.

The first presidential and National Assembly elections under this Constitution shall be held not later than June 30, 1981.

Article 3.

The term of office of the President incumbent at the time this Constitution enters into force shall terminate upon the election of the first President under this Constitution.

Article 4.

The National Conference for Unification, existing at the time this Constitution enters into force, shall be abolished upon the entry into force of this Constitution and the term of office of its members shall terminate upon its abolition.

Article 5.

(1) The term of office of the members of the National Assembly incumbent at the time this Constitution enters into force shall terminate upon the entry into force of this Constitution.

(2) The term of office of the members of the first National Assembly elected under this Constitution shall commence on the date of its first convening.

Article 6.

(1) The Legislative Council for National Security shall assume and exercise the functions of the National Assembly from the date this Constitution enters into force to the day prior to the first convening of the National Assembly under this Constitution, at which time the Legislative Council for National Security shall cease to exist.

(2) The Legislative Council for National Security shall be composed of representatives from all walks of life, and its organization, operation and other necessary matters shall be prescribed by law.

(3) Laws legislated by the Legislative Council for National Security and trials, budgets and other dispositions effected thereunder shall remain valid, and may not be litigated or disputed for reasons of this Constitution or other reasons.

(4) In order to renovate the political climate and realize ethical politics, the Legislative Council for National Security may legislate laws regulating political activities of persons conspicuously responsible for political or social corruption or chaos prior to the entry into force of this Constitution.

Article 7.

In order to establish a new political order, political parties existing at the time this Constitution enters into force shall be dissolved upon the entry into force of this Constitution. However, guarantees for the establishment of new political parties shall be provided not later than three months prior to the date of the first presidential election under this Constitution.

Article 8.

(1) Public officials whose election procedures or appointing authorities are changed by this Constitution, the Chief Justice and Justices of the Supreme Court, the Chairman and members of the Board of Audit and Inspection, and the members of the Constitution Committee shall remain in office until such time as their successors are chosen under this Constitution, and their terms of office shall terminate the day before the installation of their successors.

(2) Those provisions of this Constitution which prescribe the terms of office of public officials or which restrict the number of terms that public officials may serve shall take effect upon the dates of the first elections or the first appointments of such public officials under this Constitution.

Article 9.

Laws, decrees, ordinances and treaties in force at the time this Constitution enters into force shall remain valid unless they contradict this Constitution.

Article 10.

Local councils prescribed by this Constitution shall be established on a phased basis taking into account the degree of financial self-reliance attained by local governments and the dates for their establishment shall be determined by law.

STATEMENTS BY CHUN DOO HWAN

13. INAUGURAL ADDRESS, SEPTEMBER 1, 1980

Today, as this ceremony opens a new chapter in our history, I wish first to express my deep sense of gratitude to the delegates of the National Conference for Unification, and to the people of Korea, for my election as President of the Republic of Korea. The duties with which I am charged at this critical national juncture have filled me with a grave sense of responsibility.

As I see it, the opening of this decade represents a crucial turning point in the course of our modern history in both domestic and international spheres. The passage of time since liberation from Japan in 1945 has seen a change in the composition of our society's driving forces, and with hindsight we can see that the unforeseen events of last Oct. 26 marked the closing of an era. All of us in contemporary life share the historic mission of boldly parting with the climate of the past to build a clean, just society in mutual trust, secured by a prosperous and strong welfare state.

When we look beyond our borders, we can realistically expect continuing turmoil on the international political and economic scene in the coming decade. As tension rises between the United States and the Soviet Union, disputes and military conflicts of every kind will continue to erupt around the globe. Indicators of a structural transition in the strategic equilibrium among the major powers seem to be appearing, especially in Northeast Asia. Such shifts and developments among the major powers, as always, tend to aggravate the tensions in and around the Korean peninsula.

Nor can the world economy escape the disruptions stemming from the persisting recession and the worsening shortage of resources. Thus we must shoulder the twin burdens of these circumstances: the necessity of constant vigilance and preparation against the threat of renewed aggression from the north Korean Communists, and the deteriorating international milieu. Therefore, in order to safeguard our right to survival and sustain our vision of a brighter future, we must respond to these dual challenges with firm national resolve and unity.

Source: Korea Newsreview, September 6, 1980.

We achieved an astounding measure of national development through the 1960s and 1970s in the face of myriad trials and challenges. But during the course of this accelerated development, numerous irregularities crept into our society due to the rapidity of change, typified by the accumulation of illicit wealth through the abuse of official power, the inequitable distribution of wealth, the worship of money, degenerating morality, extremism in political differences and pervasive indolence among public servants.

Some politicians garnered billions, and even tens of billions of won by abusing political power, while some of the wealthy spent lavishly and ostentatiously. Sheer selfishness became the prevalent way of thinking.

If such an irrational situation were to go unchecked, the nation's survival would be more grievously threatened by internal conflict and disruptions than by the ever-present specter of external aggression. This would be the irony of the lion, the most kingly of beasts, falling prey to internal parasites or disease rather than to battle with his foes.

This land belongs to the nation of people who preserved it with their blood and built it with their toil. It is not the nation of a privileged few. Therefore, in the 1980s we ought to shake off the residual ills of the past and construct a genuinely democratic welfare shate.

That goals means, first of all, the cultivation in this land of a democracy suited to our political climate; secondly, the attainment of a genuine welfare society; thirdly, the realization of a just society and, fourthly, a renaissance of patriotic and civil spirit through educational reform and enhancement of cultural values. As President, I will endeavor to lay a foundation on which we may achieve these national goals.

The task of accumulating truly democratic strength lies immediately before us. Democracy is now regarded as a universal good; however, it is not indigenous to Korea, but was introduced only after liberation from Japan. Therefore, despite this nation's various efforts to practice democratic politics, we have repeatedly paid the price of trial-and-error in the absence of a foundation on which democracy could materialize.

The democratic system is a complex and elaborate political institution, one which can hardly function satisfactorily until, and unless, the conditions of maturity it requires are at hand. The government will therefore tackle one by one the tasks required to build that foundation.

We intend to prepare an efficient Constitution that can be relied upon to prevent the past politics of confrontation and reform the political climate—in other words, one that recognizes and addresses our reality. The draft Constitution will be put to a referendum in October at the latest.

Thus we plan to conduct elections under the new Constitution in the first half of the coming year to inaugurate a new government, as has been repeatedly made clear. Political activities will be allowed to resume as shortly as practicable after the new Constitution is adopted. Martial Law will be lifted once the political situation has stabilized and there is no longer any danger of disturbances.

Elections under the new Constitution will be conducted in free and fair competition, with unproductive overheated campaigning forestalled, respect for the law ensured and a free atmosphere guaranteed by circumstances in which Martial Law is no longer required.

In order to carry out this schedule, the active cooperation of the people is necessary and I have every confidence it will be forthcoming. I wish to clarify that the political schedule announced by former President Chol Kyu-hah could be advanced substantially if this cooperative atmosphere matures satisfactorily.

If true democracy is to be rooted in this land, the political climate must first be improved. A climate fraught with agitation, irrationality, factionalism, intrigue, irregularities, and corruption, as was the case in the past, can scarcely nurture democracy. In recent months, we have exposed a considerable number of past-era politicians who were responsible for the prevalence of such malpractices. Further, it is my belief that we cannot risk putting the helm of state in the hands of such politicians.

I am convinced, therefore, that the renovation of our political circles and a change of generations among politicians are unavoidable. I expect these changes to gradually neutralize and reform the political extremism exhibited in the past.

The democracy we establish must be based on the concept of individual liberty, but also guarantee our survival and safety. It must include institutional devices to eliminate inefficiency in national administration and be capable of supporting qualitative economic development under the principles of free competition. Above all, it must conform with our long-enduring national traditions and cultural heritage.

Under such a system, the President especially should work with the attitude of service rather than rule. I believe he who holds this office must realize that its authority is not an instrument forged for his personal benefit, but rather a sacred trust given for a limited period of time. To extend the roots of democracy in this land, I will establish a tradition of peaceful transfer of power through due constitutional processes. In this regard, I was deeply moved by the example set by President Chol Kyu-hah in mid-August.

However, true democracy cannot be attained solely through the efforts of the government or of politicians. I believe the road to a democratic society can be traveled, by every citizen establishing and practicing in his daily life the clearly visualized concept of a healthy, democratic citizen, and by extending that concept from public morality to affairs of state.

We can fairly say that one of our most pressing tasks is to imbue the postwar generation, which has not experienced the miseries of war, with a firm sense of values and a thorough awareness of national security, with which they can overcome the Communist threat.

The next imperative for the founding of a welfare society is to pursue sustained economic development on the basis of a free economic system. Social welfare obviously presupposes economic development, and therefore the government will respect and encourage creativity among business enterprises, and guarantee free and unhampered business activities to the fullest practicable extent.

On the other hand, the government will abolish the previous overprotection of enterprises, reexamining and modifying support measures in order to strengthen the organization of business and industry as a whole.

In other words, private initiative will be at the heart of the nation's economy. An economic environment will be sought which prompts enterprises both big and small to hold themselves finally responsible for the results of their management.

In the international area, we will endeavor to strengthen the competitiveness of our enterprises by maintaining an open trade situation and by boldly importing foreign capital and technology when necessary. At the same time, the economic activities of foreign organizations and individuals in this country will be induced and encouraged, with their legitimate interests fully guaranteed.

Our social welfare policy gives priority to the increase of job opportunities through increased public investments, so that all citizens can lead a satisfying and dignified life. The government will continue to seek improvements in working conditions, to close the wage gap, to provide economic security for workers and to establish cooperative labor-management relations for their mutual prosperity.

It will continue prompting the Saemaul Undong (New Community Movement) to increase farmers' incomes and accelerate rural modernization, while also extending the movement to cities and factories. It will seek to improve the international competitiveness of the heavy and chemical industries, and exports in general, while pushing ahead to institute fair banking and marketing practices. Immediate measures will concentrate on stabilizing prices and improving the supply of daily necessities.

Sustained economic growth and development are not only the basic ingredients of a welfare state, but are also fundamental to the strong, self-reliant defense we have so far pursued and will continue to pursue. Needless to say, the maintenance of firm military strength is an indispensable prerequisite to crushing Communist north Korea's ambition to communize the country by force, ignoring peaceful solutions to the problems on the Korean peninsula.

To further strengthen our self-reliant defense posture, I will continue promoting the development of our military into a finely honed force, stimulate the morale of our officers and men, and steadily develop the defense industry. Attempting to realize a democratic welfare society without the support of a self-reliant defense would be building on sand.

A climate of mutual trust and confidence among the people is the only path to the creation of a just society. Distrust among the people is a problem at present, but the people's distrust of the government is more serious. The primary responsibility for this, in my opinion, lies with the government and public servants.

I will not in the future tolerate irregularities, either in myself or in those around me. Corruption among public servants will be systematically eliminated so that the basis of the people's distrust is removed as rapidly as possible. I firmly believe that this course of action is the only way for the government to recover the people's trust in its honesty.

In every age and country, many social reforms have started out with great zeal and a sense of justice, but with the lapse of time have lost the original vision and sense of mission, so that they again invited the distrust of the people. We must not repeat such failures in our coming new era.

If we are to open a truly new era, the outlook of every citizen must be changed and a new sense of values established. "New values" does not necessarily denote a sophisticated or difficult concept. It simply means a resolve to remedy one by one such evil habits as ignoring regulations, breaking promises, slandering others, telling lies, seeking unearned income, indulging in luxury and waste, expecting money to open every door, and seeking concessions through improper pressures.

The government will promote the nationwide social reform campaign already underway in tandem with the Saemaul Undong to make these new values a national trait and materialize a just society. The social reform campaign has so far been limited to the removal of negative aspects, but in the future must go beyond this to encourage positive contributions.

If the campaign is to succeed, the spirit of honesty, order and creativity must be learned and practiced from childhood. This is the proper function of our homes and schools. This may require generations to take root but it is my inflexible determination to make a good start at it here and now. For this purpose, the reform of education and the cultivation of national culture in the broadest sense are necessary.

Education in the past tended to focus on the mere infusion of knowledge. This must be changed with an emphasis on the improvement of those traits required from democratic citizens, the cultivation of character, the establishment of an awareness of national security needs, and the development of creativity—in other words, the education of a well-rounded person. To that end, we will endeavor to make compulsory education more substantial, eradicate the impoverishing practice of extracurricular tutoring and recover the people's trust and respect for schools.

The university is an elite place of learning which should produce men of ability to take leading roles in the society of the future. Therefore, the government will fully guarantee the freedom to study and learn in the university. However, collegiate involvement in practical politics or acts destructive of social order cannot be tolerated, if only for considerations of national security.

For the development of culture in the new era, the government will endeavor to preserve, refine and transmit valuable aspects of our traditional cultural heritage, while actively supporting the activities of independent and creative artists.

Our determination to build a democratic welfare state is ultimately linked to the goal of peaceful unification of our homeland. The government will conduct the south-north dialogue with tenacity in order to achieve this paramount national task, concentrating on settling the most tractable problems first.

I expect to speak of this south-north issue in more detail at another time. For the moment, I wish to express my conviction that war must be prevented on the Korean peninsula and that national and territorial unification must be achieved only through peaceful means.

Similarly, the construction of a democratic welfare state will also elevate our nation's stature in the international community. The government, while further consolidating the Korea-U.S. mutual defense arrangement, will continue to foster and expand cooperative relations with the United States, Japan and all other friendly nations to keep pace with or increasing significance as a trading partner in international affairs. It will remain our policy to keep the door open to countries with different ideologies and systems on the principle of reciprocity. We will continue promoting substantial, cooperative relations with nonaligned nations.

I hereby assure all of you that I will work diligently to translate into action and reality all the ideas and aspirations on national administration I outlined for you here on the occasion of my inauguration as President. No one can frustrate our national will to create a new historic era, or block the progress of our national destiny. There is nothing before us but resolution, participation and glory.

Let us bear in mind that we all exist within the state, and that the state exists through each of us. Let us all stop to think, with a modest sense of service and humility, what we can do for the country and the people, and then march hand-in-hand toward a bright new age.

This solemn national resolve should become the driving force that opens a new chapter of national history.

In closing, I pray that happiness, prosperity and God's blessing will always be with our people at home and abroad.

Thank you.

14. PRESS CONFERENCE, OCTOBER 16, 1980

Opening remarks by Dean of the Press Corps: Thank you for taking the time to speak with us. I am sure you must be extremely busy.

President Chun: However busy I may be, I must respond when you request such meetings, because the press is the voice of the people and plays an important role.

Question: We asked for this direct meeting because there are many issues to discuss, including the new politics, new order and new history, and in relation to these there are several questions to be answered concerning the political situation.

Answer: As I have addressed these matters of interest to the people at every opportunity, you may already have a basic grasp of the issues we face. But feel free to ask any questions you might have, and I will answer to the best of my knowledge.

Q: It has been 46 days since your inauguration, and in that time you have received regular reports from government ministries and agencies. You toured provincial areas and offices and are continuing to do so. You have seen with your own eyes the lives of ordinary citizens, as in your visit to the coal mine area. So I think you may have some impressions and reactions from what you have seen. Could you relate those to us?

A: What I feel most strongly, from my time so far as President, is that I bear the gravest responsibility, and should do my utmost to serve the nation and people with devotion, passion and loyalty. My determination to do so has been renewed during this time.

Q: In regard to the proposed Constitution now before the public, the interest of the people is focused on the timing of the revocation of the ban on political activities, the lifting of martial law, and presidential and National Assembly elections. In other words, their interest is focused on the political schedule. Although you have provided a rough outline of that schedule in your inaugural address, and also somewhat more comprehensively in the Supplementary Provisions to the proposed Constitution, could you be more specific now?

A: My present thinking is that political activities should resume after the constitutional referendum and upon the legislation and promulgation of laws relevant to political activities and political parties. Therefore, I generally envision that

Source: Seoul: Korean Overseas Information Service, October 16, 1980.

political activities can resume sometime between the end of November and mid-December. That is my current approximation.

As to the lifting of martial law, which was extended nationwide on May 17, I plan to return to limited martial law at 00:00 hours October 17 and I plan to lift martial law completely before the presidential election.

I also think the presidential election under the new Constitution will be held after the laws on presidential and National Assembly elections have been revised. But I do not think there is any reason to delay the presidential election for long, so I plan to hold the presidential election by March next year following finalization of the presidential election law.

If matters progress as I am outlining them here, National Assembly elections could be held in late April or May next year, and by the end of June we should be able to launch a new government. This is the general outline.

Q: It seems to me that most people lack a clear grasp of the differences between the presidential electoral college provided for in the new Constitution and the National Conference for Unification. Can you give us an explanation of the differences?

A: I think people will understand the differences clearly once the law on presidential election is finalized. But for the present let me provide you my basic concept of those differences.

A major difference is that members of political parties were ineligible to run in National Conference for Unification delegate elections, but persons who are members of or affiliated with political parties will be eligible for electoral college elections. That is the major difference. Another salient feature is that members of the electoral college can announce or otherwise make clear who they intend to support among the various presidential candidates.

Another difference lies in the fact that currently presidential candidates can only be nominated by the National Conference for Unification. But under the new Constitution, presidential candidates can be nominated by political parties or by the support of three hundred members of the electoral college. This is to guarantee political freedom to independents.

These are the major, distinctive features, which I feel are not normally found in other countries. I believe the system is essentially democratic. The functions of the two bodies will also differ, and the electoral college will be disbanded soon after the election of a president.

Q: A new political package appropriate to the new age is expected upon the establishment of a new Constitution through the upcoming national referendum. How, in your view, would political parties come into being in this new package? We also wonder if Your Excellency will be a member of one of the new parties. In this connection, there is much discussion as to whether there will be a two-party or multi-party system in the new age. Would you discuss how our political party system should be developed to make it better suited to the new age?

A: I can say that when the new Constitution is confirmed the existing political parties must be dissolved and, therefore, it is inevitable that new parties should come into existence. The question of whether it should be a two-party or multi-party system may well hinge upon how those involved in political parties actually operate their parties. Undoubtedly, our past experience has shown that a bi-partisan system led to public distrust of political parties and politicians. The two-party system prompted political polarization and confrontation, effectively immobilizing politics and the National Assembly, as well as precluding a climate conducive to compromise and cooperation.

My personal opinion, therefore, is that the existence of a number of political parties, each with different policy ideas, could neutralize the past tendency to polarization.

As to whether the President would be affiliated with a political party, I think it would be natural to do so in view of the fact that democratic politics is essentially partisan politics. It would also be necessary to allow the President to embody governmental responsibility under the presidential system of government. But since the draft Constitution being put to a national referendum calls for a single, seven-year term for the President, I think it might also be desirable for the President to conduct state affairs from a position beyond any partisan affiliation.

I have my own ideas with respect to this issue. But since any judgment would require a deeper grasp of public opinion and the views of various circles, I do not think that at this stage I can elucidate on whether the President will have political party membership.

Q. I understand that the Government is considering a political reform law. I am curious as to what degree such a law would prohibit the political activities of the old-guard politicians subject to its control, as well as the rest of its contents. In addition, please explain Your Excellency's opinion and policy on the future renovation of the political atmosphere.

A: To improve the political atmosphere, utmost efforts are being made to perfect a system, by incorporating the lessons learned from the merits and demerits of our political history, so that the new politics will not revert to past practices. Presently the relevant offices are studying the issue of establishing universal and objective criteria to improve the political atmosphere in the spirit of the new age and destiny.

I believe that rules and norms for fresh political activities should be established on a preferential basis to facilitate the rooting of sound and stable democratic politics. I can answer the question by saying that the pertinent authorities are studying the issue of political reform by establishing universal and objective criteria.

Q: Would you explain what progress has been made toward the formation of the Legislative Council for National Security, and what direction it will take when, after the adoption of the new Constitution, it will legislate such auxiliary laws as those on political reform and the elections of the President and National Assembly, while exercising other legislative functions?

A: I think that the proposed Legislative Council for National Security will incorporate every stratum of society so that it can fully reflect the people's views even more fully, in one sense, than any past National Assembly and effectively perform its duties. The organization and membership of the Legislative Council will be made public upon the confirmation of the new Constitution in the national referendum.

Q: We anticipate great economic difficulties in the days to come due to the global recession, the oil problem caused by the Iran-Iraq war, and reduced harvests owing to the cool weather this summer. Your Excellency, would you explain what policies, if any, the Government will implement to ensure economic stability, particularly for low-income people?

A: The Government fully realizes the cool weather will cause a decline in this year's autumn harvests. Therefore, the Government is taking various steps to cope with the food-supply situation. The people, on their part, should refrain from hoarding foodstuffs. This is important for the stabilization of grain prices. I would like to say that the Government is taking every available step toward a solution.

As was announced by the pertinent minister earlier, steps are being taken to ensure assistance to those in areas where cool-weather damage was particularly serious. I would like to take this occasion to ask the people for their positive cooperation in this regard, for the success of the measures taken by the Government depends on the people's cooperation.

The economic recession we face has resulted chiefly from the weakening of the international competitiveness of Korean industry, mainly caused by rising oil prices, continuing inflation and recent wage increases. I am of the opinion, therefore, that attempts to stimulate business activity simply by printing more money would only make the recession worse by fueling inflation and blunting our competitive edge even further. Accordingly, the Government is now in the process of instituting various measures to rationalize the economy, including the program to restructure business corporations, and to thus enhance our competitiveness.

Fortunately, overseas orders for Korean products have been rising since last September. So I am confident that the slump is now bottoming out. It is predicted that the competitive edge of Korean industry will be sharpened in the course of the next year, with exports again becoming brisk. This should lead to an overall upturn in the Korean economy.

It is true that the world oil market is threatened with possible disruptions owing to the war between Iran and Iraq. Fortunately, however, the Government has made adequate arrangements to maintain an equilibrium between domestic oil demand and supply. So the Korean people at present need not worry about the oil situation here at home. But I must emphasize the necessity of stepping up our efforts to conserve energy and make the most efficient use of available energy resources, especially in light of the possibility that the Iraqi-Iranian war might become protracted, with the Middle East situation deteriorating more seriously than is currently anticipated.

The Government is preparing short- and long-term policies of a permanent nature to effectively aid needy families in terms of education, housing, health and so forth. Similarly, measures are being readied to prevent natural disasters and aid disaster victims.

Q: We believe one major concern of the Korean people is the situation in colleges and universities. Recently, normalcy has been restored on most campuses and students are studying hard. But it is understood that there are some exceptions to the general trend. In this connection, would you please comment on what measures the Government is taking to settle the overall problem of potential student unrest?

A: Currently, tranquility is prevailing on campuses throughout the country and all students are intent on their academic pursuits. I think this is a very heart-warming, fortunate development. In the recent past, in an extremely small number of colleges—say, two or three in Seoul and one or two in other parts of the country—a few students scattered seditious leaflets or did something of a similar nature. These students were caught by their fellow students and their teachers, and subjected to disciplinary action by their schools. They are also being investigated by the authorities concerned. If I remember the date correctly, on October 8 some students at the Hankuk Theological Seminary—which I understand has a total enrollment of about 200—distributed seditious leaflets and started a commotion. The school authorities thereupon voluntarily suspended classes for an indefinite period and reported to the law-enforcement authorities the eight students who created the disturbance. They also are now under investigation. I can say that, apart from those incidents, an atmosphere of serious study has been maintained throughout the country ever since colleges were reopened last summer.

Fundamentally, however, I have no intention of deviating from my long-standing conviction that the democratization of academic institutes, a climate suitable for serious study, and the freedom of pure research activities must be guaranteed. Such matters will continue to be guaranteed in the future as well.

In order to establish a clean society, vigorous campaigns are being waged to uproot illegalities and injustices. National unity is called for more than ever in order to overcome various extraordinary difficulties that could confront the nation in the course of the 1980s. I think that we cannot tolerate, at this important juncture, young men and women, who should devote themselves to the pursuit of truth, failing to respond to the challenge of the new era, but rather continuing to create instability; to do so would be to ignore their role as students. Accordingly, the Government intends to take resolute steps against such student behavior in the name of the entire Korean people. Such an unhappy state of affairs, if it should recur, would be painful not only to individual students, but also to school authorities and parents. I hope that everybody concerned will exert self-restraint and positive leadership. I also want to urge intelligent students, who will be the masters of the new era, to see to it that none of them will have to be expelled.

Q: Please allow me to ask one more question. The details of the proposed new Constitution have already been announced and the national referendum is only a week or so away. On this occasion, have you anything else to say to the Korean public in connection with the current domestic and world situation, including the war between Iran and Iraq?

A: At the very beginning of the 1980s we are faced with a period of tough and overwhelming transition. But I believe that an individual or a nation can become truly great only when hardships and adversities are overcome. So I ask that the Government and the people renew their conviction and confidence that any difficulty can be surmounted if we really work hard at it, and that the nation strive in concert and harmony to overcome adversities and nurture national strength. As matters stand now, the Iraqi-Iranian war is not likely to be brought to an early end, contrary to initial expectations, and it is hard to predict how the Persian Gulf crisis will develop. In my view, this could be a typical example of the difficulties that might befall us in the course of the 1980s. If we are to overcome such difficulties and achieve sustained national prosperity, we must enact a new Constitution based on consensus so that the groundwork can be laid for concerted national efforts to shape a new historic era.

Only when the wishes of the entire people fill the ballot boxes of the national referendum to overflowing, will the new Constitution be accorded a propitious birth and be assured of healthy growth. In that way, we must achieve a Constitution that is solid, respected and faithfully observed, with the aim of laying the cornerstone for the just welfare state to which we aspire. I hope, therefore, that all eligible voters will participate in the October 22 referendum in order to exercise their sovereign rights, and that there won't be a single abstention.

Once the Constitution is established, my long-standing conviction is that it should not be changed frequently for expediency's sake, even if some inconveniences arise in the course of its implementation. I do not favor frequent revisions to the Constitution.

15. INTERVIEW WITH JAPANESE NHK CORRESPONDENT, NOVEMBER 1980

Question: I am very grateful of you, Mr. President, for the time you have spared for this interview despite your busy schedule of state affairs.

As Korea's new Constitution was promulgated Oct. 27, I would like to hear something from you about the spirit of the Constitution of the Fifth Republic and the move toward democratization.

Answer: First of all, I would like to thank you for visiting me. As you know, our Constitution of the Fifth Republic was adopted by absolute majority national support which I think was a result of the democratic caliber of our people and their wise judgment. I firmly believe that this was a manifestation of national unity and a concentrated will toward the construction of a new history and a democratic welfare state.

Accordingly, I, as the President who initiated the new Constitution, feel acutely a great responsibility imposed upon me.

The basic goal of the new Constitution, above all, is to have "democracy in Korea" take root here.

Regrettably, we have never changed the governmental power in a peaceful manner in our Constitutional history. Therefore, we have adopted a single seven-year term for future Presidents in the new Constitution in order to prevent them from remaining in power for an extended period and in order to realize peaceful transfer of governmental power.

The Constitution stipulates that any President trying to revise the mother law cannot benefit from the amendment he initiates.

Now about the operation of the National Assembly. In the past, we adopted the parliamentary system of some advanced countries. But, because of the difference in political climate, this brought forth extreme confrontations between ruling and opposition parties.

Therefore, the National Assembly operated without receiving public confidence and respect. My conviction is that the future National Assembly should become an efficient and productive legislative branch through constructive dialogue and thus gain public confidence and respect.

If the National Assembly is operated this way, a true democracy will take root in Korea in a short period of time.

Q: When the Constitutional draft was announced Sept. 29, I read it and found out that it had the words "democracy" or "democratization" in 12 or 13

Source: Korea Newsreview, November 22, 1980.

places. With this, we can come to understand the zeal for democratization Your Excellency has. Would you please explain in detail about the future political schedule?

A: I have disclosed the timetable in my inaugural address and during my interview with Korean pressmen. As scheduled, we held a national referendum Oct. 22. In the conduct of the referendum, there were many difficulties such as lack of time. But, we did it in order to live up to our public promise.

The Legislative Assembly, organized under the new Constitution, has been dealing with the Presidential Election Law, National Assembly Election Law, Political Party Law and other laws as scheduled so that political activities can be resumed by early December or by the middle of December at the latest.

If the election laws are completed, we plan to hold a Presidential election by March next year. In April or May, we plan to hold a parliamentary election. In this way, we can inaugurate a new government in June as has been announced. It must be known that Martial Law will be lifted before the Presidential election in order to hold the election in a free atmosphere.

Q: Now let me touch on economic issues such as balance of payments, expansionary money supply, inflation and increase of unemployment which I think are global problems. I understand that the Korean economy is also in a difficult situation. Will you please, Mr. President, elaborate on your domestic policy guidelines with emphasis on these economic problems?

A: Frankly speaking, I have no professional knowledge about economics and that is why I am seriously learning economics from the economists in order to grasp the real economic situation. It is my understanding that there are two major dimensions of the current difficult economic situation. The two are external and domestic. As you pointed out, the external factor is the increase of crude oil prices to which all countries are exposed.

On the domestic front, the assassination of President Park Chung Hee on Oct. 26 last year had a profound impact on the economy. The excessive investment made in Korea's heavy and chemical industry sector could be cited as another major problem the Korean economy is facing now.

The poor fall harvest caused by the unfavorable weather conditions throughout last summer has also dealt a blow to the Korean economy.

As far as food grain is concerned, we don't have any serious problem at the moment as we have enough food grain stocks to meet the domestic demand thanks to the cooperation of friendly nations.

Fortunately, the nation's merchandise export performance started to pick up again after September following the stabilization of the domestic political and social situation. I think that the profit ratio of corporations will be improved while investment activities will gain momentum. Consumer demand is also expected to increase steadily against this background.

Q: It is our understanding that there is no easy prescription for inflation. The inflationary trend, we understand, cannot be brought under control within one or two years with short-term measures. At least three or four years of long-term planning is necessary to curb inflation. Do you have, Mr. President, any blueprint for solving the inflation and unemployment problems? If so, please tell us.

A: According to analyses made by economic experts, the Korean economy is expected to gain momentum toward the latter half of next year for recovery from the prolonged recession. And I am very much optimistic about Korea's economy personally.

For this, I'd like to cite three major factors. One of them is Korean businessmen who have shown a strong will to push ahead with economic development projects, not to mention their outstanding managerial ability and plentiful experience. The immense potentiality and ability of Korean businessmen will surely contribute to Korea's economic development.

Secondly, we do have, as you know, a diligent and sincere work force. Such an able work force with strong patriotic feeling and highly sophisticated technical ability could be cited as a national treasure and potentiality. Third and lastly, we do have highly educated and efficient technocrats in officialdom, particularly at economic ministries, who were educated in the United States, Europe and Japan. As they have solid academic backgrounds coupled with experience, they can cope with any difficulty with effective and positive countermeasures. This is also a potentiality and ability of Korea.

If and when these three strengths of Korea are well combined, we can cope with the current economic difficulty and eventually paint a rosy picture of Korea's future economy. I predict that Korea's economy will return to normalcy toward the latter half of next year, at the latest.

Q: The year 1980 is a year that a new government was inaugurated in this nation. In Japan, a new cabinet was born following the sudden death of former prime minister Masayoshi Ohira. A new president was also elected in the United States and the "Reagan administration" will be launched next January.

In other words, the heads of these three allied nations have been replaced in this year. Mr. President, what is your opinion of the "international situation of Korea" in this context?

A: I do not think there will occur any change in Korea's friendly relations with the United States and Japan whatever government may be installed in those latter countries because we have maintained traditional friendly ties with these nations regardless of who were the leaders of the two at any given time.

I hope the relations among the three nations would be further strengthened and I am going to make efforts in that direction.

In short, I firmly believe that there will not be any change. Rather, the cooperative relations will be strengthened even more.

Q: Mr. President, I understand that the Kim Dae-jung trial has ended at the appeals court and the sentence was confirmed.

We feel that there are some differences in views on Kim's trial between Koreans and some people in foreign nations. Mr. President, what do you think about this issue?

A: The case of Mr. Kim is fundamentally that of a criminal offense and not a political crime. The difference in views is attributable to the fact that they (foreigners) regard Kim as a political criminal.

The Kim Dae-jung case, as you said, is pending before the court. We have to wait for the outcome of the trial by the Supreme Court.

As in Japan and other democratic countries, in Korea, the independence of the judiciary is maintained. No one has a right to say anything that may affect the trial. No one must make such comments.

As President, I have no right to say anything about the trial. I am not in rivalry with Kim Dae-jung politically. I have not met him. He committed a crime in which he attempted to grab government power by using violence. Many Koreans were sacrificed because of him.

His trial under law is unavoidable.

A similar case in any other country would have to be tried.

Talking about the possible outcome of the Kim Dae-jung case would influence the trial.

As I said earlier, it would be prudent to wait for the outcome of the trial.

Q: After the Supreme Court passes judgment on the case, I think you, as President, can make a certain decision about it. The new ROK Constitution provides for Presidential amnesty. People in Japan and the United States expect that you will make a certain decision as President, after the Supreme Court passes its judgment on the case.

Although you have already said you will not say anything that may affect the outcome of the trial, I wonder if you are considering making any decision. Would you answer that question?

A: As I explained earlier, I think it inappropriate to say anything now because the case is still pending.

Q: The north Korean Workers (Communist) Party held its sixth congress around Oct. 19. It is said subjects related to the Third World were discussed. At the same time, during the congress, Kim Chong-il emerged as de facto successor to Kim Il-sung.

This is a matter of great interest. What is your view of the latest political, economic and international situation of north Korea?

A: According to foreign press reports and north Korea watchers, the sixth congress of the north Korean Workers' Party, which recently convened in Pyongyang, named Kim Il-sung's son, Chong Il, an heir to Kim's throne.

At this critical juncture, we should refrain from making any premature judgments as to the future behavior of north Korea.

As you well know, the Korean peninsula was divided to accommodate the interests of the powers following the end of World War II.

I believe the Korean people are a creative race with cultural homogeneity and political independence throughout most of its long history. I am convinced that we have to achieve a peaceful unification, putting an end to the tragic division.

Q: Contrary to your ardent wish, north Korea is striving to garner international support for its cause at the United Nations with the help of Third World nations. Though we sympathize with your hopes for unification, unification is an extremely complicated issue. Do you have any concrete ideas for approaching the problem?

A: You are well versed on this matter. As you know, there has been no change of north Korean leadership during the past three decades. The north Koreans have been exploiting the inter-Korea dialogue as a means of political propaganda.

As a result, we cannot trust north Korea and we realize how hard it is for a free society to conduct negotiations with a totalitarian society.

I'd like [to] call your attention to the fact that north Korea, which proposed a meeting of south and north Korean premiers in the wake of the death of President Park Chung Hee in October of last year, has boycotted the conference, now that we, in the south, have achieved stability.

Without citing further examples, I would say this is typical of north Korean behavior.

Unifying the Korean peninsula is an extremely difficult task but we cannot give it up because of its difficulty.

First, a gradual exchange should be initiated between south and north Korea in such areas as sports, culture, arts and education. Then we could proceed with the reunion of separated families at a place like Panmunjom as has been between the two Germanies.

By tackling easy issues first, we can gradually proceed to the ultimate business of unification, which, by then, will have appeared less hopeless than at the beginning.

Q: Do you have any plans to visit Japan and the United States? Japan now has a new government and the United States will inaugurate a new president next January.

A: I do not have any such plans for the moment. But I think it would be useful for heads of state of not only Japan and the United States but other friendly nations and myself to visit each other and exchange views on matters of common interest. I think Korean and Japanese leaders could exchange views on the regional situation in Northeast Asia and world peace as a whole. But I don't have any plans for such a meeting at the moment.

Questioner: Thank you very much, Mr. President.

16. NEW YEAR POLICY STATEMENT, JANUARY 12, 1981

Fellow citizens.

I hope the New Year finds you well and brings happiness and good luck to all of you and your families, and blessings to society as a whole.

I am here to explain in detail the basic policies of my Administration and to ask for your cooperation and active participation in our plans and blueprints for the future.

Let me first talk about political development.

The Fifth Republic will be formally launched during the first half of this year. The political timetable for instituting the Government of the new republic is being implemented without any setback, as I have repeatedly pledged.

The two major tasks that remain are the presidential and National Assembly elections. The fact is that the presidential election can be carried out anytime now, once the various political parties and candidates have completed the necessary preparations. Laws and decrees pertaining to the presidential election have already been finalized and promulgated.

It is beyond any doubt that the people, in their concern for stability above all else, can hardly wait to see the Government of the Fifth Republic come into being. Now that overall domestic stability has been restored, there is no reason to delay. Accordingly our plans are to hold the presidential election in February, earlier than originally envisioned, but still well within the spirit of the Supplementary Provisions of the new Constitution which stipulates that the resumption of political activities must be allowed at least three months prior to the presidential election. In such an event, I think it is desirable to hold the National Assembly elections one or two months earlier than originally scheduled.

In keeping with my repeated pledges, the forthcoming elections will be held after Martial Law has been lifted so that the free will of the people may be fully expressed. Thus Martial Law will be repealed in its entirety prior to the electoral college elections to facilitate the conduct of the presidential election.

The forthcoming elections, the symbolic events that will formally usher in the new era, must be conducted in a fair and just manner to ensure their moral legitimacy. To do otherwise would not only affect the qualification of the few successful candidates involved; it would also inflict a decisive blow to the moral underpinning and rationale of the Fifth Republic. We must never fail to achieve fair and clean elections.

Source: New Year Policy Statement by President Chun Doo Hwan, January 12, 1981, Seoul: Korean Overseas Information Service, 1981.

There is a possibility that old-style politics may be rekindled with the newly emerging political parties. The Government, however, will redouble its efforts to prevent any recurrence of old political habits. In particular, I will see to it that political organizations with pro-government leanings will serve as models for the new era by abiding by the principles of fair and clean elections.

Now I would like to turn to the economic situation.

I am fully aware that in the past year, the people, as well as the nation, have been beset by economic difficulties. As the President, responsible for the economic well-being of the nation, I share the pain of all Koreans suffering economic hardships. I am filled with a resolve to overcome these difficulties together, discussing the matter with the people and sharing their concerns.

The economic difficulties we are faced with today have resulted from a complex combination of internal and external causes. Accordingly, we cannot rid ourselves of them with a single sweep of the hand or the pressing of a button. Nonetheless, we must meet the present challenges, no matter how difficult the task.

To that end, I want to ask certain things of the people, while expressing my own thoughts about the situation.

First, let us strengthen our determination and confidence that the Korean economy will not fail to achieve a second takeoff. Over the past decade or so, the Government, the entrepreneurs and the workers have worked in concert with a strong determination to pull ourselves up by our own bootstraps—and achieved some considerable successes. However, in the course of doing so, we also created various side-effects and complex problems. Accordingly, I am convinced that we now stand at the crossroads, from which the Korean economy can either sink into a quagmire or travel toward tomorrow's takeoff point, depending on whether we can regain our determination and confidence.

Second, we must renew the realization that stability is the key to economic progress. Our current economic difficulties are eloquent testimony to how political and social instability can adversely affect the economy.

One lesson of experience should suffice; we cannot afford to learn the same costly lesson all over again. On this occasion, I want to assure you that we can safely be optimistic about the prospect of maintaining stability. This is because the overwhelming majority of the people desire stability, and the Government is fully determined and competent to preserve stability.

Third, the Government will devote its best efforts to stabilizing prices to speed economic recovery. Nothing hinders steady economic progress more than inflation.

Stable prices will strengthen the competitiveness of Korea's export products, leading to greater foreign sales, which, in turn, will make sustained economic growth possible.

In years past, the Government was in the habit of announcing, at the beginning of each year, a projected level above which prices would not be allowed to rise. But, if I remember correctly, such "price-holding lines" rarely held firm, with the result that the people's mistrust in professed government policy kept mounting.

Accordingly, I will not give any specific figure as a price stabilization target; instead, I want to underscore the Government's resolve by declaring that price stability will be fundamental to all economic policies.

Fourth, the Government takes the position that the economy must, in principle, be run by private initiative.

Only then will Korean business be able to gain greater resilience and display greater creativity, thereby acquiring the capabilities required to successfully compete on international markets. Only then will it be possible to resolve various contradictions bred by the past government-led economic system. But it is not practicable to convert the government-led system into a private-led system overnight. With this fact in mind, we must wisely overcome the difficulties which accompany the transition.

Fifth, I wish to ask all citizens to share the necessary work and sacrifices.

An old saying goes: "Even a sheet of paper can be carried more easily by four hands working together." The greater our difficulty, the greater our spirit of sharing the sacrifices and burdens should be, so that the painful period may be shortened. The sense of unity thus created will be a powerful tool with which to tackle the tough situation.

Fellow citizens.

Perhaps I have asked too much, appealing for cooperation too many times. But these are tasks we cannot shun, if we are to advance toward a second takeoff after extricating ourselves from the grip of the present economic difficulties. Let us all exercise a bit more endurance and effort. Exports are expected to increase rapidly beginning next autumn as the world economy recovers. This will stimulate capital investments by Korean enterprises, with our factories operated more fully, resulting in increased output and employment. I can confidently assure you that the Korean economy will then return to a pattern of sustained growth.

Political and social stability is an essential precondition to the resuming of sustained economic growth. Only sustained economic growth will make possible the national strengthening of security which is indispensable to the survival of our country and our people. Sustained economic progress is also essential to continued improvement in the position of the Republic of Korea within the community of nations.

In the past year alone, many momentous changes transpired around the world, deeply affecting the international situation and warranting our close attention. By coincidence, leadership changes have occurred in close succession in the United States, Japan, and Mainland China—the three foreign powers with the greatest interest in the Korean question. It remains to be seen how those changes will affect our problems.

The war between Iran and Iraq, the price increases effected by one oil-producing nation after another, and the trend toward greater protectionism among developed countries plagued by a worldwide recession, are all strong indications that the nations of the world are experiencing a resurgence of nationalist sentiments and interests.

In view of these international developments, this Administration will take the following points into active consideration in pursuing its foreign and defense policies in the New Year.

First, it must be emphasized that an independent diplomacy and self-reliant defense are now more important than ever before. Today's chilled international political order does not allow us to depend on others to create conditions favorable to our national security and progress. We must be keenly aware that we alone are ultimately responsible for the nation's survival and happiness.

World history shows beyond any doubt that a weak people never enjoy prosperity and glory. We must ensure our proud existence in the current of world history through foreign and defense policies that serve to nurture national strength.

Yet we must also realize that the principles of independent diplomacy and self-reliant defense do not mean underestimating the importance of relations with our allies. On the contrary, the existence of trustworthy allies makes our independent diplomacy and self-reliant defense even more credible and effective. Accordingly, the utmost emphasis must be placed on relations with our allies.

This year marks the centennial of the first treaty of friendship between Korea and the United States of America. Our relationships must be further developed into a mature and intimate partnership by building upon the cordial friendship that has grown between our two nations over the past 100 years.

The cooperative relationships between Korea and America have evolved far beyond the simple military alliance, with deep roots in economic, cultural and other fields. I want to make it clear that continuing programs will further solidify and develop the close and extensive relations that exist between our two nations.

At the same time, cooperative relations between Korea and Japan should be established with a broader perspective. Korea-Japan relations have already reached a high level of interdependence in cultural traditions, economic exchanges and security concerns.

Taking the unhappy past as an object lesson, our two nations must become genuinely good neighbors, friends who work together and progress on the basis of mutual respect and understanding.

The Government will step up its efforts to develop closer relations with the United States, Japan and other friendly nations under the principles of mutual understanding and mutual respect for sovereignty.

Efforts to broaden and diversify our external relations will be intensified, especially by promoting amicable and cooperative relations with European countries, as well as with Mideast countries which have recently emerged as our close friends.

This Administration also plans to bolster its efforts to improve Korea's relations with non-hostile Communist countries as well as with non-aligned countries, irrespective of different ideologies and socio-political systems. In this connection, freedom of travel to countries with ideologies and political systems that differ from ours will not be restricted so long as the personal safety of Korean travelers is not threatened.

Furthermore, the Government has already taken steps to permit unrestricted home visits by those overseas Koreans who had been denied entry to their homeland. The government will continue its efforts to promote ties between overseas Koreans and their home country, and to protect their interests.

It is now 36 years since Korea was liberated from the yoke of Japanese colonial rule. During this time, yet another major tragedy—another stain—has appeared upon the nation's history with the division of our homeland upon liberation.

A fratricidal war, deepening national heterogeneity, strife in the international arena, and an intermittent dialogue are but a few examples of the many spiritual and material wounds inflicted upon us by the territorial partitioning.

It is the paramount national task to reunify our homeland, characterized by a single people, language and culture, into a unified, independent and democratic nation-state.

Looking back on the past decade, we cannot find any improvement in the relations between the two halves of Korea, in spite of the South-North Joint Communique of July 4, 1972. It must be recognized that both sides have consistently engaged in a war of words and vain expositions of unilateral proposals.

We have no use for empty agreements, which without embodying the will to translate them into action are not worth the paper they are written on. What is truly needed is a firm resolve on both sides to honor even the smallest agreement already reached.

Breaching various agreements contained in the July 4 Joint Communique, the North Korean Communists have continually sent armed agents into the South, demonstrating that they have not given up their scheme to communize the entire Korean peninsula by force of arms. They are intensifying their slander of the Republic of Korea through radio broadcasts of the so-called Voice of the Unification-Revolution Party, as well as through loudspeakers strung along the entire length of the Armistice Line. They also incessantly attempt to subvert the Republic of Korea Government by organizing and funding anti-ROK organizations abroad.

But their scheme to communize the entire Korean peninsula has been totally frustrated by the iron-clad security of the ROK Armed Forces and the firm resolve of the people to defend their country, which is growing steadily stronger.

Can the Korean people—who have lived for the past 36 years under two different sets of ideologies, ideals and political systems—be unified again? Is it inevitable that we should continue to live in a divided land? The answer to these questions depends, above all else, on whether a sense of trust can be restored.

Accordingly, I have formulated an epochal proposal to the North Korean authorities, with the aim of finding an avenue to the solution of the unification question that takes into account the prevailing circumstances.

Thus far, a dialogue has been conducted on an on-and-off-again basis at various levels and in various formats. But nothing ever ensued that could contribute to the substantive improvement of relations. The only result has been the wasting of a great deal of time and energy. Even the working-level contacts that began last year to pave the way for a South-North Prime Ministers conference were unilaterally suspended by Pyongyang. As we all know, again there is no South-North dialogue.

Once again, I emphasize that the path to unification is not paved by unilateral proposals rich only in rhetoric, nor by written promises that are not kept; it is paved by the restoration of trust.

But it is not my intention today to argue over things past. To provide decisive momentum to creating mutual trust between the South and the North of Korea, epochal momentum to preventing a recurrence of tragic, fratricidal war, and historic momentum to paving the way to peaceful unification through unconditional resumption of the suspended dialogue, I hereby solemnly propose that the highest authorities of the South and the North exchange visits.

I invite President Kim Il-sung of North Korea to visit Seoul without any condition attached and free of any burden.

I will ensure that his personal safety is fully guaranteed during his stay in Seoul. I will extend all possible cooperation to him if he wishes to travel to any place of his choice in order to take a first-hand look at the actual situation in Seoul, other cities, or rural areas.

I also want to make it clear that I am prepared, at any time, to visit North Korea if he invites me on the same terms as I offer.

I am convinced that any problems between the South and the North can be resolved if we work strenuously to narrow our differences following the historic exchange of visits between the highest authorities, thus creating mutual trust precluding a fratricidal war and contributing to peaceful unification through a resumption of the dialogue.

The day of reunification, our nation's long-cherished goal, will not be far away, if only both sides begin reaching agreement on the most amenable matters in the least sensitive areas and progress toward the more difficult ones.

Another important task of the Government is to progressively expand social welfare policies. A just welfare society is an urgent goal of both this Administration and the Korean people.

All citizens should have equal opportunities to participate in economic and civic activities according to their inherent qualities and abilities. The basic precondition for building a just society is the creation of a climate in which honesty and diligence are duly rewarded.

Toward that end, the Government will do its best, first of all, to create jobs and reduce unemployment by further increasing public investments.

Second, government spending on education, housing, health care and other basic needs will be gradually increased.

Third, more effective measures will be taken to protect the low-income families and destitute persons who are suffering most from the current recession.

Such measures will include public works programs and vocational training designed to fundamentally increase their wage-earning abilities.

Fourth, better medical care is desired by all. But we must admit that our medical facilities are, if only in their number, far from adequate. Therefore, the Government will steadily expand medical facilities to the greatest possible extent, while expanding and improving programs of preventive medicine and medical insurance.

Housing is yet another important element in this Administration's welfare policy. Food, shelter and clothing are widely recognized as the three basic needs of man. The problems of food and clothing have been resolved to a considerable extent, thanks to the economic growth of the past decade or so. But the housing problem remains unresolved.

In view of this state of affairs, the Government has decided to continue boosting public investments in housing in order to supply housing units in the large numbers still needed in this country.

In the field of industrial relations, both entrepreneurs and workers should realize that the coexistence and mutual prosperity of labor and management are basic to industrial development and national harmony. Both parties should strive to cultivate an atmosphere in which solutions to labor-management problems are sought through dialogue and cooperation.

To that end, this Administration will encourage the establishment and functioning of labor-management councils in accordance with recent legislation, while furthering the activities of company-level labor unions.

One major goal of the new era is a society governed by justice, order, law and common sense, along with the progressive advancement of material welfare.

An object lesson of the history of mankind—universally and inexorably applicable—is that a society that fails to remedy injustice, corruption, disorder and internal contradictions will crumble, no matter how well it grows and progresses in material terms.

The Government is determined to steadfastly implement the social reform campaigns, while ensuring that the shocks and side-effects are minimal.

Some time ago, Solzhenitsyn, the Soviet writer who has exiled himself in the United States, deplored license in the name of liberty in America and the American obsession with the notion that the "law is everything." He pointed out that the American tendency to appeal to and depend on the law for things both large and small in their daily lives is diminishing their traditional sense of ethics.

How about Korean society? Not only has a law-abiding spirit yet to take firm root but also the traditional sense of ethics is rapidly fading. Accordingly, I wish to emphasize that another major goal of the new era is a society in which the modern rule of law and the traditional sense of ethics complement each other.

The policy of normalizing education will continue to be implemented forcefully to remedy the blighted educational climate of the past. At the same time, the basic aim of education will be to produce morally-sound and competent persons to lead the shaping of the new era. For that purpose, the Government will pursue a multi-faceted educational policy centered on three basic components: ethics, science and technology, and lifelong education.

It will also be necessary to give more positive political education to the young generation that did not experience the Korean War, enabling them to correctly grasp the flaws in Communist theory, the internal contradictions manifest in Communist society and, last but not least, the realities of life in North Korea.

Science and technology play an increasingly important role in the modern world. Thus, the Government will drastically strengthen science and technology education to produce high-grade technical manpower capable of adapting to the needs of an industrializing society.

Even without citing the old saying, "No age is too old to learn," we are well aware that every citizen should continuously seek self-improvement, if he is not to fall behind in this rapidly changing modern society.

Society, therefore, must be able to furnish citizens of every social stratum and age group with educational opportunities.

This Administration will take various measures to found a program for life-long education. In particular, it plans to dramatically expand educational programs for preschool children in light of the increasing importance of early education.

Every effort will also be made to enlarge educational opportunities for the poor and disadvantaged by expanding college scholarships, providing educational assistance for working youths and eliminating institutional and social obstacles to the education of the mentally or physically handicapped.

To advance those goals, the Government will endeavor to provide comprehensive education in an effective manner by improving the educational system, including the schools themselves, along with the educational climate, curricula, and respect for teachers' authority.

The Government's cultural policy for the 1980s will basically aim at developing an independent and progressive national culture, while encouraging all citizens to actively participate in cultural and artistic activities, with the fruits of culture shared equally by all. A medium- and long-term program for that purpose will be established within the year. This program will contain, among other things, concrete measures to reaffirm the cultural identity of the nation and foster creative development of our cultural heritage.

In line with these objectives, the Government this year will provide intensive support to various academic and artistic activities designed to facilitate the preservation and modernization of traditional culture and art, while stimulating the development of local culture.

Fellow citizens,

Having consigned an era to history, we are now exploring a new era.

The conflict-laden climate of the old era has disappeared and the protagonists of those conflicts have left center stage. The time has come to kick the old quarreling habit. We must all join hand in hand under the banner of pan-national participation.

The energies that once were wasted on confrontation must now serve constructive ends. The sense of resistance once harbored by some intellectuals, students and youths must become a creative passion for the dawning era.

We should boldly and wisely sort out the good and bad legacies of the past era. It is our duty as well as our right, as masters of the national destiny, to determine what to preserve and what to reject.

Shaping a new course of national history through the creative exercise of this duty and right is the mandate of destiny that none of us in the present generation, including the President, can shirk.

Only when we squarely face this historic mandate will we be able to share together the glory and responsibility of freedom.

Thank you.

17. INAUGURAL ADDRESS, MARCH 3, 1981

Fellow citizens at home and abroad, distinguished guests, ladies and gentlemen:

Today we are gathered at the threshold of the fifth republic: beyond, the new era promises to blossom under the certain banner of creativity, renewal and progress. This marks the end of an era marred by many ordeals.

To the people I extend my abiding respect and profound gratitude. In a period of transition, a crucial, epochal phase in the nation's history, they have entrusted to me the enormous responsibility of the Presidency.

The overwhelming endorsement of my fellow countrymen in the recent election for the 12th term President of the Republic of Korea is a tremendous honor and glory: at the same time, I feel the weight this powerful mandate places on my shoulders.

I hereby pledge to the 50 million Korean people that I will devote myself wholly to the nation and faithfully carry out the momentous mission entrusted to me, so that I may live up to their expectations.

Fellow citizens,

The homeland is not ours alone. It is an invaluable bequest from our ancestors, who dedicated their blood and sweat to its preservation and development. Throughout history it has been a haven, a haven that must be handed down to the countless generations to come.

History shows that the Korean people have sustained a flourishing culture through 5,000 years of uninterrupted existence, triumphing over innumerable challenges and trials, including foreign invasions. Beyond our borders, an untold number of powerful peoples rose and fell on the continent of Asia. The histories and cultures of many have simply vanished from the earth. But the Korean people, proudly maintaining their identity, have constructed an illustrious tradition that contributes greatly to creating and nurturing the brilliance of East Asian culture.

Still, I am well aware of how Korea's history is laden with the sorrows of a small country and the angers of a subjugated people when I was born in this land, it was dominated by a foreign power as did all Koreans of my generation, I grew up in the days of harsh colonial rule. The use of our own alphabet and

Source: Korean Information Office, Washington, D.C., March 3, 1981.

language was all but forbidden. Even our names were taken from us. Should we simply accept such developments as our fate?

We must not forget the humiliations we suffered. To become the masters of our homeland, we must keep our spirit high, come what may. When that spirit weakens, we should renew our resolve by reflecting upon the shameful portions of our past. We must never again let our country fall. We must awaken and discard complacency and apathy.

Fellow citizens,

Some months ago, I proposed as national goals the development of a viable democracy, the construction of a welfare state, the realization of a just society and the promotion of innovative education and culture. I will devote my best efforts to these four major goals during my tenure, firmly laying the foundations for their full attainment. In this regard, I must address a matter of utmost importance: no matter how fine our goals, they are meaningless unless our national security is unflinchingly preserved. We must not relax our guard for even the most fleeting of moments: in light of our unique geopolitical position, we must keep an unblinking watch on the volatile situations surrounding the Korean peninsula, as well as on the unpredictable global scene in the 1980's. There is no substitute for national security: it is fundamental to national survival. The overriding importance of national security must be indelibly ingrained in our minds.

Fellow citizens,

Today, 36 years after liberation from Japanese colonial rule, which itself lasted for 36 years, the fifth republic sets sail. This coincidence of history should serve as a revelation, inspiring us to redouble our resolve to face this transition squarely. In other words, just as the hardships and adversities of Japanese occupation ended after 36 years, so the turbulence, chaos and trial and error processes which beset our endeavors to remain independent must end at this moment.

The history of modern Korea is characterized by the people's desire to regain and preserve independence. But our homeland remains divided, and we have yet to attain the goal of an industrialized welfare nation that guarantees each and every citizen a decent life. At this critical juncture, the historic task of building a prosperous and democratic nation awaits us. To lay the foundations for that nation we must achieve another great takeoff in the 1980s: to accomplish this, the 1980s should be a decade of great national progress in every field in an atmosphere of stability and harmony. All should participate in creating the foundations for affluence and well being that we shall bequeath to posterity.

In the new era that we are shaping, the government and the people of every social strata—businessmen, workers, farmers, intellectuals, educators, artists and men of letters—will focus their burning determination, wisdom, energy and concern on the building of a strong, prosperous and joyous nation. It will be an era of stupendous creation.

We are now passing the threshold of that new era for which we have all yearned so keenly. The fifth republic has been launched, in fact as well as in name, with the inauguration of the first president elected under its constitution. The old constitution, a source of political controversies, has been completely consigned to history.

But we cannot boast that a new era has begun simply because a new constitution and government have come into being. We can say a truly new era has blossomed only when a "new state of affairs" unfolds from the new constitution and government.

The solemn demand of that new state of affairs is that we must part with the doctrines which justified the former constitution and government, along with all the tribulations and passions associated with them. On this clean slate a new beginning must be made by unifying a creative will to vigorously seek new values, an innovative will to rid society of counterproductive and inefficient elements and infuse it with new vitality, and an enterprising will to develop our fine traditions and preserve the historical integrity of the nation. These should crystallize into a determined spirit to meet the challenges of historic transition into the new era.

Having weathered generations of agonies and trials we are entering a decade which should be devoted to a search for perfection through "growth and maturity." This decade has assigned to us the momentous task of perfecting a modern industrial democracy in a mature and independent nation. The birth of the fifth republic is the moment of our entry into an era of growth and maturity. Having assumed the awesome responsibilities of the presidency at the opening of a hallowed new era, I am acutely aware that my mission is to achieve that national growth and maturity.

The confusion, war and strife that marked the past 36 years were quite difficult and painful tests. All the Korean people in light of their experiences and the lessons of history, have unflaggingly sought freedom from the threat of war, freedom from poverty and freedom from political repression and abuses of power. I want to make it clear that all my ability and all my heart will be devoted to attaining the freedoms all Koreans have yearned for and sought for so long.

First and foremost, freedom from war should mean not only the prevention of war but also the absence of the fear of war. Needless to say, this requires the attainment of a lasting peace on the Korean peninsula and the normalization of living conditions for all the Korean people, eventually leading to peaceful unification. Since I have repeatedly commented on the need for lasting peace and peaceful unification, today I will discuss the quality of life.

For the past 36 years, residents of North Korea have been denied access to information about the outside world. They have been unable to enjoy even the slightest freedoms. They lead a miserable life in which their human dignity and worth are completely disregarded. They are not allowed even to express their yearning for freedom. The grim bleakness of life in North Korea, in political, economic, social, cultural and humane terms, is without parallel. As their compatriots, we cannot but feel a profound pity. The North Korean authorities should reflect upon this grim state of affairs and restore human worth to the people under their rule and improve the quality of their lives. They must be urged to do so in the name of mankind.

I take this opportunity to call, in the name of the Korean people, for an end to the total isolation imposed on North Korea and for the door to North Korean society to be opened wide as the first step toward ameliorating their plight. My proposal for an exchange of visits between the highest authorities in the South and the North, presented January 12, 1981 was aimed not only at finding a path to unification but also at stimulating the opening of North Korea to the outside world to restore human worth and improve the quality of life there.

Once it is recognized that freedom from war is essential to improving the quality of life for all Korean people, the creation of mutual trust between the South and the North is obviously a most urgent matter. Accordingly, I again urge Pyongyang to accept my January 12 proposal.

Although indications of a negative response from the North Korean side have been reported, I do not consider it a formal rejection. It is my expectation that they will someday accept this opportunity.

Second, freedom from poverty has been yearned for by the Korean people for centuries. Unendowed with significant natural resources, the Korean people once accepted poverty as their fate. But as a result of hard work for the past decade or so, the Republic of Korea is a model of growth and income distribution in the developing world. Of course, I know full well that pockets of dire poverty remain in this country.

It may be true that all citizens cannot enjoy the same high standard of living in any society: nor may it necessarily be desirable to enforce such a uniform standard of living. But there should be no citizen in this country who must worry about the basic requirements for civilized life. Everyone must work diligently and cooperatively if we are to banish the gloom of poverty that still darkens our society. Entrepreneurs should abide by ethical business standards. Workers, farmers and consumers should discharge the duties and responsibilities the times demand.

The government will give top priority to policies designed to abolish the poverty still plaguing some segments of society and meet the basic needs of all. But policies not understood and supported by the people are mere paper exercises. Therefore, I ask for the active cooperation of all citizens with these policies.

Third, to prevent the recurrence of political repression and abuses of power, I will clearly demonstrate that affairs of state will be conducted according to law and I will lead the government according to law. The key to freedom from political repression and abuses of power is faithful compliance with the constitution and the other laws of this land. Revisions of laws to serve specific persons must by all means be rejected. Abuses of power to serve special interest groups must be thoroughly precluded.

I want to emphasize that while the government should set an example of abiding by the laws of the country, it is equally important that all citizens obey them. Violations of the law could create the dangerous situation in which power is placed above the law. The rule of law cannot prevail if individuals violate the laws they do not like, or if citizens feel no pangs of conscience when they do so.

Laws must be observed by all: neither high government officials nor politicians should be exceptions. It is basic to democracy to revise a law, if it is found to be defective, through rational discussion and constructive dialogue.

Fellow citizens,

I am convinced that only by achieving freedom from these three great agonies will we be able to build a modern, industrial democracy. And thus bequeath a legacy that will promote the welfare of all for generations to come.

But the growth and maturity of a nation cannot rest in the hands of a president or a government alone. Presidents will always come and go, but the people will always exist. The government will change, but the nation will remain forever.

The days when an individual or small group of leaders could shape the course of history are gone. A great history can be fashioned only through participation by the entire people. Pan-national participation is also fundamental to ensuring peaceful changes of government, a goal long aspired to by the Korean people. We cannot let an individual or a small group alone bear responsibility for the destiny of our people or our country. New leaders must continually emerge if creative innovation and progress are to be sustained.

I want to make it absolutely clear that as a man who is stern with himself and sincere and honest with others—and as a citizen of the Republic of Korea who desires sustained progress for his country—I will not fail to establish the tradition of peaceful transfer of power, a long-delayed national task.

Fellow citizens,

We seek an open society full of vitality, a liberal democracy in which the dignity, worth and ability of man are treasured, and the freedoms and interests of individuals have the maximum guarantee. We must adjust to and integrate diverse opinions, transforming diversity into inner strength. Putting strife and partisan wrangling aside, we should continue forging the national consensus through reconciliation and discussion. The consensus so formed will drive our broadly dynamic progress along a new historic course. Trying to obstruct, rather than facilitate, the formation of consensus, of idly standing apart from the national endeavor, will never contribute to national progress.

Fellow citizens,

We are taking our first steps into the new era. We have not yet reached our goals: we have only begun to move toward them. All we have done so far is little more than to overcome a national crisis of major proportions. In fact, we must now begin everything anew. Our tasks are many and our goals are lofty and distant. I do not claim that all will be accomplished within the seven years of my new term.

But I recall the saying: "sijagi panida"—well begun is half done. If we make a good solid start, success will be but a matter of time. With conviction and determination, I will devote my energies to setting cornerstones firmly in place for development in the new era. To be honest, I am awed in assuming the highest office in the nation at this critical juncture, for I am aware of the limits of my ability.

But I am greatly encouraged by the maturity, cooperation and determination of the Korean people to shape their future. Your support and encouragement are redoubling my ability and further strengthening my resolve.

Fellow citizens,

Standing on this hallowed and symbolic dais, I firmly renew my pledges: I will be faithful to the mandate of the people, who have so overwhelmingly endorsed me. I will work with devotion for the growth and maturity of this country, which is our home. I will dedicate myself to shaping the new era that I have promised. I will be loyal to the constitution which I proposed and promulgated. As a man whose motto has been honesty, I will be true to my creed.

I am confident the Korean people will cooperate fully in transforming my renewed pledges into reality. When this transpires March 3, 1981 will be recorded forever in history as "the day the construction of a great homeland was begun." Thank you.

18. SPEECH TO THE NATIONAL ASSEMBLY, APRIL 11, 1981

The Honorable Speaker and other distinguished members of the National Assembly, ladies and gentlemen:

On this auspicious occasion, I wish to offer my heartfelt congratulations to all of those who were successful in the National Assembly elections held on March 25.

I also want to express my deep respect and gratitude to the people of Korea for having chosen untainted and competent representatives from all walks of life to form a new legislature in response to the mandate of history to forge a new era.

With the official opening of the 11th National Assembly today, the Fifth Republic has completed its preparations for the progress ahead.

This ends an 18-month period of transition that began on Oct. 26, 1979—a period marked by chaos, aimlessness, self-reflection and the search for a new course. The time has come for us to conclude an ignominious past and dedicate ourselves to creation and construction.

Honorable Assemblymen,

Our bitter past experiences have driven home the unfortunate results of wrongful politics. We have all learned a costly lesson about the great and awesome responsibility of politicians.

A new chapter of history is unfolding. But the new era will be fruitful only when a new political modus operandi is firmly established. I am convinced, therefore, that our foremost task, as we stand at a turning point in the nation's history, is to build a firm foundation for new political development.

Needless to say, the National Assembly is the rightful center of political activities. Our political development, therefore, hinges on the role to be played by the assembly.

The National Assembly is an institution created to grasp, reflect and transmit the wishes of the people. This is why assemblymen are called the spokesmen of the people, and the National Assembly is termed the hall of the popular will.

By filtering and crystalizing the popular will and adjusting and harmonizing diverse views and interests, the National Assembly should forge a national consensus on each issue. A national consensus so formed should then be reflected in government policy so that government by the will of the people will succeed.

Accordingly, the relationship between the National Assembly and the administration is one of working for common goals, a division of labor in which

Source: Korea Herald, April 12, 1981.

we translate the wishes of the people into policies. The National Assembly is thus neither a challenger nor a protagonist to the administration: it is a partner.

Honorable Assemblymen,

The National Assembly does not exist for your benefit; the National Assembly exists to ensure our society's stability, progress and prosperity.

At this juncture, I feel it is necessary for us to coolly reexamine the past legislature, to determine whether it was truly faithful to its fundamental purpose. So I would like to raise the following questions.

First, did our assemblymen in the past not let themselves become preoccupied with their own narrow interests and political parties, rather than doing their best to reflect the will of the people?

Second, were they not intent on dividing the will of the people, thereby dissipating national energies and abetting strife and confrontation, rather than on achieving national consensus by adjusting and accommodating popular wishes?

Lastly, did they not, in the course of formulating policies, try to assume the role of challenger to the executive branch in the name of checks and balances, rather than seeking to maintain a dialogue and partnership with the administration?

Lamentably, I cannot find anything in their track record to justify a negative reply to those questions.

It was especially regrettable that even in the conduct of routine business, such as the consideration of budgets and proposed laws, opposition party members often resorted to sit-ins, while government party members were not above using "surprise tactics" to pass legislation. Thus, a vicious political circle became endemic, making it virtually impossible to develop politics of dialogue or maintain normal relations between the legislature and the executive branch.

Antiquated Perception

We can think of a number of reasons why the National Assembly came to be operated in such an abnormal manner. We should look to the days of the First Republic, when Constitutional rule was introduced into this country, to find a major reason. In those days we witnessed unreasonable parliamentary politics conducted to keep a certain person in power indefinitely. This gave rise to self-serving politics, as well as the politics of confrontation. The habit persisted, perpetuating the abnormal conduct of Constitutional government.

We can also note the distorted relationships among political parties. There prevailed the antiquated perception that other political parties were the enemies of one's own party, rather than partners to dialogue and compromise.

That perception resulted in rigid, backward relations between the government party and the opposition, fundamentally subverting politics of dialogue and blocking political modernization. Such a state of affairs led to a dangerously pervasive tendency to see things only in black-and-white. That is the third reason our parliamentary government was crippled.

No national or social issue can be neatly divided into categories of absolute evil and absolute good. Few problems are susceptible to simple solutions. But the shameless predominance of thinking in primitive black-and-white terms perpetuated extreme confrontations, frictions and confusions in the political arena. Such was the deplorable political past of this nation.

Honorable Assemblymen,

In the past, we made many mistakes in the conduct of parliamentary politics. But we should not be resigned to thinking we are fated to continue such errors. Depending on our determination, we can use bad precedents and painful experience as an object lesson to correct ourselves fully.

Of course, all political ills are not easily or quickly cured. But no matter how difficult the cure may be, I believe that we can and must achieve it.

This task is for you assemblymen alone. I know full well that the executive branch must also maintain a dedicated and sincere attitude, if that task is to be accomplished. I have repeatedly pledged to do my best to firmly establish a tradition of peaceful change of government, while making democracy take hold.

On this felicitous day, I reaffirm that pledge. I want to emphasize that there will be no reason whatsoever to justify serious mistrust of the administration in the National Assembly, extreme confrontations among political parties or primitive thinking in black-and-white terms.

I want to emphasize also that the administration will not spare any cooperative effort to ensure the normal conduct of parliamentary government. If you work together with the administration with an unswerving confidence in the new political modus operandi, I am sure that our goals will certainly be attained.

Honorable Assemblymen,

The sad fact is that in the past, politics was invariably associated in the minds of the Korean public with chaos, strife, corruption, and irregularities. I believe our task is to transform that deep-seated popular mistrust into a positive view.

The new political pattern should be able to resolve chaos and strife, rather than foment them. It should be able to eradicate corruption and irregularities, rather than encourage them. The time requires us to demonstrate before history and the nation that we can meet the new political standards.

In that sense, I am convinced that the topmost political goals of the new era are stability and reform.

Stability is basic to both national security and economic progress, which can be built only upon political stability. We must not forget the fact that the past political instability bred social and economic instability, eventually weakening national security.

It is impossible to overemphasize the dire need to value and protect stability, especially in light of the fact that the north Korean Communist rulers—the world's most bellicose regime—has a huge army deployed at our very doorstep, while the volatile international situation of the 1980s threatens to explode at any moment.

But we must not commit the foolish error of equating stability with stagnation. To remain stagnant in a constantly changing world would be to retrogress.

Accordingly, we must incessantly strive to reform ourselves in order to sustain creation and progress. The National Assembly is in a position to lead the way for such reforms.

Still waters are bound to stagnate. The iron rule of human history is that corruption and irregularities, and not merely stagnation, come where there is self-reform. Accordingly, reforms must be as constant as a river flows, and pursued with concerted efforts by all. It is wrong to assume that there are forces conducting reform while other forces are subjected to it. What we are after is comprehensive reform carried out in unity by all. It is a mistake to think that we only need to achieve a single reform in the early 1980s. Reform should be a steadfast, ongoing process of self-perfection.

Honorable Assemblymen,

Stability and reform must be our constant creed in this era. The two are equally important. Stability without reform means stagnation and lethargy. Reform without stability means unrest and tension. We want neither lethargy nor tension. What we want is the harmonization of stability and reform. I pray from the bottom of my heart that the National Assembly will be the home of that harmony.

Honorable Assemblymen,

The Korean people place great hopes and expectations in the new political modus operandi for which we are striving. An enormous responsibility is thus put on our shoulders. But I am confident that all our political goals can be attained rather easily, if only we bear in mind that politics is not a profession but a vocation.

A politician is given a mandate to serve the nation during the prescribed term of office. In this regard, it is important to remember that a politician must be a thoroughly public-minded person during the prescribed term, rising above all personal interests.

Our constitutional history is full of instances of politicians behaving not as public-minded persons but as self-serving persons who spent practically all their public tenure on preparing for the next elections.

Constitutional crises, political repression, illegal amassing of wealth, influence-peddling, cunning maneuvers to curry favor with the voters, factional infighting—all these ills stemmed mostly from politicians' obsession with getting reelected. All must realize that the people will never tolerate a National Assembly plagued by a resurgence of such ills.

Accordingly, my conviction is that to achieve clean, honest and fair politics, it will be necessary for all politicians to maintain an attitude in which they will not regret being able to serve only one term, thus internalizing a sense of public service.

Honorable Assemblymen,

A new political era is dawning in response to the longing of the people. The 1980s must be recorded in our constitutional history as the landmark period in which democracy was firmly established. We must all pledge before the people and before the country that a new beginning will be made with unflagging resolve and hope.

All of us must discard narrow personal interests and partisan considerations and stratagems. We must be loyal to the principle of service to the nation and strive to win the unwavering confidence of the people.

Only when we do so will both the Fifth Republic and the 11th National Assembly be recorded forever as great and glorious monuments in the history of our nation.

Thank you.

19. PRESIDENT CHUN ON THE PACIFIC DOCTRINE

Question: It is understood that Your Excellency broached the idea of a Pacific summit conference with Australian Prime Minister Malcolm Fraser when he visited Seoul last May. Could you explain the concept behind this proposal as well as concrete plans to implement it?

President: The sea has played an important role in the evolution of civilization since time immemorial. It will most likely continue to do so in the future. As you know well, the center stage of world affairs first shifted from the Aegean Sea to the Mediterranean and then to the Atlantic. Following World War II, however, the focal point of world events has been moving toward the Pacific. I think the Pacific will emerge as the undisputed center stage of world affairs following the 1980s.

As is well known, the Pacific-basin region is laden with various impediments to its development into a single cooperative community. These include the vastness of the area, ethnic and cultural diversity, and different degrees of economic development.

Such obstacles, however, are now being resolved one after another, thanks to the advancement of transportation and communications and increasing exchanges of various forms among the nations in the region. It is true that these impediments seemed in the past to be insurmountable barriers. But the barriers are rapidly diminishing in height, and I believe they will be gone altogether in the not so very distant future.

If we can say that the Atlantic age represented in the main the stage of civilization at which ships played the key role, it may be said that aircraft symbolize the Pacific age. In this sense, I am convinced that the time has come for Pacific-basin nations to devote concerted efforts to the creation of a great Pacific era in which peace and prosperity will prevail throughout the region. I wish to take this opportunity to discuss in some detail my thinking about a Pacific summit meeting.

First, I believe that the most expeditious way to triumph over various constraints, obstacles and challenges attendant upon the evolution of a Pacific era will be through an institutionalized, periodic summit conference of Pacific-basin nations to discuss matters of mutual interest and plans for cooperation. It is beyond question that summit diplomacy is the most effective way to resolve the most difficult and urgent international issues.

Source: President Chun Doo Hwan Meets the Chong Wa Dae Press Corps at Chinhae, Seoul: Korean Overseas Information Service, July 31, 1982.

Second, I hope that the doors of the proposed consultative body will in principle be open to all countries in the regions.

Third, relations among the nations in the region ought to be guided by the principles of mutual respect for sovereignty and independence, or reciprocity and equality, and of non-interference in domestic affairs. Hegemony by any specific nation or nations must not be tolerated. It is also my belief that the proposed body must not be politicized nor turned into a bloc.

Fourth, the basic agenda of the body should cover the questions of multi-faceted development of the limitless potential for progress in the region, expansion of trade within the region, strengthening of economic and technical cooperation, manpower development, enlargement and improvement of transportation and communications networks, and promotion of educational and cultural exchanges.

Fifth, I believe that through broader and closer cooperation between the developed and developing nations in the region and among the developing nations themselves, the proposed Pacific community will be able to serve as a model for resolving the so-called North-South question.

To bring the Pacific summit idea into reality, it will be necessary to obtain the agreement of the various countries in the region. I plan to intensify diplomatic efforts to win support and concurrence of other Pacific-basin nations by taking advantage of the ties of friendship and understanding with the leaders of the five members of the Association of Southeast Asian Nations (ASEAN) cemented through my visits with them last year.

U.S.-ROK RELATIONS

20. U.S.-ROK MUTUAL DEFENSE TREATY, OCTOBER 1, 1953

Signed at Washington October 1, 1953; Ratification advised by the Senate of the United States of America, with an understanding, January 26, 1941; Ratified by the President of the United States of America, subject to the said understanding, February 5, 1954; Ratified by the Republic of Korea, January 29, 1954; Ratifications exchanged in Washington, November 17, 1954. Proclaimed by the President of the United States of America, December 1, 1954; Entered into force November 17, 1954.

The Parties to this Treaty,

Reaffirming their desire to live in peace with all peoples and all governments, and desiring to strengthen the fabric of peace in the Pacific area,

Desiring to declare publicly and formally their common determination to defend themselves against external armed attack so that no potential aggressor could be under the illusion that either of them stands alone in the Pacific area,

Desiring further to strengthen their efforts for collective defense for the preservation of peace and security pending the development of a more comprehensive and effective system of regional security in the Pacific area,

Have agreed as follows:

ARTICLE I

The Parties undertake to settle any international disputes in which they may be involved by peaceful means in such a manner that international peace and security and justice are not endangered and to refrain in their international relations from the threat or use of force in any manner inconsistent with the Purposes of the United Nations, or obligations assumed by any Party toward the United Nations.

Source: U.S. Defense and Mutual Security Commitments in the Pacific Area, USIS Tokyo, October 1969.

ARTICLE II

The Parties will consult together whenever, in the opinion of either of them, the political independence or security of either of the Parties is threatened by external armed attack. Separately and jointly, by self help and mutual aid, the Parties will maintain and develop appropriate means to deter armed attack and will take suitable measures in consultation and agreement to implement this Treaty and to further its purposes.

ARTICLE III

Each Party recognizes that an armed attack in the Pacific area on either of the Parties in territories now under their respective administrative control, or hereafter recognized by one of the Parties as lawfully brought under the administrative control of the other, would be dangerous to its own peace and safety and declared that it would act to meet the common danger in accordance with its constitutional process.

ARTICLE IV

The Republic of Korea grants, and the United States of America accepts, the right to dispose United States land, air and sea forces in and about the territory of the Republic of Korea as determined by mutual agreement.

ARTICLE V

This Treaty shall be ratified by the United States of America and the Republic of Korea in accordance with their respective constitutional processes and will come into force when instruments of ratification thereof have been exchanged by them at Washington.

ARTICLE VI

This Treaty shall remain in force indefinitely. Either Party may terminate it one year after notice has been given to the other Party.

21. CARTER–PARK JOINT COMMUNIQUE, JULY 1, 1979

1. At the invitation of President Park Chung Hee, President of the United States of America and Mrs. Jimmy Carter made a state visit to the Republic of Korea from June 29 to July 1, 1979. In addition to consultations with President Park and other senior officials, and meetings with other prominent Korean leaders in Seoul, President Carter visited field installations of both the United States and Korean armed forces.

2. The two Presidents met at the Blue House on June 30 and July 1, 1979 to review Korea-United States relations and a variety of subjects of vital mutual interest in an atmosphere of cordial respect and confidence. Among those present at these meetings were Prime Minister Choi Kyu Hah, Minister of Foreign Affairs Park Tong Jin, Minister of National Defense Ro Jay Hyun, Presidential Secretary-General Kim Kae Won, and Ambassador Kim Yong Shik from the Korean side, and Secretary of State Cyrus R. Vance, Secretary of Defense Harold Brown, National Security Advisor Zbigniew Brzezinski, Assistant Secretary of State Richard Holbrooke and Ambassador William H. Gleysteen from the United States side.

3. President Carter outlined the policies of his Government to seek peace and the reduction of tensions around the world, including his efforts to promote a lasting peace in the Middle East and to reach agreement with the Soviet Union on limitation of strategic weapons. President Park endorsed these peace efforts and emphasized his view that the United States should continue to demonstrate its firm leadership wherever challenges to peace occurred.

4. The two Presidents reviewed the events which have significantly altered the recent political face of Asia. Among these were the normalization of Sino-American relations and the signing of the Peace and Friendship Treaty between Tokyo and Beijing. They noted that armed conflicts in Southeast Asia and the Indochina refugee problem are creating major difficulties affecting the entire region, and agreed that there is a need to prevent the extension of these conflicts to other countries. President Carter reaffirmed that the United States as a Pacific power is vitally engaged in Asia and the Pacific and will continue its best efforts to ensure the peace and security of the region.

5. On the Indochina refugee problem, President Carter outlined the discussions at the Tokyo Summit and steps being taken by the United States and other countries to deal with the situation. He stressed the need for all nations to make

Source: Korean Overseas Information Service, Seoul, July 1, 1979.

the maximum effort possible, whether by resettlement, financial contributions, or temporary shelter. President Park, noting the serious situation both in terms of individual human suffering and destabilizing impact on the directly affected nations in Southeast Asia, stated that the Government of the Republic of Korea would make an additional grant of a considerable sum to the United Nations High Commission for Refugees.

6. President Carter, referring to the basic relations between the United States and the Republic of Korea, noted the existence of strong bonds of friendship and cooperation and assured President Park that the United States will continue to support the efforts of the Government of the Republic of Korea to maintain peace and stability in Korea and sustain economic and social development. President Carter stressed the solidarity that exists between the United States and the Republic of Korea as traditional allies.

7. The two Presidents reaffirmed the importance which the United States and Korea attach to the reciprocal commitments contained in the Republic of Korea-United States Mutual Defense Treaty of 1954. They also agreed that the continued security of the Republic of Korea is pivotal to the preservation of peace and stability in the Northeast Asian region. President Park reviewed the security situation on the peninsula and the continuing threat to peace posed by the North Korean military build-up. The two Presidents agreed that ROK-US cooperation in maintaining a high degree of strength and combat readiness was an important contribution to peace and stability. They noted that the activation last November of the ROK-US Combined Forces Command had enhanced the effectiveness of the joint defense cooperation between military authorities of the two countries. President Carter reiterated the firm commitment of the United States to render prompt and effective assistance to repel armed attack against the Republic of Korea in accordance with the Mutual Defense Treaty, and affirmed that the United States nuclear umbrella provided additional security for the area.

8. President Carter expressed his appreciation for the full consultations between the two Presidents and their Defense Ministers on security issues and said that he would be consulting with United States congressional leaders on his return in the light of these detailed discussions. President Carter reaffirmed the deep interest of the United States in preventing any destabilization of the peninsula or region and assured President Park in connection with the question of further withdrawal of American ground combat forces from Korea that the United States will continue to maintain an American military presence in the Republic of Korea to ensure peace and security.

9. President Park reviewed the extensive and continuing efforts of the Republic of Korea to modernize and enhance its self-reliant defense capabilities and the progress achieved in the first five-year Force Improvement Plan which is nearing completion. President Carter expressed United States agreement with the objectives of the force improvement program and reaffirmed the readiness of the United States to continue to support the successful implementation of the

program. President Carter assured President Park that the United States will continue to make available for sale to Korea appropriate weapons systems and defense industry technology necessary for enhancing Korea's ability to deter or defeat aggression and for the development of appropriate defense industries in the Republic of Korea.

10. The two Presidents agreed on the priority need to continue the search for means to reduce tensions on the Korean peninsula. President Park explained the recent efforts of the Republic of Korea Government, beginning with his initiative of January 19, 1979, to resume productive dialogue with North Korean authorities. President Carter assured President Park of United States support for these efforts and expressed the hope that meetings between the responsible authorities of the South and the North of Korea would become possible.

11. In view of the importance of this issue for peace and stability on the Korean peninsula and in the region, and as a testament to the personal commitment of the two Presidents to seek honorable means to promote dialogue and reduce tensions, President Park and President Carter have decided jointly to propose the convening of a meeting of senior official representatives of the South and the North of Korea and the United States to seek means to promote dialogue and reduce tensions in the area. In order to promote this effort and to prepare for the meeting which it is hoped can be arranged, the two Presidents have directed the Foreign Minister and the Secretary of State to communicate jointly with the Foreign Minister of North Korea in this regard in an appropriate manner.

12. The two Presidents agreed that any arrangement that would reduce tension and establish lasting peace leading ultimately to the peaceful unification of the Korean people should result from dialogue between the two responsible authorities of both the South and the North of Korea. President Park noted the consistency with which the Republic of Korea has pursued efforts at dialogue and the reduction of tensions as exemplified in the policies which he announced on June 23, 1973.

13. President Carter stated that if and when North Korea's principal allies are prepared to expand relationships with the Republic of Korea, the United States is prepared to take similar steps with North Korea. President Carter also noted that unilateral steps toward North Korea which are not reciprocated toward the Republic of Korea by North Korea's principal allies do not improve stability or promote peace in the area.

14. The two Presidents shared the view that the admission of both the South and the North of Korea to the United Nations as an interim measure pending their eventual unification would provide authorities of both Korean parties with broader opportunities for dialogue aimed at the resolution of their differences.

15. The two Presidents noted the importance to all nations of respect for internationally recognized human rights. President Carter expressed the hope that the process of political growth in the Republic of Korea would continue commensurate with the economic and social growth of the Korean nation. In this connection,

President Park explained his view on this matter together with the current unique circumstances confronting the Republic of Korea.

16. President Carter expressed to President Park his great admiration for Korea's remarkable record of achievement in sustained economic development over the past fifteen years under his leadership in the face of various obstacles and adverse conditions, thus offering a model and an inspiration for other countries as an example of economic growth and equity. President Park acknowledged with appreciation the United States' contribution to Korea's development in the economic, scientific, and technological areas, and affirmed his intention to continue to give high priority to economic and social goals. The two Presidents shared the view that possible cooperative efforts between the two Governments should be explored to enhance assistance to third countries.

17. President Park and President Carter also reviewed the current international economic situation, and President Carter reported on the discussions at the Seven-Nation Economic Summit just completed in Tokyo. President Park expressed concern about the world energy problem in particular and the two Presidents shared the view that there is an urgent need for concerted international efforts to arrive at a reasonable solution to the problem.

18. The two Presidents expressed satisfaction at the rapid expansion in scope of the economic relations between the Republic of Korea and the United States, and confidence that this mutually beneficial trend will continue. They noted the advantages which accrue to the people of both nations when the freest possible system of trade exists, and they pledged their mutual efforts to promote and preserve an open world trading system. President Carter noted the commendably progressive import-liberalization and other measures that the Government of the Republic of Korea had recently taken with a view to developing a more balanced trade with the United States. These actions and the recent buying mission to the United States will help promote export of American products to Korea. President Park expressed his hope that the United States would continue its efforts to promote, in the MTN and elsewhere, a freer trading system, and to preserve fair access to the United States market for Korean goods. The two Presidents agreed that further efforts to expand trade and economic cooperation between their two countries will be highly beneficial to their respective peoples.

19. Noting that their meeting had deepened understanding and cooperation on many matters of mutual interest, the two Presidents recognized that, at a time when the Republic of Korea and the United States have entered into a new era of mature partnership based on mutual respect and confidence, there remains need for further promotion of mutual understanding and exchanges between the two peoples. As evidence of their joint desire to deepen the contact and understanding between the two nations, the two Presidents agreed that cultural and educational exchanges should be expanded. The two Governments agreed to enhance these exchanges by supporting the activities of organizations such as the Korean-American Educational Commission and to establish a Korean-American Cultural Exchange Committee to be funded jointly by the two Governments.

The Committee would be designed to stimulate activities in both countries aimed at furthering mutual understanding and to endorse mutually agreed programs of this nature. Details will be worked out through diplomatic channels.

20. President and Mrs. Carter, on behalf of themselves and all the members of their party, expressed their deepest thanks to President Park and the people of the Republic of Korea for the warmth of their reception and the courtesies extended to them during the visit.

21. President Carter cordially invited President Park to visit the United States of America and President Park accepted the invitation with pleasure. They agreed that the visit would take place at a time of mutual convenience. Both Presidents expressed their desire to maintain close personal contact in order to preserve and further cultivate close partnership existing between their two countries.

22. REAGAN–CHUN JOINT COMMUNIQUE, FEBRUARY 2, 1981

1. At the invitation of President Ronald W. Reagan, the President of the Republic of Korea and Mrs. Chun Doo Hwan made an official visit to Washington, D.C. from February 1 to 3, 1981.

2. The two Presidents met at the White House on February 2 to exchange views on the current international situation and to discuss matters of mutual interest in an atmosphere of friendship and cordial respect. Among those present at the meeting were Vice President Bush, Secretary of State Alexander Haig, Secretary of Defense Caspar Weinberger, Counsellor to the President Edwin Meese III, Chief of Staff James Baker III, Assistant to the President for National Security Affairs Richard Allen, and Ambassador William Gleysteen from the American side; and Deputy Prime Minister Shin Byong Hyun, Foreign Minister Lho Shin Yong, Minister of National Defense Choo Yong Bock, Ambassador Kim Yong Shik, and Secretary General to the President Kim Kyong Won from the Korean side.

3. The two Presidents reviewed the world situation and reaffirmed the critical importance of maintaining peace on the Korean peninsula and in Northeast Asia. President Reagan and President Chun pledged to uphold the mutual obligations embodied in the United States-Korea Mutual Defense Treaty of 1954. President Reagan affirmed that the United States, as a Pacific Power, will seek to ensure the peace and security of the region. President Chun expressed his full support for United States policies directed toward these ends and emphasized his view that the United States should continue to exercise firm leadership in world affairs.

4. President Reagan and President Chun reviewed the security situation on the Korean peninsula and the continuing threats to peace in the area. President Reagan assured President Chun that the United States has no plans to withdraw U.S. ground combat forces from the Korean peninsula. The two Presidents pledged to seek to strengthen US-Korean cooperation in deterring and defending against aggression as an indispensable contribution to peace and stability in Northeast Asia.

5. President Chun outlined the continuing efforts of the Republic of Korea to enhance its self-reliant defense capabilities through the modernization of its armed forces. President Reagan commended the Republic of Korea for its significant continuing efforts and confirmed that the United States will make available

---

Source: White House release, February 2, 1981.

for sale appropriate weapons systems and defense industry technology necessary for enhancing Korea's capabilities to deter aggression.

6. President Chun was assured of United States support for the efforts of the Republic of Korea to resume a constructive dialogue with North Korea in order to ease tensions and build the framework for peaceful reunification of the peninsula. President Reagan commended President Chun for the far-reaching proposal made on January 12, 1981 calling for an exchange of visits by the Presidents of the South and the North of Korea. President Reagan reaffirmed that the Republic of Korea must be a full participant in any United States negotiation with North Korea. The two Presidents shared the view that any unilateral steps toward North Korea which are not reciprocated toward South Korea by North Korea's principal allies would not be conducive to promoting stability or peace in the area.

7. Noting the strong ties of traditional friendship, alliance, and cooperation which have existed between the United States of America and the Republic of Korea, the two Presidents announced that they would resume immediately the full range of consultations between the two governments.

- US–ROK Security Consultative Meetings will be resumed promptly at a mutually convenient time later this spring.
- Annual U.S.-Korean Economic Consultations covering the entire range of our economic relations will resume. The Under Secretary of State for Economic Affairs will lead a U.S. delegation to Korea to initiate these consultations before mid-year.
- Annual U.S.-Korea policy planning talks will be resumed at a mutually convenient time this year.

8. President Reagan and President Chun expressed their satisfaction at the continuing expansion in the scope of economic relations between the two countries, and agreed to seek to foster a freer international trading system.

9. Presidents Reagan and Chun noted with satisfaction that mutually profitable U.S.-Korea trade had grown dramatically from $531 million in 1970 to $10 billion in 1980, and that the Republic of Korea is now the United States' twelfth largest trading partner. President Reagan emphasized in particular the importance of Korea as the fifth largest market for American agricultural exports. President Chun welcomed the positive response of the United States in meeting Korea's special needs this year for rice imports.

10. The two Presidents reaffirmed the close cooperation of the two countries on energy issues. The United States will seek to assist Korea to obtain energy supplies in the event of an emergency affecting our mutual security interests. Korea will explore long term arrangements for importing American coal. President Reagan promised that the United States would remain a reliable supplier of nuclear fuel, generation equipment and power technology.

11. The two Presidents recognized that there remains a need for further promotion of mutual understanding and exchanges between the two peoples both through private and public channels, and they agreed to an early activation of the Korean-American Cultural Exchange Committee to be funded jointly by the two Governments.

12. President Reagan expressed special appreciation for the significant contribution to the Smithsonian Institution which President Chun presented on behalf of the Korean people for the construction of a new Museum of Eastern Art on the Mall in Washington. This museum will further enhance inter-cultural understanding and appreciation between the people of America and the peoples of Asia.

13. Pledging their mutual efforts to expand international cooperation throughout the Pacific Basin, the two Presidents expressed their intent to maintain close communication with each other and with other friends and allies in Asia. President Chun invited President Reagan to visit the Republic of Korea at a time of his convenience, and President Reagan accepted the invitation with pleasure.

14. President and Mrs. Chun, on behalf of themselves and the members of their party, expressed their deep appreciation to President and Mrs. Reagan and also to the people of the United States for the warmth of their friendly reception and the many courtesies extended to them both during the official visit to Washington and during their visits to other cities during their trip to the United States.

23. U.S.-ROK DEFENSE MINISTERS' JOINT COMMUNIQUE, APRIL 30, 1981

The 13th Annual Security Consultative Meeting between the Republic of Korea and the United States was held in San Francisco, Calif., on April 29 and 30, 1981.

Minister of National Defense Choo Young-bock and Secretary of Defense Caspar Weinberger led their respective delegations, which included Gen. Lew Byong-hion and Gen. David C. Jones, the chairmen of the joint chiefs of staff of both countries and other senior foreign affairs and defense officials.

The two delegations reviewed the security situation in Asia and the Pacific area with particular emphasis on matters affecting the Korean peninsula.

In particular, they agreed that the continuing military build-up of north Korea posed a serious threat to the security of the Republic of Korea.

The two sides reaffirmed the letter and spirit of the Feb. 2, 1981 meeting between President Chun Doo Hwan and President Ronald Reagan. They agreed that the security of the Republic of Korea is pivotal to the peace and stability of Northeast Asia and, in turn, vital to the security of the United States.

Secretary Weinberger confirmed that the United States intends to remain a Pacific power and reiterated the firm commitment of the United States to render prompt and effective assistance to repel armed invasion against the Republic of Korea—which represents a common danger—in accordance with the Mutual Defense Treaty of 1954. He also reconfirmed that the United States nuclear umbrella will continue to provide additional security to the Republic of Korea.

The two delegations welcomed President Reagan's assurance in February 1981 that the United States had no plans to withdraw U.S. ground combat forces from the Republic of Korea and agreed that it not only provides tangible evidence of the United States' firm resolve to help defend the Republic of Korea, but will make a significant contribution to the peace and stability of Northeast Asia.

Minister Choo explained in detail the progress of the Republic of Korea's force improvement program. Secretary Weinberger gave his assurance that the United States, subject to consultation with and the approval of the Congress, will continue to provide a wide range of support, including appropriate sophisticated technology, the sale of equipment, and improved FMS credits for the enhancement of the defense of the Republic of Korea.

Source: Korea Herald, May 1, 1981.

In this regard, Minister Choo and Secretary Weinberger expressed their satisfaction with the ROK–U.S. cooperation to date in the development of Korea's defense industry and Secretary Weinberger assured Minister Choo that the United States would continue such broad cooperation in a positive manner.

Secretary Weinberger welcomed Minister Choo's proposal for the use of Korean facilities for the maintenance of U.S. equipment. It was agreed that the proposal would be studied jointly.

Minister Choo and Secretary Weinberger expressed satisfaction with the state of defense cooperation and renewed their pledge to exert their efforts toward the further enhancement of combined ROK–U.S. defense capabilities and the Combined Forces Command.

Secretary Weinberger assured Minister Choo that the United States would continue to modernize the U.S. forces in Korea and in this regard noted ongoing efforts to upgrade the Second Infantry Division, the deployment of A10s and the prospective deployment of F16s to bases in Korea.

The two sides agreed on the need for improving early warning capabilities, for broadening the scope of information exchange, and for improving the structure of the Combined Forces Command.

Minister Choo and Secretary Weinberger shared the view that joint ROK–U.S. military exercises had contributed significantly to the combat readiness of U.S. and ROK forces and served significantly to deter aggression, and agreed to continue such exercises for further improvement.

Minister Choo and Secretary Weinberger agreed to continue to support jointly the supply and stockpile of war reserve material including POL resupply with a view to maintaining and enhancing combat readiness in the event of a contingency on the Korean peninsula.

Minister Choo and Secretary Weinberger agreed to continue the development of the current Wartime Resupply Requirements Study.

Minister Choo and Secretary Weinberger agreed that lasting peace of the Korean peninsula could only be achieved through a reduction of tension and through a dialogue between the responsible authorities of the Republic of Korea and north Korea. They expressed their full support for the Jan. 12, 1981 proposal of President Chun Doo Hwan for an exchange of visits between the highest authorities of the Republic of Korea and north Korea.

Minister Choo and Secretary Weinberger reconfirmed the continuing impor- of the effective functioning of the peacekeeping machinery of the U.N. Command to enforce the Armistice agreement.

Both sides reaffirmed the importance of the annual Security Consultative Meeting and agreed to hold the next meeting in 1982 in the Republic of Korea.

Minister Choo expressed the sincere appreciation of the Korean delegation for the courtesy and hospitality of the government of the United States and for the excellent arrangements which led to a productive and successful meeting.

NORTH KOREA

24. SOVIET-NORTH KOREAN TREATY OF ALLIANCE, JULY 6, 1961

The Presidium of the USSR Supreme Soviet and the Presidium of the DPRK Supreme People's Assembly, striving to develop and strengthen the friendly relations between the Soviet Union and the DPRK, relations based on principles of socialist internationalism; wishing to contribute to the maintenance and consolidation of peace and security in the Far East and throughout the whole world in accordance with the aims and principles of the United Nations; fully determined to render assistance and support to each other in case of an armed attack by some state or a coalition of states on one of the contracting parties; certain that the strengthening of friendship, neighborliness, and cooperation between the Soviet Union and the DPRK meets the vital interests of the peoples of both states and will in the best way help their further economic and cultural development, have resolved to conclude this treaty, and have appointed as their plenipotentiaries:

The Presidium of the USSR Supreme Soviet—Nikita Sergeyevich Khrushchev, chairman of the USSR Council of Ministers;

The Presidium of the DPRK Supreme People's Assembly—Kim Il-song, chairman of the DPRK Council of Ministers.

Both plenipotentiaries, after exchanging their credentials, which were found to be in due form and full order, agreed on the following:

Article 1—The contracting parties declare that they will continue to take actions aimed at insuring peace and security in the Far East and throughout the world, and will make their contribution to the cause of the accomplishment of these lofty tasks.

In case one of the contracting parties becomes the object of an armed attack by some state or a coalition of states and thus finds itself in a state of war, the other contracting party will immediately render it military and other assistance with all means at its disposal.

Source: Tass, July 6, 1961.

Article 2—Each of the contracting parties undertakes to conclude no alliance or participate in no coalitions or actions or measures directed against the other contracting party.

Article 3—The contracting parties will consult each other on all important international issues affecting the interests of both states, being guided by an effort to contribute to the consolidation of peace and general security.

Article 4—Both contracting parties undertake, in the spirit of friendship and cooperation in accordance with the principles of equality and mutual respect for state sovereignty, territorial integrity, and noninterference in each other's internal affairs, to develop and strengthen economic and cultural contacts between the USSR and the DPRK, to render each other all possible assistance, and carry out necessary cooperation in the economic and cultural fields.

Article 5—Both contracting parties maintain that the unification of Korea must be carried out on a peaceful and democratic basis and that such settlement is in line both with the national interests of the Korean people and the cause of maintaining peace in the Far East.

Article 6—The treaty goes into force on the day of the exchange of the instruments of ratification, which will take place in Pyongyang. The treaty remains in force for 10 years. If one of the contracting parties does not declare one year before the expiration of this term its desire to denounce the treaty, the treaty will continue in force for the next 5 years and will be prolonged in accordance with this rule.

Done in Moscow 6 July 1961 in two copies, each in the Russian and Korean languages, with both texts equally valid.

Signed: For the Presidium of the USSR Supreme Soviet, N. S. Khrushchev; for the Presidium of the DPRK Supreme People's Assembly, Kim Il-song.

25. CHINESE-NORTH KOREAN TREATY OF ALLIANCE, JULY 11, 1961

The Chairman of the People's Republic of China and the Presidium of the Supreme People's Assembly of the Democratic People's Republic of Korea, determined, in accordance with Marxism-Leninism and the principle of proletarian internationalism and on the basis of mutual respect for State Sovereignty and territorial integrity, mutual non-aggression non-interference in each other's internal affairs, equality and mutual benefit, and mutual assistance and support, to make every effort to further strengthen and develop the fraternal relations of friendship, cooperation and mutual assistance between the People's Republic of China and the Democratic People's Republic of Korea, to jointly guard the security of the two peoples, and to safeguard and consolidate the peace of Asia and the world, and deeply convinced that the development and strengthening of the relations of friendship, cooperation and mutual assistance between the two countries accord not only with the fundamental interests of the two peoples but also with the interests of the peoples all over the world, have decided for this purpose to conclude the present treaty and appointed as their respective plenipotentiaries:

The Chairman of the People's Republic of China: Chou En-lai, Premier of the State Council of the People's Republic of China,

The Presidium of the Supreme People's Assembly of the Democratic People's Republic of Korea: Kim Il Sung, Premier of the Cabinet of the Democratic People's Republic of Korea,

Who, have examined each other's full powers and found them in good and due form, have agreed upon the following:

Article One

The contracting parties will continue to make every effort to safeguard the peace of Asia and the world and the security of all peoples.

Article Two

The contracting parties undertake jointly to adopt all measures to prevent aggression against either of the contracting parties of any state. In the event of

---

Source: New China News Agency, July 11, 1961.

one of the contracting parties being subjected to the armed attack by any state or several states jointly and thus being involved in a state of war, the other contracting party shall immediately render military and other assistance by all means at its disposal.

Article Three

Neither contracting party shall conclude any alliance directed against the other contracting party or take part in any bloc or in any action or measure directed against the other contracting party.

Article Four

The contracting parties will continue to consult with each other on all important international questions of common interests to the two countries.

Article Five

The contracting parties, on the principles of mutual respect for sovereignty, non-interference in each other's internal affairs, equality and mutual benefit and in the spirit of friendly cooperation, will continue to render each other every possible economic and technical aid in the cause of socialist construction of the two countries and will continue to consolidate and develop economic, cultural, and scientific and technical cooperation between the two countries.

Article Six

The contracting parties hold that the unification of Korea must be realized along peaceful and democratic lines and that such a solution accords exactly with the national interests of the Korean people and the aim of preserving peace in the Far East.

Article Seven

The present treaty is subject to ratification and shall come into force on the day of exchange of instruments of ratification, which will take place in Pyongyang.

The present treaty will remain in force until the contracting parties agree on its amendment or termination.

Done in duplicate in Peking on the 11th day of July, 1961, in the Chinese and Korean languages, both texts being equally authentic.

Plenipotentiary of the People's Republic of China	Plenipotentiary of the Democratic People's Republic of Korea
(signed) Chou En-lai	(signed) Kim Il Sung

26. KIM IL SONG ON UNIFICATION, OCTOBER 10, 1980

Comrades, it is the most important revolutionary task of our party to win the cause of national reunification, the greatest desire of the entire Korean people.

During the period under review our party, conscious of its important mission entrusted by the country and the nation and firmly determined to reunify the country in our generation, put forward an absolutely correct line and policy on reunifying the country and strove for their implementation.

Reflecting the fundamental stand our party had invariably maintained on the question of national reunification and the requirements of the fast-changing situation at home and abroad at the beginning of the 1970s, we advanced the three principles of independence, peaceful reunification and great national unity as the basic programme of national reunification.

Our party took the initiative in proposing for meetings and negotiations among representatives of political parties, social organizations and individual persons from the North and the South as a decisive step to open the way to independent and peaceful reunification and made all sincere efforts to bring them about. Thanks to our initiative in making the proposal and to our strenuous efforts, the door which had stood tightly closed between the North and the South for a long time was opened at last and the North-South dialogue was held, which resulted in the publication of the historic North-South joint statement. With the publication of the joint statement, the basic message of which is the three principles of independence, peaceful reunification and great national unity, the three principles of national reunification advanced by our party became the nation's single common programme of reunification jointly confirmed and solemnly proclaimed internally and externally by North and South.

The holding of the dialogue and the publication of the joint statement was a step forward towards national reunification, and after that, the trend to reunification quickly mounted on a nationwide scale. Patriotic youth and students, democrats and all other sections of people in South Korea, to say nothing of the people in the northern half of the republic, rose bravely in the struggle to reunify the country.

Alarmed at the soaring fighting spirit of the entire people in North and South Korea determined to reunify the country independently and peacefully, the U.S. and South Korean authorities came out with the "two Koreas" policy to delay Korea's reunification and perpetuate her division.

Source: Kim Il Song's speech to the Sixth Congress of the Korean Workers Party, October 10, 1980 (in part); Korean Central News Agency, October 10, 1980.

The United States tried in various ways to carry out their policy for "two Koreas" which they had set as their basic strategy towards Korea, and even actively mobilized their allies and followers for the move.

At the instigation of U.S. imperialism, the South Korean authorities became the shock force in implementing the separatist line against their national conscience as Koreans and against the pledge they had given to the nation in the North-South joint statement. In order to suppress the ever-growing trend of the South Korean people to national reunification and to realize their design of national division, they rigged up the fascist "yusin system" by mobilizing armed forces and police, the "Central Intelligence Agency" and other repressive means, and brutally cracked down on the South Korean patriots and democrats who called for national reunification and democratic liberties and rights. The South Korean authorities not only frustrated the North-South dialogue which was under way amidst great expectation and concern of the entire nation, but clamoured for "simultaneous entry into the UN" and "cross recognition" in accordance with the libretto of U.S. imperialism and made frantic efforts to put them into effect.

The separatist moves of the United States and the South Korean authorities and the latter's traitorous acts threw a serious stumbling block in the way of the country's reunification. Therefore, thwarting the separtists' moves to create "two Koreas" and democratizing South Korean society became the central task in the struggle to end the tragedy of division of the territory and the nation and to realize the national liberation of the South Korean people. Thus began the serious confrontation and struggle between the forces of national reunification and the forces of separatism, between the democratic and the fascist forces, and between patriots and traitors. This was a struggle to choose between the reunification of the North and the South into one Korea and their permanent division into "two Koreas," between democracy and fascism, and between the complete national liberation and independence and the relinquishment of half the land as a permanent colony of imperialism.

The South Korean people rose in a patriotic struggle and bravely fought to abolish the fascist "yusin" system of dictatorship, an obstacle to the reunification of the country, and to democratize South Korean society, thereby dealing a heavy blow at the enemies of democracy and national reunification. The gallant struggle of the people which started in October last year and raged in Pusan, Masan, Seoul, Kwangju and many other parts of South Korea brought about the destruction of the notorious traitor and chieftain of the "yusin" dictatorship and gave a serious warning to his surviving minions. In particular, the heroic popular uprising in Kwangju last May when large numbers of people rose as one and fought bravely with arms in their hands, shook the fascist rule of South Korea to its very foundation and sent the U.S. imperialists and the military fascists, their stooges, atremble with anxiety and fear.

In South Korea today a very grave situation is prevailing due to the manoeuvrings of the U.S. imperialists and the military fascist clique, their lackeys.

The military fascists who got hold of power by conspiratorial means after the "October incident" last year, have been making vicious attempts to hinder social democracy and national reunification. They proclaimed an "emergency martial law" throughout South Korea, banning all political activities including those of parties and social organizations and unhesitatingly perpetrating savage repressions even the notorious former dictators had not dared to commit.

Other instructions from the "Korea-U.S. Combined Forces Command," the military fascist blackguards of South Korea called out heavily armed units of the puppet army and indiscriminately arrested and imprisoned and brutally murdered patriotic citizens, youths and students in Kwangju who turned out in defence of their right to live and democracy. And they threw into jail all the prominent democrats and political figures who demanded social democracy and national reunification and brought false charges of "fomenting rebellion," "violating the anti-communist law," and what not against them in their vicious efforts to finish them off. South Korea has now become a living hell, the most gruesome of all scenes in the latter part of the 20th century, where atrocious massacres are carried out openly and the people's freedoms and rights are trampled upon miserably.

As regards the brutality of the despotic repression they are perpetrating, the present military fascists of South Korea put all the fascist dictators of the world into the shade. History does not know yet such hangmen as the South Korean military fascist rulers who massacred thousands of their compatriots by arms at a time and cruelly removed their political opponents.

For 35 long years the United States has been occupying and maintaining harsh colonial rule in South Korea, and egged its dictators on to trample mercilessly on the people's democratic freedoms and rights. The United States that took under its wings the former quisling dictators of South Korea is now again giving active protection to the new military fascist dictator who is following the fascist policy of his predecessor.

All the barbaric acts of the South Korean military fascist elements that stir up the towering indignation of the world public now are committed under the manipulation and aegis of the United States. It is the United States that masterminded the beastly pogrom against the patriotic people who rose in revolt in Kwangju; it is the United States that instigated the cruel suppression of the South Korean democrats; and it is also none other than the United States, the wirepuller, that has rigged up the military fascist dictatorial "government" in South Korea and put a hangman at its head.

Although the U.S. authorities try to play innocent, ostensibly expressing "regret" and "concern" over the South Korean situation, they cannot conceal by any means their secret intention as aggressors and their true colours as fascist executioners. The United States is the culprit who smothers democracy and human rights in South Korea and the wirepuller for the slaughtering of South Korean people. With no artifice the United States can escape the responsibility for the present situation in South Korea where such a heinous fascist dictatorial "government" has been knocked up and shocking bloodshed has been enacted. [sentence as received]

The tragic developments in South Korea and the disasters suffered by its people today immediately represent the distress of the entire Korean nation, and this is precisely the bitter outcome of the partition of the territory and division of the nation. Anyone who is of Korean blood cannot remain a passive onlooker to the unhappy state of affairs today, and cannot but think soberly of the destiny of our nation.

We must do away with the colonial fascist rule of the U.S. imperialists and their stooges in South Korea and reunify the country, and thus end the distress and tragedy of our fellow countrymen and carve out a bright future for our nation.

If reunification does not come quickly and division continues, our nation will remain bisected forever, and the South Korean people will be unable to cast off the yoke of colonial slavery. Failing reunification at the earliest possible date, it will be difficult even to defend the independence and sovereignty of our country.

On the international arena today, antagonism and conflict between great powers scrambling for spheres of influence are aggravated daily. History shows that whenever great powers struggled for expanding their spheres of influence, small nation's interests were harmed and they were victimized. At present, the interests of many nations are entangled with one another and military confrontation between great powers is aggravated with each passing day. If in this situation our country is not reunified but remains divided into North and South, our people may again fall a victim to foreign forces and become colonial slaves. We must not repeat our bitter lot of the past when the destiny of our country and nation was toyed [with] by foreign powers in their interests and our people were forced to live as a homeless race. For this purpose, we must reunify the divided country as soon as possible.

Division is the road to slavery and national ruin; reunification alone will lead us to independence and prosperity. For our nation today nothing is more precious than reunification and there is no more pressing task than reunifying the country. The people in North and South and the entire Korean nation must rise up as one in the struggle for the country's independent, peaceful reunification.

In order to achieve the independent, peaceful reunification it is imperative to eliminate military fascist rule and democratize society in South Korea. As long as democracy is stamped out and harsh military fascist rule is maintained in South Korea as today, there can be no national rapprochement and solidarity nor can the country be reunified by peaceful means. The "anticommunist law," "national security law" and other fascist laws must be abolished and all the apparatuses of tyrannical rule be eliminated there. Meanwhile, all the political parties and social organizations must be legalized and the free political activities of these parties and organizations and individual persons guaranteed; and the democrats and patriotic people who have been unwarrantedly arrested and imprisoned must be released and all the penalties imposed on them must be made null and void. After the elimination of the "yusin system" in South Korea, the military fascist "government" should be replaced by a democratic government which will defend and speak for the will and interests of the broad masses of people.

The country's independent, peaceful reunification requires easing the tensions and removing the danger of war. In our country the massive armed forces of the North and the South stand face to face across the military demarcation line now, and there are tens of thousands of American troops stationed in South Korea. Because of the ceaseless provocations of the U.S. imperialists and South Korean military fascists, the situation in our country is as strained as ever and there is a constant danger of war breaking out at any moment. Today the situation is most tense and acute in Korea of all parts of the world. This is arousing deep concern not only among the Koreans but among the people of our neighbouring countries and the rest of the world.

Our people do not want war; they want to evade a fratricide and reunify the country peacefully at all costs. Eliminating the military confrontation between the North and the South and obviating the danger of war is the prime requisite for the peaceful reunification of the country. As long as the North and the South stand levelling guns at each other and the menace of a fratricidal war is hovering, no contact or dialogue will bear good fruit and bring about genuine concord and unity of the nation.

The question of easing the tensions and removing the danger of war in our country can be solved only by replacing the armistice agreement with a peace agreement. We have already proposed more than once to the United States to hold a dialogue and conclude a peace agreement between Korea and the United States. This proposal of ours is the most reasonable one for the independent and peaceful reunification of Korea and for world peace. It fully agrees with the interests and desire of the American people, too. The United States, however, has not yet accepted our just proposal; it keeps its troops in South Korea and is seriously jeopardizing peace.

We propose once more to the United States to negotiate on the question of replacing the Korean armistice agreement with a peace agreement. How the U.S. authorities respond to our proposal will clearly provide their answer to the question of war or peace. They should reflect seriously on this matter, and accept our just proposal in a sincere and conscientious attitude and withdraw their troops from South Korea as soon as possible, thus meeting the unanimous aspiration and desire of the people the world over including the United States.

For the independent, peaceful reunification of our country it is necessary to check the machination of the United States for "two Koreas" and do away with its interference in the internal affairs of Korea. Today the U.S. machination for "two Koreas" is the main obstacle to our country's independent and peaceful reunification. The U.S. policy of bisecting our homogeneous nation for good by creating "two Koreas" goes against the unanimous aspiration of the Korean people and the trend of the times, and nothing can justify this policy. Further, the policy of interference in the internal affairs of South Korea pursued by the United States which has turned it into a colony and is giving active protection to its military fascists, impedes the democratic development of South Korean society and the reunification of Korea, and it will adversely affect the development of the relations between the Korean and American peoples.

The United States should not pursue the separatist "two Koreas" policy any longer, but work to facilitate Korea's reunification instead of obstructing it. The United States should refrain from backing the military fascists of South Korea and desist from all acts of interference in Korea.

We hold that the country must on all accounts be reunified on the three principles of independence, peaceful reunification and great national unity. The question of Korea's reunification resolves itself into the question of ending foreign domination and interference, winning the complete sovereignty of the Korean nation, removing distrust and antagonism between North and South, and achieving national unity. Our country should be reunified independently by the efforts of our own people, free from any foreign interference, peacefully through North-South contact and dialogue without recourse to arms, and on the principle of great unity of all Korean nationals from the North and the South and abroad as one nation, irrespective of the difference in their ideas and social systems.

Based on the lofty ideas and principles laid down in the July 4 North-South joint statement, and proceeding from our country's actual conditions in which different ideologies and social systems exist in the North and the South, we must find out the shortest and surest way to national reunification and reunify the country by positive efforts.

Our party considers that the most realistic and reasonable way to reunify the country independently, peacefully and on the principle of great national unity is to bring the North and the South together into a confederal state, leaving the ideas and social systems existing in North and South as they are.

For a long time, ever since liberation, different social systems have existed and different ideas are prevailing in the North and the South. If in these circumstances the country is to be reunified through national union, neither side should regard its own ideology and social system as absolute. If any of the North and the South should consider its own ideology and social system absolute or try to force them on the other side, it will inevitably lead to confrontation and conflicts, and this will lead to further aggravation of division. Since the entire people regard national reunification as the supreme task, the difference in ideology and system cannot be an insurmountable barrier to reunification. People with different ideas can live in one country, and different social systems can coexist in a unified country. We will never force our ideas and social system upon South Korea but will subordinate everything to the interests of national union and reunification.

Our party holds that the country should be reunified by founding a confederal republic through the establishment of a unified national government on condition that the North and the South recognize and tolerate each other's ideas and social systems, a government in which the two sides are represented on an equal footing and under which they exercise regional autonomy respectively with equal rights and duties.

It will be reasonable that the unified state of a confederal type form a supreme national confederal assembly with an equal number of representatives from the North and the South and an appropriate number of representatives of overseas nationals and that a confederal standing committee be organized in the aforesaid assembly to guide the regional governments in the North and the South and to administer all affairs of the confederal state.

The supreme national confederal assembly and the confederal standing committee, its permanent organ, should as the unified government of the confederal state discuss and decide on political affairs, national defence problems, foreign affairs and other questions of common concern related to the interests of the country and the nation as a whole, on a fair principle and in accordance with the desire for national unity, collaboration and reunification; push forward the work of uniform development of the country and the nation; and realize unity and collaboration between the North and the South in all spheres. The unified government of the confederal state should respect the social systems, and the wishes of administrative organizations, every party, every group, and every section of people in the North and the South and prevent one side from forcing its will on the other.

Under the leadership of the confederal government the regional governments in the North and the South should follow an independent policy within the limits consistent with the fundamental interests and demands of the whole nation, and strive to narrow down the differences between the North and the South in all spheres and to achieve a uniform development of the country and the nation.

It will be a good idea to call the confederal state Democratic Confederal Republic of Koryo [DCRK], after the name of a unified state that once existed in our country and is well known to the world, and by reflecting the common political aspirations of the North and the South for democracy.

The DCRK should be a neutral nation which does not participate in any political-military alliance or bloc. Since the two parts of the country, North and South, with different ideas and social systems are to be united into a single confederal state, it is necessary and most reasonable in reality that the DCRK should be a neutral state.

The DCRK, as a unified state embracing the whole of the territory and people of our country, should pursue a policy which agrees with the fundamental interests and demands of the entire Korean people.

Our party deems it appropriate that the DCRK should put forward and carry out the following policy: First, the DCRK should adhere to independence in all its state activities and follow an independent policy. Independence is the basic emblem of an independent state; it is the life and soul of the country and the nation. Only when a state exercises sovereignty with firm independence in its activities can it uphold the nation's dignity and honour and ensure the development and prosperity of the country in keeping with the desire of the people. The DCRK should be a fully independent and sovereign state and a non-aligned nation which is not a satellite of any other nation and does not depend on any foreign forces. The DCRK should oppose all forms of foreign interference and dependence on foreign forces, exercise complete sovereignty in its internal and external activities and solve all questions arising in state politics independently to suit the fundamental interests of the Korean nation and the actual conditions of our country.

Second, the DCRK should effect democracy throughout the country and in all spheres of society and promote great national unity. Democracy is a common political idea congenial and acceptable to people with differing thoughts and political views, and is a sacred right due to people from all walks of life as masters of the state and society. The DCRK should fully develop a democratic social and political system which opposes dictatorship and intelligence government and firmly guarantees and defends the liberties and rights of the people.

The confederal state should ensure the freedom of forming political parties and social organizations and their free activities, the freedoms of religious belief, speech, the press, assembly and demonstration, and guarantee the rights of the people in North and South to travel freely across the country and to conduct political, economic and cultural activities freely in any areas.

The confederal government should follow a fair policy which will equally guarantee the interests of the two regions, two systems, different parties, groups, classes and circles in the country without bias to either side. All the policies pursued by the confederal government should proceed from the principle of great national unity and contribute to the uniform development and prosperity of the country through the strengthening of national unity and collaboration.

The confederal government should not question the past records of any organization or individual in the North and the South that works for the development of the unified state, but should join hands with them, and should not allow any form of political reprisal or persecution.

Third, the DCRK should bring about economic cooperation and exchange between North and South and ensure the development of an independent national economy. In the two parts of our country there is a wealth of natural resources for continued exploitation and also the economic foundations that have been built in the past years. If the North and the South develop the natural resources jointly and use the existing economic foundations effectively through cooperation and collaboration when the country is reunified, our national economy will be able to develop at a great pace, and our people will all be able to enjoy as good a life as any other people.

Economic collaboration and exchange between North and South should be realized on the basis of recognizing the different economic systems and diverse economic activities of enterprises in the two parts of the country. The confederal government should recognize and protect state, cooperative and private property in the North and the South as well as personal effects, and refrain from restricting or encroaching upon the property of capitalists and their business activities so long as they help develop the national economy without engaging in monopolist and comprador activities.

The confederal state should see to it that the north and the south jointly develop and exploit mineral, marine and other natural resources, and further the division of labour and trade extensively on the principles of cooperation and mutual accommodation, while properly coordinating the economic activities of all production units and enterprises in keeping with the interests of different classes and circles. It will be advisable that the authorities or enterprises in the North and the South organize and run joint companies, common markets and the like rationally.

The confederal state should develop the economies of the North and the South into an organically interlinked independent national economy through extensive collaboration and exchange between the two parts of the country.

Fourth, the DCRK should realize North-South exchange and cooperation in the spheres of science, culture and education and ensure uniform progress in the country's science and technology and in national culture, arts and education. Our people have time-honoured, resplendent traditions of national culture. Resourceful and talented, our nation has admirably developed science, technology, culture and arts since the olden times. Since liberation, large numbers of competent scientists, technicians, and talented cultural workers and artists have grown up in the North and South of our country. If they pool their efforts and talents through exchange and cooperation, our science and technology, national culture and arts will flourish more resplendently.

The confederal state should ensure that the scientists and technicians in North and South make joint scientific researches and widely exchange their achievements and experiences so as to develop our science and technology quickly.

The confederal state should actively encourage exchange and cooperation between the artists and sportsmen in the North and the South and see to it that the scientists in the two zones jointly discover and take good care of the cultural heritages of our nation and that they study and develop our unique written and spoken language. Thus, our national culture and arts should be brought into full flower and the unique nature of our people as a homogeneous nation should be preserved.

Education is a very important undertaking which decides the fate of the nation. The confederal government should train large numbers of competent technical experts and steadily raise the cultural and intellectual levels of the entire people by developing an educational system of a popular character and giving active state and social support to education work.

Fifth, the DCRK should reopen the suspended traffic and communications between North and South and ensure free utilization of the means of traffic and communications in all parts of the country. Traffic and communications constitute the artery and nervous system of the country. Because the territory has been bisected and traffic and communications cut off, our people cannot see or hear from their families and relatives, though living within easy reach. This is a tragedy. Restoring the broken traffic and communications between North and South is the only way to end the national tragedy and fully realize political, economic and cultural exchange and cooperation.

The confederal state should restore the railways and motor roads linking the North and the South and open ship and plane services to realize free traffic by land, sea and air between the two zones. Further, steps should be taken to open telegraph and telephone services and unrestricted postal exchange between all areas of the North and the South.

The confederal government should see to it that the North and the South use the means of transport and the post and telegraphic facilities in common and, further, gradually go over to their joint operation, so that in the future the traffic and communications of the whole country are unified.

Sixth, the DCRK should see to the stability of livelihood for the entire people including the workers, peasants and other working masses and promote their welfare systematically. The working masses are the masters of the state and society and creators of all material wealth. Guaranteeing a stable life for the working people and steadily enhancing their welfare should be the most important principle of activity for a democratic state serving the people, and this is also a national duty devolving on the unified government.

In all its activities the confederal state should give preference to the work of stabilizing the lives of people of all social strata including the workers, peasants, and other sections of working people and of promoting their welfare. It should provide a decent life to all the people by guaranteeing adequate living conditions for the entire working people in respect of food, clothing and shelter and by raising the living standard of the poor to that of the middle class.

The confederal state should find jobs for all able-bodied people, provide sufficient conditions for work and rest and introduce a wage system, a price policy and an equitable tax system which can ensure a stable livelihood for the working people. Steps should be taken for various enterprises including small and medium ones to carry on productive activity on a normal basis and to guarantee the working people's livelihood and, in particular, the state should give active support to the husbandry of the poor peasants and fishermen, small merchants and handicraftsmen.

The confederal state should pay deep attention to the education of the working people and the promotion of their health and adopt adequate measures to this end, so that all the working people and their families can receive education and medical assistance.

Seventh, the DCRK should remove military confrontation between North and South, organize a combined national army and defend the nation against invasion from outside. Military confrontation between North and South with huge armed forces gives cause for mutual misunderstanding and mistrust, discord and menace to peace.

The confederal state should cut the military strength of both sides to 100,000–150,000 respectively in order to end the military confrontation between North and South and bring the fratricidal strife to a close for good. At the same time, it is imperative to abolish the military demarcation line which comes between the North and the South, dismantle all the military installations in its vicinity, dissolve militia organizations in both parts and forbid military training of civilians.

The confederal state should amalgamate the Korean People's Army and the "national army" of South Korea and form a single combined national army. As a national army of the unified state independent of either side, North or South, the combined national army should perform the duty of national defence under the unified leadership of the confederal government. All the expenses for the up-keep of the combined national army and the defence of the country should be borne in common by the North and the South.

Eighth, the DCRK should defend and protect the national rights and interests of all the overseas Koreans. Today large numbers of our Korean compatriots are living abroad. As their motherland, the DCRK should assume the responsibility and duty of defending and protecting their national rights and interests. The DCRK should make vigorous efforts to enable all the Korean nationals abroad to enjoy their internationally accepted legal rights and liberties, and give them strong support and encouragement in their struggle for democratic national rights. The confederal government should guarantee the rights for all our overseas compatriots to travel freely to their motherland or to return home and live and act freely at any place they please.

Ninth, the DCRK should deal properly with the foreign relations established by the North and the South prior to reunification, and should coordinate the foreign activities of the two regional governments in a unified way.

Only when the foreign relations built up by the North and the South before the achievement of national reunification are handled in the right manner is it possible to adequately ensure both the interests of the whole nation and the interests of the two zones within the framework of the unified state and to enable the confederal state to develop friendly relations with various countries of the world on an equitable footing. Further, in view of the fact that even after reunification the North and South will maintain foreign relations separately with other nations on a limited scale, the confederal government needs to coordinate the foreign activities of the two regional governments properly in a unified way.

The DCRK should repeal all treaties and agreements with other countries detrimental to national amity including military treaties concluded separately by the North and the South prior to reunification. Of the foreign relations formed by the North and the South, those relations including economic relations not inimical to the common interests of the nation should be maintained continuously.

The confederal state should permit the North and the South to cooperate economically with other countries irrespective of the social system. It should leave intact the capital invested by other nations in South Korea prior to the reunification of the country and continue to ensure their concessions.

The DCRK should permit the governments of the two parts of the country to establish bilateral relations with other countries. The confederal state will have to coordinate properly the foreign relations of the North and the South to make it sure for the two regional governments to keep in step with each other in the foreign activities.

Tenth, the DCRK should, as a unified state representing the whole nation, develop friendly relations with all countries of the world and pursue a peaceful foreign policy. The DCRK should be the only representative of the entire Korean nation in foreign relations. The confederal state should represent the entire Korean nation in the United Nations and other international organizations and will have to send a single delegation to all international functions where the whole nation should be represented.

The DCRK should stick to the line of neutrality, follow the policy of non-alignment and develop friendly relations with all nations on the principles of independence, non-interference in internal affairs, equality, mutual benefit and peaceful coexistence. In particular, it should actively develop good neighbourly relations with adjacent countries.

The DCRK should be a peace-loving nation and pursue a peaceful foreign policy. A unified Korea will not threaten aggression against neighbouring countries and any other nations of the world and will not be a party to or cooperate in any international act of aggression. The confederal state should make the Korean Peninsula a permanent peace zone and nuclear-free zone. To this end, it should prohibit the presence of foreign troops and establishment of foreign military bases in our territory and ban the production, introduction and use of nuclear weapons.

The ten-point policy of the DCRK accurately reflects the common aspirations and demands of the entire Korean nation and illumines the road ahead of a unified Korea. The plan for national reunification and the ten-point political programme of the unified state newly proposed by our party this time will win active support and approval of all the Korean people and receive warm welcome from the people of the world.

Our party will strive with might and main to put the new plan for national reunification into effect as soon as possible and satisfy the ardent desire of our 50 million brethren to live happily in a unified homeland.

In order to found a confederal republic and bring about national reunification as proposed by our party, all the Korean nationals in North and South and abroad should fight firmly banded together in a grand national united front under the banner of national reunification, regardless of the difference in ideology, social system, party affiliation and political view.

The road ahead of our party and people striving for the country's independent and peaceful reunification is still beset with many a difficulty and obstacle. But we will pull through them at all costs and finally accomplish the historic cause of national reunification by the united efforts of the whole nation.

When the DCRK is founded and the country is reunified through the unity of the whole nation and cooperation of North and South, our country will make its appearance on the world arena with great dignity and authority as an independent and sovereign state with its 50 million population, brilliant national culture and powerful national economy, and an ever-prosperous peoples paradise will be built in our land of three thousand ri.

SUGGESTED READING

The following suggestions of books on Korea in English are intended to be helpful without of course pretending to be exhaustive.

An excellent introduction to the people and culture of Korea, with emphasis on the premodern period, is Cornelius Osgood, *The Koreans and Their Culture* (Tokyo: Tuttle, 1951). There is a careful, highly critical, study of Japanese rule and its effects: Andrew J. Grajdanzev, *Modern Korea* (New York: John Day, 1944). A prominent U.S. scholar of Korean origin, Chong-Sik Lee, has written a standard study of the Korean political response to Japanese domination in *The Politics of Korean Nationalism* (Berkeley: University of California Press, 1963). George M. McCune, *Korea Today* (Cambridge, Mass.: Harvard University Press, 1950) is a good study of the occupation period by a well-known U.S. authority, now deceased. More specialized, and also useful, is E. Grant Meade, *American Military Government in Korea* (New York: King's Crown Press, 1951). The best book on the Korean War is the excellent one by David Rees, *Korea: The Limited War* (New York: St. Martin's Press, 1964). The massive work of Robert A. Scalapino and Chong-Sik Lee, *Communism in Korea*, 2 vols. (Berkeley: University of California Press, 1972) is the standard study of its subject. A declassified intelligence study, *North Korea: A Case Study in the Techniques of Takeover* (Washington, D.C.: Department of State, 1961) is especially valuable and interesting because it is based largely on information collected in Pyongyang during the brief period in 1950 when it was not under North Korean control—the only case to date of a liberated Communist capital city.

A good brief introduction to contemporary Korea by a qualified U.S. scholar is David Steinberg, *Korea: Nexus of East Asia* (New York: American-Asian Educational Exchange, 1968). There is an excellent official handbook, full of information although of course never critical of the government, on the Republic of Korea: *A Handbook of Korea* (Seoul: Korean Overseas Information Service, 1979).

There is a very valuable book on modern Korean politics: Gregory Henderson, *Korea: The Politics of the Vortex* (Cambridge, Mass.: Harvard University Press, 1968). At one point (p. 191), Henderson expresses a cautiously favorable view of Park Chung Hee's regime, but he later retracted this and became an articulate critic of it and its successors. There is a somewhat more specialized, and unfortunately unpublished, but also very useful work by a highly competent observer, Donald S. Macdonald, *Korea and the Ballot: The International Dimension in Korean Political Development as Seen in Elections* (Ph.D. dissertation, George Washington University, 1977).

Fortunately, there are some good studies of Korean political development in English by Koreans, outstanding among them being Sungjoo Han, *The Failure of Democracy in South Korea* (Berkeley: University of California Press, 1974) on the First and Second Republics; and Se-Jin Kim and Chi-Won Kang, eds., *Korea: A Nation in Transition* (Seoul: Research Center for Peace and Unification, 1978).

On the emergence of the Fifth Republic there is an excellent study by David Rees, *Crisis and Continuity in South Korea* (London: Institute for the Study of Conflict, *Conflict Studies*, no. 128, March 1981).

Of the various comparative studies of North and South Korea and of their relations with one another, many of them by Koreans, two are especially valuable: Hak-Joon Kim, *The Unification Policy of South and North Korea: A Comparative Study* (Seoul: Seoul National University Press, 1977); and Young Hoon Kang and Young Soon Yun, *Politics of Korean Reunification* (Seoul: Research Center for Peace and Unification, 1978).

A useful study of the two Koreas in relation to their external environment, by U.S. authors, is William J. Barnds, ed., *The Two Koreas in East Asian Affairs* (New York: New York University Press, 1976). The military aspects of this question have been addressed, again from a U.S. perspective, in Ralph N. Clough, *Deterrence and Defense in Korea: The Role of U.S. Forces* (Washington, D.C.: Brookings Institution, 1976); Ralph N. Clough et al., *The United States, China, and Arms Control* (Washington, D.C.: Brookings Institution, 1975, chap. 6); and Joseph A. Yager, *Nonproliferation and U.S. Foreign Policy* (Washington, D.C.: Brookings Institution, 1980, chap. 3).

Two polemics by U.S. authors with varying official connections against the government of the Republic of Korea (mainly that of President Park), on human rights and related grounds, are Robert Boettcher, *Gifts of Deceit: Sun Myung Moon, Tongsun Park, and the Korean Scandal* (New York: Holt, Rinehart and Winston, 1980); and

Donald L. Ranard, "Korea, Human Rights and United Foreign Policy," in *Toward a Humanitarian Diplomacy: A Primer for Policy*, ed. Tom J. Farer (New York: New York University Press, 1980). A much more balanced treatment of U.S.-Korean relations is Richard L. Sneider and William Watts, *The United States and Korea: New Directions for the '80s* (Washington, D.C.: Potomac Associates, 1980). An interesting study of U.S. public attitudes toward Korea and the rest of Asia is William Watts, *Americans Look at Asia: A Need for Understanding* (Washington, D.C.: Potomac Associates, 1980).

Korean war, 8, 10; aftereffects, 11;
    postwar U.S. contacts, 18; prison-
    ers, 10
Koreans: discrimination against, in
    Japan, 83; leftist activities, in
    Japan, 83; overseas, 225; physical
    characteristics, 2
Korean Workers Party, 26
Kungchong-dong, 123
Kwangju: political unrest in, 53;
    street violence in, 147; student
    demonstrations in, 146

labor management, 207
labor unions, 227
labor unrest, 52
Lee Bum Suk, 23
Lee Hu Rak, 35
Lee Hui Sung, 50
Lee Ki Boong, 30
Lee Kwang-pyo, 151
Lew Byong-hion, 253
Lho Shin Yong, 250
Liberal party, 28
local self government, 172; election,
    172

MacArthur, Douglas, 8
Manchu dynasty, 3
Manchurian Koreans, 7
martial law, 107; lifting of, 62, 63,
    153, 205, 211; people's coopera-
    tion, 153; political activity ban,
    130; politics of, 58; press censor-
    ship, 130; proclamation of, 130
martial law commander, statement of,
    117
martial law government, in South
    Korea, 52, 53
Marxism–Leninism, 257
maturity, national, 232
medical care, 227
medical insurance, 227
military, political role of, 94
military coup, 31, 32

military employee, 158
military leadership, in North Korea, 27
Ming dynasty, 4
Ministry of National Defense, 107
modernization, 37
Mongolia, 25
Mongols, 4
Moon, Sun Myung, 19
Mun Hong-ku, 127
Mun Ik-hwan, 143, 144
mutual defense treaty, 16
Myon, Chang, 30

Nam Duck Woo, 59
national administration, 206
national army, combined, 269
National Assembly, 62, 190; arrest of
    members, 166; attendance, 167;
    bills, 167, 192; and budget, 167,
    168; declaration of war, 168; disso-
    lution of, 186, 187; duties of, mem-
    bers, 191; elections, 211; extra-
    ordinary sessions, 166, 191; finan-
    cial decisions, 168; inaugural ses-
    sion, 68; internal regulations, 195;
    legislative power, 166; members,
    160, 166, 190; prime minister,
    removal of, 194; proceeding rules,
    195; public confidence, 216; quali-
    fication of, members, 169; removal
    of, members, 169; speaker, 166;
    state affairs, 194; taxation law,
    193; treaties, 194
national bonds, 168
National Budget Bill, 193
national confederal assembly, 265
National Conference for Unification,
    159, 211; chairman, 159; delegates,
    159; election of president, 160
national culture, 208
national defense, 224; citizens' duties,
    182
national referendum, 155, 205, 215;
    and amendments to 1980 constitu-
    tion, 201

national security, 131; council, 189; legislative assembly for, 59; legislative council, 202, 212; special committee for, 131; standing committee, 131; subcommittees, 131
National Security Law, 71
national stability, 153; maintaining, 154
national unity, 204, 223
natural resources: and economy, 199; laws, 172; licenses to exploit, 199; protection of, 173; utilization of, 173, 199
New Democratic Party, 34, 134; confrontation with government, 46; control of, 135; elections, 45
Nixon, Richard, 33
Nixon Doctrine, 17
Nonproliferation Treaty, 41
North Korea, 259-271; access to information, 232; armed forces, 86; attack on South Korea, 10; communism, 25; freedom, 232; military buildup, 27; quality of life, 233; relations with United States, 247; reunification policy, 259-271; Soviet influence, 26; Soviet invasion, 14; Soviet military assistance, 255; Soviet military withdrawal, 26; Soviet occupation, 7, 26; as totalitarian state, 92
North Korean threat, 86-87
North-South joint statement, 259
Northeast Asia, 1, 2; stability, 13
nuclear power, 41

oil prices, 213

Pacific countries, 241; relations among, 242; summit conference of, 88, 241
Pacific doctrine, 241
Paekche, 2
Pak Hung-Chu, 102, 105
Pakistan, 96
Park Chung Hee, 32; assassination of,

[Park Chung Hee]
21, 48; and Carter, joint communique, 245-249; dictatorship, 35; and economic growth, 33; economic policies of, 41; invitation to United States, 249; opposition to, 35
Pak Hung-chu, 103
Park Tong Jin, 245
parliamentary politics, 237
peace, preservation of, 243
peace agreement, 263
People's Alliance, 133; involvement in student disturbances, 138; reorganization of, 137
Persian Gulf crisis, 215
Pohang Iron and Steel Company, 42
political education, 228
political parties: merging of opposition parties, 34; president affiliation, 212; relations among, 237
political system, renovation of, 206
politics: activities, 211; extremism, 206; instability, 222; of reconciliation, 69
population, rural, 40
poverty, 233
power, abuse of, 233
president: authority, 206; candidate eligibility, 184; declaration of martial law, 186; election of, 153, 183, 211; electors, 183, 184; inauguration, 232; oath of, 184; proper use of authority, 206; successor, 184
Presidential Security Force, 121
press censorship, 35
press strike, 141
preventive medicine, 227
price stabilization, 74, 207
prime minister: appointment of, 187; removal of, 169
private enterprises, 173
proletarian internationalism, 257
propaganda material, 140
public housing, 227

public investment, 226; in housing, 227
public officers, corruption of, 207
Pusan, 40; student demonstrations, 142

Reagan–Chun joint communique, 250
Reagan–Suzuki communique, 82
recession, 204
reforestation, 40
reform law, political, 212
repression, political, 233
Republic of Korea, *see* South Korea
reunification, confederal state, 264
revenues, account of, 165
revolution 1960–61, 30
Rhee, Syngman, 6, 28; and National Assembly, 29; politics under, 28; resignation of, 30; South Korea and, 28–30
Ro, Jay Hyun, 245
rural modernization, 207
rural population, industrial development, 40

science and technology, 228
Security Consultative Meeting, 13th Annual, 253
self reliant, defense, 224
Seoul, political disturbances in, 148
Seventh Fleet, modernization program, 81
Shim Jae-Kwon, 143
Shin Byong Hyun, 250
Shin Hyon Hwack, 51
Shufeldt, Robert W., 13
Silla, 2
Singlaub, John K., 21
Sino-American relations, 245
Sino–Japanese War, 3, 5
Sino–Soviet border, 80
social instability, 222
social reform, 208
social security, 182
social transformation, 43

Socialist internationalism, 255
Song Ki-won, 143
South Korea: agriculture in, 40; armed forces, 86; armed forces modernization, 18; Carter's visit, 21; defense expenditures, 18; democratic party, 29; diplomatic relations, 96; disasters, 262; economic growth, 19; educational system, 43; election in, 15, 29; and European countries, 224; and France, 89; governments, comparison of, 92; industrial development, 41; internal stresses, 15; international relations, 79, 209, 218; invasion by North Korea, 16; and Japan, 19, 33; leftist activity, 28; loan from Japan, 89; martial law in, 22, 29; meeting with North Korea, 247; and Mideast, 224; military leaders, 97; military role of, 93; natural resources, 37; and North Korea, comparison to, 91; North Korea view, 261, 262; nuclear weapons, 87; official power, abuse of, 205; oil policy, 39; and Pakistan, comparison to, 96; parliamentary democracy, 97; political development, 91; political record, judgment of, 96; political system, 19; protest against Japan, 83; relations with Japan, 83, 218; relations with North Korea, 219; security, 87; social welfare policy, 207; and Southeast Asia, 84; strategic importance, 79; student demonstration, 30; and Taiwan, comparison to, 94; trade with Japan, 83; transportation, 40; U.S. defense, 16; U.S. economic aid, 16; U.S. military government in, 15; U.S. occupation, 8, 15; U.S. public image, 20; U.S. role in security, 87; U.S. troop withdrawal, 15, 20, 34, 81; viability of, 97

ABOUT THE AUTHOR

HAROLD C. HINTON is Professor of Political Science and International Affairs and a member of the Institute for Sino-Soviet Studies at The George Washington University. He has traveled and lectured widely in Asia and has made nine visits to Korea, the first in 1945 and the latest in 1982. He has published many books and articles on East Asian politics and international relations, including *Three and a Half Powers: The New Balance in Asia* (1975).